YES I AM A MEMBER OF PARLIAMENT

Tool kit for Parliamentarians

DR. MAN MOHAN SINGH

INDIA • SINGAPORE • MALAYSIA

ISBN

Paperback 979-8-89475-393-5

Hardcase 979-8-89498-338-7

DISCLAIMER:

My Mentor

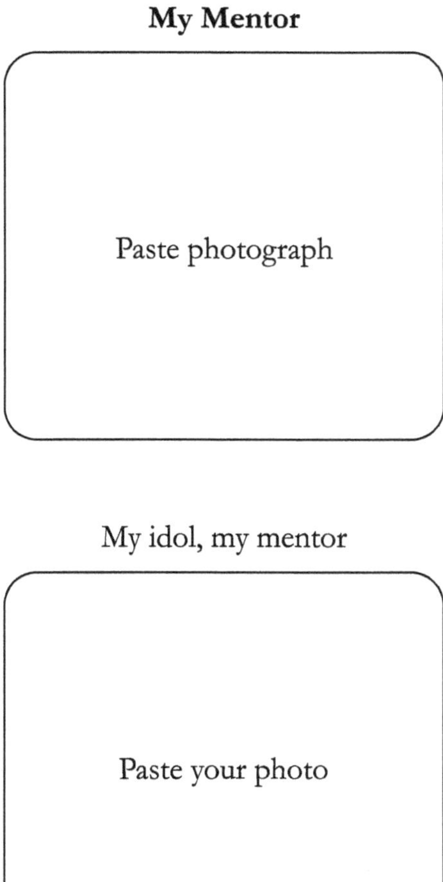

Yes I can do it,

I am the most successful Member of Parliament.

MP PRAYER

I lift up my voices in prayer as 'Member of Parliament'. Grant me guidance and clarity as I navigate the responsibilities entrusted to me by the people. May I be filled with compassion and empathy, seeking the common good in all my actions.

Grant me the strength to uphold justice and integrity in my decisions, to champion the voices of the marginalized, and to work tirelessly for the welfare of all citizens.

Bless me with discernment to distinguish truth from falsehood, humility to listen to differing perspectives, and courage to stand firm in my convictions for the betterment of society.

May I be a beacon of hope and a force for positive change in our community and nation. Surround me with support and encouragement, and protect me from harm as I serve with dedication and commitment.

In your mercy, hear my prayer. Amen. (OM)

O Divine Source of Wisdom

CONTENTS

Thank You

"It's about face time. Voters are not difficult people. If you promise it, do it! [Citizens] like when MPs go to their constituency to see their faces. MPs should always be with constituents, live in the constituency and be part and parcel of them. Whatever you do matters in elections. You can bring development but if they don't see you, then electors will not remember."

– First-term MP, Malawi

"Members of Parliament are first and foremost representatives of the people. They are elected or appointed to serve the interest of the public generally, and the interest of the constituency, in accordance with the greater good of the society or community and keeping with the laws and the constitution. This public role requires them to be mindful that conduct in their personal capacity must uphold integrity, dignity and professional stewardship befitting the public office. The ultimate exercise of the representatives' role of Member of Parliament is to pass laws for the good government of the country and advancing our interests."

In this book, we will read the roles, responsibilities, and challenges faced by Members of Parliament (MPs) in serving their constituents and representing their interests in legislative bodies. It's important to understand the vital role that MPs play in our democratic system. MPs are elected representatives chosen by the people to voice their concerns, advocate for their needs, and make decisions on their behalf in the halls of parliament. Throughout history, MPs have been the driving force behind transformative legislative changes, championing causes that improve the lives of citizens and uphold the values of democracy, justice, and equality. As a Member of Parliament, you have a significant opportunity to make a positive impact on your constituents and contribute to the governance of your country.

One of the most fundamental roles of an MP is to be the bridge between the citizens and the government. This involves actively listening to the needs and grievances of constituents, whether they are individuals, businesses, or communities, and advocating for policies and initiatives that will improve their lives. It is a role that requires empathy, integrity, and a deep commitment to public service.

Being an MP is about making decisions that impact the future of our country. It means engaging in debates, scrutinizing proposed legislation, and working with colleagues from different political persuasions to find solutions that benefit the greater good. This includes scrutinizing the implementation of policies, ensuring transparency in decision-making processes, and speaking out against injustices or abuses of power when necessary. Upholding democratic values and protecting the rights of all citizens are at the heart of this oversight function.

Beyond the legislative chamber, being an MP involves being a community leader and a representative on the world stage. It means attending local events, meeting with constituents, and being accessible to those who seek assistance or guidance. It also means engaging with international counterparts, participating in diplomatic efforts, and representing our country's interests in global forums.

"Member of Parliament" is both a privilege and a responsibility of the highest order. It is a commitment to serving the people, upholding democratic values, and working towards a better, more prosperous future for all. By following these suggestions and leveraging your position as an

MP, you can make a meaningful and positive impact on the lives of your constituents and contribute to the betterment of your country. Here are a few suggestions to help you effectively fulfill your role:

- **Listen to Your Constituents**: Actively listen to the concerns, needs, and aspirations of your constituents. Regularly engage with them through public meetings, town halls, and other forums to understand their priorities and represent their interests effectively.
- **Advocate for Your Constituents**: Be a strong advocate for your constituents' interests and concerns in parliament. Use your position to push for legislative changes, policies, and initiatives that address the needs of your constituents and improve their quality of life.
- **Stay Informed**: Keep yourself informed about key issues, legislation, and developments at the national, regional, and local levels. Stay abreast of current events, research relevant topics, and seek expert advice to inform your decisions and positions on various issues.
- **Build Relationships**: Build positive relationships with your colleagues, both within your party and across party lines. Collaboration and cooperation with fellow MPs are essential for advancing legislative priorities, building consensus, and achieving meaningful outcomes.
- **Be Transparent and Accountable**: Practice transparency and accountability in your actions and decisions as an MP. Communicate openly with your constituents about your activities, positions, and the reasons behind your votes. Be accessible and responsive to their inquiries and feedback.
- **Engage in Legislative Process**: Actively participate in parliamentary debates, committees, and other legislative processes. Contribute constructively to policy discussions, propose amendments to legislation, and hold the government accountable through oversight and scrutiny.

- **Promote Inclusivity and Diversity**: Advocate for inclusivity, diversity, and equality in all aspects of governance. Ensure that the voices and perspectives of marginalized communities, minorities, and underrepresented groups are heard and considered in parliamentary deliberations and decision-making.
- **Address National Issues**: Address national-level issues and challenges facing your country, Work collaboratively with your colleagues to develop and implement effective solutions to these issues.
- **Stay Connected**: Stay connected with your constituents through regular communication, updates, and outreach efforts. Use traditional and digital platforms, including social media, newsletters, and constituency offices.
- **Lead by Example**: Lead by example and uphold high standards of integrity, ethics, and professionalism in your conduct as an MP. Demonstrate a commitment to public service, honesty, and accountability in all your actions and interactions.

He, who reads, understands and avails of the valuable knowledge within this book will have no further need of instructions from any one. He will be his own master. In fact, who has once read this book will say that he has never seen or heard of this. Some of the most mighty and powerful politicians in the world have become so through a thorough understanding of the rules contained within this book

Take this book. Keep it near you always. Read, refresh whenever you get time. Refer to it I need. Let it help you in every way. Let the secret knowledge contained in the book and the pages inspire you to ever greater deeds and endeavors and bring you parallel to none. These rules have worked for others. They will work for you. **I am interested in your success.**

Reading is essential for MPs to fulfill their responsibilities effectively, stay abreast of current developments, and contribute positively to democratic governance. It enables MPs to be well-informed representatives who can advocate for the interests of their constituents, engage in informed debates, and contribute to the overall progress of their country.

Chapter 1
INTRODUCTION

"While we talk at the beginning of our term about electoral promises, it is difficult to meet expectations – they are ever increasing. The task becomes more difficult as time goes on. Expectations increase and communication moves fast. As citizens get more involved, they become more demanding."

– Veteran MP, Algeria

"We are 44,098 parliamentarians globally. Can't we do something individually and collectively that can change the lives of mothers and children? We have the power. We have the voice. Do we have the courage? Dr. Gertrude Mongella

We have many MPs who understand the weight of their roles as legislators and do their best in their work. They try to highlight issues on the floor of Parliament so as to establish their grasp on certain issues to not only their colleagues in Parliament, but also to the larger world. Remember they are not responsible for the implementation relating to civic issues. MPs need to perform their actual duties well.

Constructive parliamentarian: A constructive parliamentarian is one who actively contributes to the legislative process, fosters collaboration, and works towards positive outcomes for society. By embodying these qualities and behaviors, a constructive parliamentarian can make a meaningful and positive impact on the legislative process and contribute to the well-being of society.

- **Commitment to Public Service**: A constructive parliamentarian is driven by a genuine desire to serve the public interest and improve the lives of constituents.
- **Knowledge and Expertise**: They possess a deep understanding of legislative procedures, policy issues, and the needs of their constituents. They continuously educate themselves on relevant topics to make informed decisions.
- **Collaborative Approach**: They collaborate across party lines and with stakeholders to find common ground, build consensus, and advance legislative agendas that benefit society as a whole.
- **Effective Communication**: They communicate effectively with colleagues, constituents, and stakeholders, listening actively and expressing their views clearly and persuasively.
- **Constructive Criticism**: They provide constructive criticism when necessary, offering alternative solutions and suggestions for improvement rather than simply opposing or obstructing.
- **Commitment to Ethics and Integrity**: They uphold high ethical standards, integrity, and transparency in their conduct as parliamentarians, avoiding conflicts of interest and unethical behavior.
- **Respect for Democratic Institutions**: They respect the institutions of democracy, including parliament, the rule of law, and the separation of powers, and work to strengthen and defend them against threats.
- **Advocacy for Marginalized Groups**: They advocate for the rights and interests of marginalized and underrepresented groups, ensuring their voices are heard and their needs addressed in legislative debates and policy decisions.

- **Focus on Solutions**: They focus on finding practical solutions to pressing issues, rather than engaging in partisan politics or ideological battles that hinder progress.
- **Accessibility and Accountability**: They are accessible to constituents, listening to their concerns, responding to inquiries, and keeping them informed about legislative activities and decisions. They hold themselves accountable for their actions and decisions.
- **Empathy and Compassion**: They demonstrate empathy and compassion towards those affected by legislative decisions, considering the human impact of policies and striving to mitigate harm.
- **Long-Term Vision**: They have a long-term vision for the betterment of society, recognizing that meaningful change often requires persistence, patience, and collaboration over time.

- **Essential Leadership Qualities:**
    - **Self-Awareness**: While this is a more inwardly focused trait, self-awareness and humility are paramount qualities of leadership. The better you understand yourself and recognize your own strengths and weaknesses, the more effective you can be as a leader.
    - **Respect**: Treating people with respect on a daily basis is one of the most important things a leader can do. It helps ease tensions and conflict, fosters trust, and improves your effectiveness. Creating a culture of respect is about more than just the absence of disrespect. Respectfulness can be shown in many different ways, but it often starts with showing you truly value others' perspectives and making an effort to build belonging in the workplace both critical components of supporting equity, diversity, and inclusion.
    - **Compassion**: It is one of the most powerful and important acts of leadership. It's more than simply showing empathy or even listening and seeking to understand, as compassion requires leaders to *act* on what they learn. After someone shares a concern or speaks up

about something, they won't feel truly heard if their leader doesn't then take some type of meaningful action on the information, our researchers have found. This is the core of compassionate leadership, and it helps to build trust, increase collaboration, and decrease turnover across organizations.

- **Vision**: Motivating others and garnering commitment are essential parts of leadership. Purpose-driven leaders ensure they connect their team's daily tasks and the values of individual team members to the overall direction of the organization. This can help employees find meaning in their work — which increases engagement, inspires trust, and drives priorities forward.
- **Communication**: Effective leadership and effective communication are intertwined. The best leaders are skilled communicators who can communicate in a variety of ways, from transmitting information and storytelling to soliciting input and using active listening techniques. They can communicate well both orally and in writing, and with a wide range of people from different backgrounds, roles, levels, geographies, and more.
- **Learning Agility**: Learning agility is the ability to know what to do when you don't know what to do. If you're a "quick study" or are able to excel in unfamiliar circumstances, you might already be learning agile. But anybody can foster and increase learning agility through intentional practice and effort.
- **Collaboration**: The most effective leaders can work with a variety of colleagues of different social identities, locations, roles, and experiences. As the world has become more complex and interconnected, good leaders find themselves spanning boundaries and learning to work across various types of divides and organizational silos. When leaders value and embrace collaboration, whether within their teams or cross-functionally, several benefits arise — including increased innovation, higher-performing teams, and a more engaged and empowered workforce.

- **Influence**: As a leader, you must be able to influence others to get the work done. Being able to persuade people through thoughtful use of appropriate influencing tactics is an important trait of inspiring, effective leaders. Influence is quite different from manipulation, and it needs to be done authentically and transparently. It requires high levels of emotional intelligence and trust.
- **Integrity**: Integrity is an essential leadership trait for the individual and the organization. It's especially important for top-level executives who are charting the organization's course and making countless other significant decisions. Reinforce the importance of honesty and integrity to managers at all levels.
- **Courage**: Courage is a key leadership trait — it takes courage to do what's right! Leaders who promote high levels of psychological safety in the workplace enable their people to speak up freely and share candid concerns without fear of repercussions. This fosters a coaching culture that supports courage and truth-telling. Courage enables both team members and leaders to take bold actions that move things in the right direction.
- **Gratitude**: Being thankful can lead to higher self-esteem, reduced depression and anxiety, and better sleep. Sincere gratitude can even make you a better leader. Yet few people regularly say "thank you" in work settings, even though most people say they'd be willing to work harder for an appreciative boss. The best leaders know how to show frequent gratitude in the workplace.
- **Resilience**: Practicing resilient leadership means you'll project a positive outlook that will help others maintain the emotional strength they need to commit to a shared vision, and the courage to move forward and overcome setbacks. A good leader focuses on resilience, both taking care of themselves and also prioritizing leading employee wellbeing, too — thereby enabling better performance for themselves and their teams.

- **Good leaders are made, not born.** Leadership is a social process. It's also essential to recognize that **leadership is less about one strong or charismatic individual, and more about a group of people working collectively to achieve results** together. If you demonstrate several of the characteristics of a good leader, but fail to grasp this key point, chances are you won't get very far on your own. You may be well-liked and respected, but it will be challenging to accomplish team or organizational goals.
- **Good leadership never stops.: Leadership isn't a destination, it's a** *journey* — it's something that you'll have to work at regularly throughout your career, regardless of what level you reach in your organization or what industry you work in. Different teams, projects, and situations will provide different challenges and require different leadership qualities and competencies to succeed. So you will need to be able to continue to apply these leadership characteristics in different ways throughout your career. Just continually keep learning and growing, and you'll be an agile learner with a long career.

The importance of Member of Parliament can be seen as they serve as the link between the citizens and the government. They are elected to represent the interests and concerns of their constituents in the legislative process. Through regular interactions, public forums, and constituency visits, MPs gather feedback and understand the issues that matter most to the people they represent. This direct connection ensures that the government remains accountable and responsive to the needs of the population.

MPs are essential because they bridge the gap between citizens and government, ensure effective governance, and uphold democratic norms. Their role is not only to legislate and govern but also to represent and empower the people they serve. Without MPs, the democratic process would lack representation, accountability, and the diversity of perspectives necessary for inclusive and responsive governance. Thus, their presence is vital for the functioning and advancement of democratic societies worldwide.

A politician running for office was asked about his policy on liquor. He answered, "If you mean the demon drink that poisons the body, ruins the mind, destroys the family and creates criminals, and then I'm against it! But if you mean the beautiful drink used for a wedding toast, the foundation of a fun Friday night and the biggest source of tax revenue to fund needy orphans, then I'm for it! And I won't change my mind, no matter what you say."

Chapter 2
ROLE OF M.P.

"We must show voters that we're normal people. We are not corrupt or criminals. It is a job like any other. You must take the time to speak with them and listen to them, in the market, on the street. That is how you will convince them."

– Veteran MP, Croatia

A Member of Parliament (MP) holds a crucial position in a parliamentary democracy such as India. With 543 Lok Sabha (Lower House) MPs representing more than 1.2 billion people, a Lok Sabha MP represents more than 2.2 million people on average. He is more than just a representative elected by the people; they are entrusted with the vital task of shaping the legislative landscape and advocating for the interests of their constituents. The role of an MP is multifaceted, encompassing legislative responsibilities, constituent service, oversight of the government, and community leadership.

MPs are elected to represent the diverse voices and concerns of their constituents. They serve as the link between the people and the government, this legislative function requires them to possess a thorough understanding of a wide range of issues—from healthcare and education to economic policy and environmental sustainability. They play a crucial role in addressing the needs of individual constituents and communities.

They serve as advocates for those seeking assistance with government services, navigating bureaucratic processes, or voicing concerns about local issues. This requires them to be accessible, responsive, and empathetic to the needs of their constituents.

MPs participate in parliamentary committees, and are community leaders who engage with local organizations, attend public events, and collaborate with stakeholders to address community challenges and promote civic engagement. Effective MPs must possess strong communication skills to articulate their constituents' concerns persuasively, negotiation skills to navigate political complexities and build consensus, and a commitment to ethical leadership that prioritizes the public good over personal or partisan interests.

The role of an MP demands resilience and dedication. It involves long hours, extensive travel, and the ability to balance competing demands from constituents, party obligations, and parliamentary duties. However, it is also a role that offers immense opportunities to make a positive impact, shape national policy, and contribute to the democratic process. MPs are entrusted with representing the interests of their constituents, shaping legislative decisions, holding the government accountable, and serving as community leaders. It is a role that requires dedication, integrity, and a deep commitment to public service, with the ultimate goal of advancing the welfare and prosperity of the nation as a whole. The broad roles of the Members of Parliament are the following:

- **Legislative role:** Passing Laws of India in the Lok Sabha.
- **Oversight role:** Ensuring that the Executive (i.e., Government) performs its duties efficiently.
- **Representative role:** Representing the people's views and aspirations of their constituencies in the Parliament of India (Lok Sabha).
- **Power of the Purse role:** Approving and overseeing government-proposed revenues and expenditures.

- The Union Council of Ministers, also Members of the Parliament, bear the additional responsibility of the Executive.

- **Legislative Role:** First and foremost, an MP is a legislator. In the case of ordinary bills (Article 100), more than 50% of MPs present in the house need to vote in favor of the Bill for it to become an Act. Deemed passed by that House. The Constitutional Amendment Bill under Article 368 requires at least two-thirds of the MPs present and 50% of the strength of the House to vote on it for it to become an Act. MPs also need to debate on various provisions of the Bill, and then propose amendments if they wish to.

- **Delegated Legislation:** After a bill is signed into a law, the power to make detailed regulation rests in the hands of the executive. That's when the role of an MP comes into play, wherein he/she keeps a check on the executive and ensures the power is not abused by the Govt.

- **Deliberative Role:** As per the Indian constitutional scheme, the Executive is accountable to the legislature. This is maintained partly by MPs, as they are to ask questions to government ministers. The procedures in both Houses of Parliament have rules for a 'Question Hour' and a 'Zero Hour'. Here there are starred and un-starred (oral and written questions which can be asked by MPs). These questions and debates are vital as they allow an MP to be an active voice of their constituency. Other role an MP carries to exercise power over the executive are to initiate Adjournment Motion, No-Confidence Motion, and Calling Attention Motion etc., if necessary.

- **Electoral Role:** An MP also plays a vital role in electing the President and Vice-President of a country. Lok Sabha MPs also have the power to elect the Speaker and Deputy Speaker of the house, whereas a Rajya Sabha MP elects the Vice-Chairman of the house.

- **Power of the Purse Responsibility:** No tax can be levied and no expenditure incurred by the government except with the approval of the Parliament. The Budget is therefore presented to the Parliament. Every MP is the voice of his/her constituency.

- **Developmental Role:** A MPs developmental role in their State or constituency is important. They generally fulfill these roles through these provisions:
    - **Representation in local bodies**: Panchayats and municipalities play a key role in bringing development to the grassroots. The provisions of Part IXA of the Constitution outlines how the Legislature of a State can provide for the representation of an MP at the intermediate and District level Panchayats. It also states how the State legislature can provide for the representation of MPs in municipal bodies within the constituency. Moreover, MPs can be nominated to District Planning Committees.
    - **Vigilance and monitoring of government schemes**: MPs play important roles in monitoring of some Centrally Sponsored Schemes in their States. Beyond these responsibilities, MPs can work towards catalyzing schemes of the State and Central government in their own constituencies. This requires a proactive engagement with public officials at both the Central and State levels. It also requires greater interaction with constituents in order to better understand their needs and concerns. Since they are elected representatives, they have legitimate political authority for direct engagement with the private or corporate sector to ensure the industrial development of their constituencies.

The powers of our Members of Lok Sabha are conferred on them to ensure that the Lok Sabha functions for the purpose that it has been set up for. The main functions of the Lok Sabha are:

- **Legislative**: Lawmaking is the main function of the Parliament. All types of bills can originate in the Lok Sabha and if a bill is moved in and passed by the Rajya Sabha, it has to come to the Lok Sabha for its approval. If there is any disagreement between the two Houses, the Lok Sabha will prevail in the joint sitting with the Rajya Sabha because it has more members than the other House of the Parliament.

- **Financial**: The next important role of the Lok Sabha and its members is fiscal responsibility. The Lok Sabha exercises control over the finances and have to approve the budget presented by the Government in power and ensure that money is allocated adequately and appropriately for the business of Governance. In financial matters, the Lok Sabha has a distinct superiority over the Rajya Sabha. The Money Bill can be introduced only in the Lok Sabha and cannot be moved in the Rajya Sabha.

- **Control over Executive**: The Council of Ministers is collectively responsible to the Lower House of the Parliament. Thus, the government is accountable to the Lok Sabha for its acts of omission and commission. The Rajya Sabha cannot hold the government accountable to it. It is only the Lok Sabha which can force the Council of Ministers to resign by passing a vote of no-confidence against it.

- **Constitutional**: The Lok Sabha shares with the Rajya Sabha the power to amend the constitution.

- **Electoral**: The Lok Sabha takes part in the election of the President and the Vice-President. It elects the Speaker and the Deputy Speaker and its members are also elected to different Committees of the Parliament.

- **Judicial**: The Lok Sabha has power to punish a person on the ground of breach of privilege. It takes part in the impeachment proceedings against the President of India, and it shares power with the Rajya Sabha to remove the Judges of the Supreme Court and the Judges of High Courts.

- **Ventilation of Grievances**: The members of the Lok Sabha are elected from different parts of India. They try to remove the difficulties of their respective constituencies by stating their grievances on the floor of the Lok Sabha.

- **Imparting Education on Democracy**: The Lok Sabha discussions would help in raising the political consciousness of people. As the discussions in the Lok Sabha are directly telecast, the people are able to learn of different aspects of Indian politics.

- **Other Functions**: The Lok Sabha discusses reports submitted by the Union Public Service Commission (UPSC), Comptroller and Auditor-General of India (CAG), Finance Commission etc.
- **Working in the Parliament** Members' parliamentary functions may include:
    - Enacting and debating proposed new legislation
    - Scrutinizing the actions of the Government and government departments as members of parliamentary committees.
    - Participating in general debates in the Chamber.
    - Attending parliamentary party meetings and
    - Performing other duties within the parliamentary complex such as Deputy Speaker roles.
    - Participating in general debates in the Chamber is a major parliamentary occupation.
    - Members regularly speak either in support of, or in opposition to, a piece of legislation. In Parliament,
    - Members may also address constituent concerns during debates, ask questions of Ministers during Question Time and work to create or amend laws.
    - They may also seek to have matters referred to a parliamentary committee for investigation
- **Member of a political party** Most Members of Parliament belong to a political party and are expected to contribute to the development and amendment of their party policies. At the start of each parliamentary sitting week, MPs (with the exception of Independent members) will attend their respective party meetings where they will:

- Plan strategies
- Develop policies
- Scrutinize proposed legislation and
- Discuss parliamentary business.

- **In their electorates**, Members' party responsibilities may include:
    - Attending branch party meetings
    - Keeping their fellow party members well informed on policy decisions and other relevant information
    - Participating in party debate at branch level and
    - Generally representing the party at the electorate level.
- **Privileges and Responsibilities:**
    - MPs actively participate in formulation and amendment of laws.
    - They can propose bills, discuss them in Parliament, and contribute to shaping the legal framework of the country.
    - MPs represent their constituencies in the Lok Sabha (House of the People). They voice concerns, aspirations, and needs of their constituents during parliamentary debates and discussions.
    - MPs receive a salary, allowances, and other perks. The salary is subject to revision from time to time.
    - Additionally, they have access to various allowances for travel, accommodation, and office expenses.
    - After serving a certain number of terms, MPs are eligible for pension. This ensures financial security after retirement. While performing their duties, MPs enjoy parliamentary immunity.
    - This means they cannot be held legally accountable for their statements or actions within Parliament.

- MPs have access to government information, data, and reports. This keeps them informed about various issues affecting the nation.
- An MP can allocate funds from MPLADS which directly contributes to local development.
- Serving as an MP provides opportunities to network with other politicians, bureaucrats, and influential individuals.
- This enhances their influence and impact.
- MPs can use their position to advocate for specific causes, raise awareness, and drive positive change.
- They can champion issues related to education, healthcare, infrastructure and more.
- Being an MP brings social recognition and prestige.
- It is a position of authority and respect within the community but they also have significant responsibilities towards their constituents and the nation.
- They are accountable for their actions and decisions during their tenure in office.
- MPs also enjoy immunity and freedom of speech on the floor of the House.
- They cannot be prosecuted for having said anything on the floor of the House.
- During session the members cannot be arrested in any civil cases.
- Participation of an MP in Lok Sabha. The work in Lok Sabha begins at 11 am and is ordinarily scheduled to be worked until 6 pm, with a lunch break from 1 pm to 2 pm. If the House decides, it can be worked through the lunch break or be worked beyond 6 pm.

Chapter 3
DUTIES & RESPONSIBILITIES

"An MP's duties and responsibilities are not merely to represent their constituents in parliament, but to be their voice, their advocate, and their champion. It is a sacred trust bestowed upon them by the people, demanding unwavering dedication, integrity, and service to the common good."

Common good." "An MP's duties and responsibilities are not merely to represent their constituents in parliament, but to be their voice, their advocate, and their champion. It is a sacred trust bestowed upon them by the people, demanding unwavering dedication, integrity, and service to the common good."

MPs are entrusted with a range of duties and responsibilities that are essential for the effective governance of their constituencies and the nation as a whole. One of the primary responsibilities of an MP is legislative. MPs participate in the law-making process by proposing, debating, and scrutinizing legislation in the parliament. They represent the interests and concerns of their constituents by advocating for policies that address local issues, promote economic development, safeguard public health, and protect the environment. Through their legislative role, MPs contribute to shaping the legal framework that governs society, ensuring that laws are fair, just, and responsive to the needs of the people.

MPs play a crucial role in holding the government accountable. Through parliamentary debates, question periods, and participation in parliamentary committees, MPs scrutinize the actions and decisions of the government, ensuring transparency, accountability, and adherence to democratic principles. MPs have the power to question government ministers, investigate matters of public interest, and advocate for reforms that promote good governance and prevent abuses of power.

Important responsibility of MPs is to represent their constituency's interests on a national and international level. MPs participate in parliamentary committees, where they contribute to the formulation of policies and strategies that address national challenges and promote the country's interests abroad. MPs also engage in diplomacy, representing their constituency in international forums and negotiations, advocating for policies that enhance global cooperation, promote human rights, and address global challenges such as climate change and international security.

Besides their formal duties, MPs are also community leaders and role models. They engage with local organizations, attend public events, and collaborate with stakeholders to address community issues, promote civic engagement, and foster a sense of unity and solidarity within their constituency. MPs serve as advocates for marginalized groups, championing social justice initiatives and promoting inclusive policies that ensure equal opportunities and protections for all citizens.

The duties and responsibilities of Members of Parliament are diverse and far-reaching. MPs play a crucial role in the legislative process, representing the interests of their constituents, holding the government accountable, and advocating for policies that promote the well-being and prosperity of the nation. As elected representatives, MPs are entrusted with the sacred duty of upholding democratic values, protecting the rights of citizens, and contributing to the advancement of society through effective governance and responsible leadership.

MPs play a crucial role in the functioning of a democratic society by representing the interests of their constituents, making laws, and holding the government accountable. The duties and responsibilities of a Member of Parliament (MP) can vary depending on the country's political system, but generally include:

- **Legislative Functions**: MPs participate in the process of making laws by proposing, debating, and voting on legislation in the parliament or legislative assembly.
- **Representation**: MPs represent their constituents in parliament by voicing their concerns, opinions, and interests on various issues, legislation, and policies.
- **Constituency Work**: MPs are responsible for addressing the concerns and needs of their constituents by helping them navigate government services, advocating for local projects and initiatives, and attending to individual concerns.
- **Committee Work**: MPs often serve on parliamentary committees where they examine specific issues in detail, scrutinize government policies, and contribute to the development of legislation.
- **Oversight of Government**: MPs hold the government accountable by questioning ministers, scrutinizing government actions, and participating in debates on matters of public interest.
- **Policy Development**: MPs may engage in policy research, analysis, and advocacy to develop and promote legislative proposals and policy initiatives.
- **Representation of Political Party**: MPs typically belong to a political party and are expected to support party policies, participate in party activities, and contribute to the party's objectives.
- **Constituency Outreach**: MPs communicate with constituents through various means such as public meetings, town halls, social media, and newsletters to keep them informed about parliamentary activities and seek their input on important issues.

- **Public Advocacy**: MPs often engage in public advocacy on behalf of their constituents or on issues they are passionate about, both within and outside of parliament.
- **Constituency Development**: MPs may work towards the development and improvement of their constituencies by advocating for infrastructure projects, economic development initiatives, and social welfare programs.
- **Constituency Representation**: MPs represent their constituents' interests and concerns within the parliamentary chamber, ensuring that their voices are heard and their needs addressed in the legislative process.

PARLIAMENTARY DUTIES OF A MEMBER OF PARLIAMENT:

- Writing to or organizing meetings with relevant ministers
- Speaking in Parliament during a debate
- Asking questions during Prime Minister's Questions (PMQs)
- Introducing Members Bills on topics of concern to their constituents
- Lobbying other organizations (such as local councils, health boards) and individuals on behalf of their constituents
- Raising the profile of an issue in the media
- Involvement in committees which scrutinize new legislation or question the work of the government.
    - **Whips: MPs from the government party who ensure their colleagues support the government and vote for their policies are called 'whips'. Sometimes the views of the party may come into conflict with the views of constituents**
- **The responsibilities of an MP are multifaceted.**
    - He/she actively engages in parliamentary debates on proposed bills, amendments, and other legislative matters.

- MPs vote on various issues, including budgetary allocations, constitutional amendments, and policy decisions.
- He/she represents the interests, concerns, and aspirations of the constituents in Lok Sabha.
- They advocate for policies and projects that benefit their constituencies.
- MPs scrutinize the functioning of the government, ensuring transparency and accountability.
- They can question ministers during Question Hour, seeking clarifications on government actions.
- They work to improve infrastructure, healthcare, education, and other essential services in their constituencies.
- MPs serve on various Committees, such as, Standing Committee, Select Committees to examine bills, policies, and administrative matters.
- They raise awareness about social issues, promote public welfare, and address community concerns.
- They interact with constituents, attend public meetings, and address grievances, participate in budget discussions, ensuring that public funds are allocated appropriately.
- They scrutinize government spending and financial decisions.
- MPs contribute to policy formulation by suggesting reforms, improvements, and innovative solutions and discuss critical national issues affecting citizens.
- MPs engage in international forums, representing India's interests and building diplomatic ties.
- As constitutional duties are concerned, MPs participate in the electoral process in electing the President and Vice President of India.

- MPs play a role in impeachment proceedings against constitutional functionaries.
- MPs must balance their duties to the nation, their party, and their constituents while upholding democratic values and principles.

- **Duties of Member of Parliament:** The duties of a Member of Parliament (MP) vary depending on the country's political system, these duties collectively contribute to the functioning of democracy, ensuring that citizens are represented, laws are made in the public interest, and the government remains accountable to the people. They include:
  - **Representation**: MPs represent the interests and concerns of their constituents in the legislative process. They listen to their constituents' issues, raise them in parliamentary debates, and advocate for solutions.
  - **Legislation**: MPs participate in the creation, debate, and voting on laws. They may propose bills, scrutinize government legislation, and contribute to shaping new laws or amending existing ones.
  - **Constituency Work**: MPs engage with their constituents through regular surgeries, meetings, and events. They help constituents navigate government services, address concerns, and advocate on their behalf.
  - **Scrutiny of Government**: MPs hold the government to account by questioning ministers, scrutinizing government policies, and participating in parliamentary committees. This oversight ensures transparency and accountability in governance.
  - **Policy Development**: MPs contribute to policy development within their political party. They may serve on policy committees, draft party manifestos, and advocate for specific policies aligned with their party's values and goals.
  - **Public Engagement**: MPs communicate with the public through speeches, media interviews, and social media. They explain

government policies, respond to public inquiries, and engage in public debates on various issues.

- **Representing Parliament**: MPs may represent their country or parliament in international forums, diplomatic missions, or parliamentary delegations. They participate in discussions on global issues, treaties, and international cooperation.
- **Budgetary Oversight**: MPs review and approve government budgets, ensuring that public funds are allocated appropriately and effectively. They may scrutinize budget proposals, question government spending decisions, and propose amendments.
- **Contribution to Committees**: MPs often serve on parliamentary committees, where they delve deeper into specific policy areas, conduct inquiries, and make recommendations to the government.
- **Contribution to Debates**: MPs participate in parliamentary debates on various issues, expressing their views, questioning government decisions, and advocating for their constituents' interests.

- **Responsibilities of Member of parliament:** The responsibilities of a Member of Parliament (MP) can vary somewhat depending on the specific political system, the role of an MP is multifaceted, requiring a combination of legislative, representative, oversight, and advocacy responsibilities to effectively serve both their constituents and the broader interests of the nation, they may include:
    - **Legislation:** MPs participate in the drafting, debating, and passing of laws. They may propose bills, scrutinize government legislation, and vote on proposed laws.
    - **Representation:** MPs represent the interests and concerns of their constituents in the legislative process. They listen to the needs of their constituents, address their grievances, and advocate on their behalf.
    - **Oversight:** MPs hold the government accountable by monitoring its actions, policies, and expenditures. This involves questioning

government ministers, participating in parliamentary committees, and conducting inquiries into government activities.

- **Constituency Work:** MPs provide assistance and support to their constituents on various issues, such as accessing government services, resolving problems, and advocating for local projects.
- **Policy Making:** MPs contribute to the development of public policy by researching issues, participating in parliamentary committees, and proposing legislative solutions to societal problems.
- **Representation of the Political Party:** MPs often belong to a political party and are expected to represent its values, principles, and policies in parliament.
- **Debating:** MPs participate in parliamentary debates on a wide range of topics, including proposed legislation, government policies, and current affairs.
- **Public Engagement:** MPs communicate with the public through speeches, public appearances, social media, and other means to inform constituents about parliamentary activities and seek their input on issues.
- **Constituency Development:** MPs may work on projects and initiatives to promote the economic, social, and cultural development of their constituencies.
- **Constituency Advocacy:** MPs may lobby the government on behalf of their constituents to secure funding for local projects, infrastructure, and services.

- **MP looks after:**
  - **The legislative role**: The primary role of an MP is seen as that of a legislator. According to Article 111 of the Constitution of India, any Bill is transformed into an Act only when it is passed by both houses of Parliament and is given assent by the President. In the case of ordinary bills, a simple majority (more than 50%)

of the members (MPs) present in the house needs to vote in favor of the Bill for it to be considered as passed by that House (Article 100). In the case of a Constitutional Amendment Bill under Article 368, a special majority of the MPs. This is among the primary Responsibilities of MP.

- **The deliberative role in the life of a Member of Parliament.:** In the Indian constitutional scheme, the Executive (government) is made accountable to the legislature. This principle of accountability is partially realized by government ministers, including the Prime Minister, being questioned by elected representatives (MPs) in Parliament. The rules of procedure in each House of Parliament contain provisions for a Question Hour and a Zero Hour during which written and oral questions can be posed by MPs. These questions may encompass topics specific to the State or the constituency represented by them.
- **Developmental role in the life of a Member of Parliament.:** The developmental role of an MP is highlighted, in addition to their parliamentary responsibilities, as a vital aspect of their respective State or constituency. This role out of all the responsibilities of an MP can be fulfilled with the assistance of the following provisions:
    - **MPLADS** – The Member of Parliament Local Area Development Scheme (MPLADS), introduced in 1993, allots an annual budget of Rs 5 crore to each MP for the initiation of developmental projects within their constituency. The scheme's administration falls under the purview of the Ministry of Statistics and Programme Implementation (MoSPI), which prescribes guidelines concerning the permissible works and activities under MPLADS. The allocation of funds through MPLADS is carried out by the relevant implementing agencies at the district level. Further details on the scheme and the types of permissible projects are elaborated upon later in this document.

- **Representation in local bodies** – The Constitution, in Part IXA, includes provisions that enable the Legislature of a State to facilitate the representation of MPs at the intermediate and District level Panchayats (Panchayat Samiti and Zila Parishad). Similarly, Part IXA of the Constitution empowers the State legislature to facilitate the representation of MPs within municipal bodies situated in their respective constituencies. MPs may also receive nominations to District Planning Committees (DPCs), constitutional bodies responsible for the formulation of development plans for the district. For instance, in Maharashtra, the State government appoints MPs and MLAs to the DPC.
- **Vigilance and monitoring of government schemes** – MPs have been entrusted with a significant role in monitoring several Centrally Sponsored Schemes within their respective districts. For example, the National Rural Drinking Water Programme (NRDWP) mandates the establishment of District Water and Sanitation Missions (DWSMs), of which all MPs and MLAs from the region become members. The DWSM assumes responsibility, among other things, for the formulation, management, and monitoring of projects related to drinking water security. It also oversees the evaluation and approval of schemes submitted by the Block Panchayat/ Gram Panchayat, as well as the coordination of matters concerning water and sanitation across various departments. Similarly, under the National Rural Health Mission (NRHM), MPs are expected to be included as members of the District Level Vigilance and Monitoring Committees (DVMC) tasked with reviewing the progress in the implementation of the scheme.

"For Success as Politician"

- **Authenticity and Integrity**
- **Effective Communication**
- **Listen and Connect**
- **Build Coalitions and Collaborate**
- **Stay Informed and Educated**
- **Adaptability and Resilience**
- **Focus on Solutions**
- **Transparency and Accountability**
- **Empathy and Empowerment**
- **Persistence and Patience.**

Chapter 4
CHARACTERISTICS OF M.P.

"An MP should possess the integrity of a judge, the wisdom of a sage, the humility of a servant, and the courage of a lion, for they are entrusted with the solemn duty of representing the hopes, dreams, and aspirations of an entire nation."

Members of Parliament (MPs) are entrusted with significant responsibilities in representing their constituents, participating in legislative processes, and contributing to the governance of their nation. To effectively fulfill these roles, MPs typically exhibit a range of distinctive characteristics that define their effectiveness and impact as public representatives.

Integrity is a fundamental characteristic of an MP. Integrity entails honesty, transparency, and a commitment to ethical behavior in all aspects of their work. MPs with integrity uphold the trust placed in them by their constituents and act with integrity in their decision-making processes, legislative activities, and interactions with fellow parliamentarians, stakeholders, and the public.

Empathy and compassion are crucial characteristics for MPs. Empathy allows MPs to understand and connect with the diverse perspectives, concerns, and needs of their constituents. By demonstrating compassion, MPs show genuine care and consideration for the well-being of the people they represent, striving to address their issues and improve their quality of life through legislative advocacy and constituent service.

Leadership is another essential characteristic of an MP. Effective MPs exhibit leadership qualities such as vision, strategic thinking, and the ability to inspire and mobilize others towards common goals. They take initiative in addressing critical issues, championing causes that benefit their constituents and the nation as a whole, and navigating complex political landscapes with integrity and foresight.

Communication skills are vital for MPs. MPs must possess the ability to articulate their constituents' concerns and advocate for their interests persuasively in parliamentary debates, committee meetings, and public forums. Effective communication also involves active listening, enabling MPs to understand diverse viewpoints, engage in constructive dialogue, and build consensus on legislative matters.

Adaptability and resilience are also important characteristics for MPs. The political landscape is dynamic and constantly evolving, presenting MPs with unforeseen challenges and opportunities. MPs who demonstrate adaptability can respond effectively to changing circumstances, adjust their strategies, and continue to serve their constituents effectively despite obstacles or setbacks. Resilience enables MPs to withstand pressure, criticism, and adversity while remaining committed to their duties and responsibilities.

MPs often exhibit a strong work ethic and dedication to public service. They are committed to working tirelessly on behalf of their constituents, investing time and effort in researching issues, drafting legislation, attending parliamentary sessions and committee meetings, and engaging with stakeholders to address pressing concerns and advocate for policy changes that benefit society.

MPs with a global perspective and a commitment to diversity and inclusivity are essential in today's interconnected world. They recognize the importance of international cooperation, diplomacy, and addressing global challenges such as climate change, human rights, and economic inequality. MPs who prioritize diversity and inclusivity strive to represent and empower marginalized communities, promote equality of opportunity, and ensure that all voices are heard and valued in the legislative process.

CHARACTERISTICS OF A MEMBER OF PARLIAMENT:

- **Integrity**: Upholding high ethical standards and demonstrating honesty and integrity in all actions is essential. MPs should act in the best interests of their constituents and the public, even when faced with difficult decisions.
- **Commitment to Public Service**: A strong commitment to serving the public and improving the lives of constituents is paramount. MPs should prioritize the needs of their constituents above personal or party interests.
- **Empathy and Compassion**: Having empathy and compassion for the diverse needs and concerns of constituents is crucial. MPs should listen actively; understand the challenges faced by individuals and communities, and advocate on their behalf.
- **Effective Communication Skills**: Good communication skills, both verbal and written, are essential for MPs to articulate their positions, engage with constituents, and collaborate with colleagues. Clear and transparent communication builds trust and fosters effective representation.
- **Accessibility and Responsiveness**: Being accessible and responsive to constituents' concerns is fundamental. MPs should maintain open lines of communication, promptly respond to inquiries, and engage with constituents through various channels, such as town hall meetings, social media, and community events.
- **Leadership and Collaboration**: Effective MPs demonstrate leadership by championing important issues, building coalitions, and working collaboratively with colleagues to achieve common goals. They understand the importance of teamwork and cooperation in achieving legislative and policy objectives.
- **Expertise and Knowledge**: Developing expertise in key policy areas relevant to constituents' needs enables MPs to make informed decisions and advocate effectively on behalf of their constituents. Continuous

learning and staying informed about legislative developments are essential.

- **Accountability and Transparency**: MPs should be accountable to their constituents and transparent in their actions. This includes disclosing financial interests, adhering to ethical standards, and being accountable for their voting records and decisions.
- **Adaptability and Resilience**: The political landscape is dynamic and often unpredictable. Good MPs demonstrate adaptability and resilience in navigating challenges, responding to changing circumstances, and finding creative solutions to complex problems.
- **Representation of Diverse Voices**: Effective representation requires MPs to understand and reflect the diverse perspectives and interests of their constituents. MPs should strive to represent all segments of society, including marginalized communities, and ensure that their voices are heard and considered in decision-making processes
- **MP's as Good politician:** A good politician is someone who effectively represents the interests of their constituents, upholds democratic principles, and works towards the betterment of society as a whole. Here are some qualities that often define a good politician:
    - **Integrity**: Good politicians adhere to high ethical standards, demonstrate honesty, and act with integrity in all aspects of their work. They prioritize the public interest over personal gain or political expediency.
    - **Empathy and Compassion**: Good politicians possess empathy and compassion for the needs and concerns of their constituents. They actively listen to diverse perspectives, understand the challenges faced by individuals and communities, and strive to address them effectively.
    - **Leadership**: Good politicians demonstrate strong leadership skills, inspiring others through their vision, integrity, and ability to bring people together to achieve common goals. They lead by example and empower others to participate in the democratic process.

- **Communication Skills**: Effective communication is essential for politicians to articulate their positions, engage with constituents, and build consensus. Good politicians are adept at conveying their ideas clearly and persuasively through various channels, including public speaking, writing, and social media.
- **Collaboration and Diplomacy**: Successful politicians understand the importance of collaboration and diplomacy in achieving legislative objectives and solving complex problems. They build relationships across party lines, work constructively with colleagues, and negotiate compromises when necessary.
- **Adaptability and Resilience**: The political landscape is dynamic and often unpredictable. Good politicians demonstrate adaptability and resilience in responding to changing circumstances, navigating challenges, and finding creative solutions to pressing issues.
- **Commitment to Public Service**: Good politicians are genuinely committed to serving the public and improving the lives of their constituents. They prioritize the common good over personal interests and work tirelessly to address the needs of society as a whole.
- **Accountability and Transparency**: Good politicians are accountable to the people they serve and operate with transparency in their actions and decision-making processes. They disclose financial interests, uphold ethical standards, and take responsibility for their decisions.
- **Strategic Thinking**: Good politicians possess strategic thinking skills, understanding the long-term implications of policies and decisions. They analyze complex issues, anticipate challenges, and develop effective strategies to address them.
- **Inclusivity and Diversity**: Good politicians value diversity and inclusivity, recognizing the importance of representing the voices and perspectives of all segments of society. They work to promote

equality, equity, and social justice for all individuals, regardless of background or identity.

Overall, a good politician is someone who embodies these qualities and strives to make a positive difference in the lives of others through their leadership, integrity, and commitment to public service.

MP QUALITIES:

- Helping councilors and candidates to represent their voters, get themselves noticed and secure the recognition & responsibility they deserve by writing and delivering World Class, memorable speeches
- **Communication skills:**
  - You need to be able to make clear points in broadcast interviews as well as at public meetings.
  - Often you have to deliver a speech at the drop of a hat, so it is important to practice creating a three minute speech from scratch with just five minutes of preparation – on any subject.
  - Clear written communication is also very important as you will have to draft letters to constituents, press statements and if you are lucky you might be asked to write a column for your local newspaper.
- **Intellect:**
  - You will need to be comfortable with complex material including budgets and academic reports.
  - Scrutiny work on select committees is an important component of a MPs role and Ministers who don't question their officials are no more use than an (expensive) empty chair.
  - It is important to understand the difference between intelligence and education. Possession of a good degree is helpful but not essential.
  - Far more important is an understanding of critical thinking and causation.

  - You also need to be enthusiastic about learning new things.
  - Experience of constantly learning and adapting is useful. Most people are uncomfortable with change but MPs can't afford to be hidebound.
- **Relate to people:**
  - As an MP, you will meet senior business figures and leaders of other countries but you will also deal with ordinary constituents every day and you have to empathize with their difficulties.
  - Far too often people regard their politicians as out of touch or 'not interested in my problems' and the recent antics in Westminster haven't helped.
  - Experience of voluntary work is a good way to demonstrate that you are comfortable with people from all backgrounds, rich and poor, friendly and hostile.
- **Leadership:**
  - During the campaign you will have to lead and motivate a team of political activists.
  - You may be seen as a great leader at work, oozing charisma, but in politics it often comes down to leading by example.
  - In essence you shouldn't expect your campaigners to do anything that you aren't prepared to do yourself.
- **Resilience:**
  - In politics there are far more lows than highs – but the highs are worth it. Most politicians lose an election before they can find a winnable seat and there are a lot of rejections along the road.
  - So you need to be able to bounce back swiftly from disappointment and defeat. It's worth considering times when you changed career or had to recover from a setback.
  - A degree of maturity and self-awareness is essential.

- **Conviction:**
  - Also remember that politics goes through changes. The ground is shifting so you need to know where you stand.
  - Demonstrating these essential attributes is vital for application CVs and interviews.
  - The good news is that I can help you – as I have already helped dozens of candidates – so drop me a message for more information.
- **Measures of success:** In carrying out their various duties, MPs must be able to balance their work in the legislative assembly, party meetings, commission rooms, and their constituency. The following are measures of success on how MPs can be effective in their dealings with constituents, staff, other parliamentarians, the media, and civil society organizations.
  - **Develop Trust and an Atmosphere of Collaboration**: In order to work well, government requires a level of trust between citizens and their representatives. Developing trust requires understanding, patience and the awareness of a common purpose and goal. Every MP should try to appeal to the best instincts in colleagues and be able to discuss the principles they stand for and objectives they intend to achieve during their term.
  - **Master the Internal Regulations of Parliament**: Being an effective MP depends on familiarity and a firm grasp of the internal regulations of Parliament. Understanding and respecting regulations gives power and legitimacy to an MP when in the legislative chamber or parliamentary commissions. New MPs should have easy access to the internal regulations so that they can refer to the regulations often.
  - **Adhere to the Code of Ethics**: The voters entrust MPs with important responsibilities and they must fulfill these obligations honorably. MPs should ensure that they understand legislative etiquette and their ethical responsibilities. Two important pointers to assist MPs in adhering to the code of ethics include:

(1) Avoid anything that could be interpreted as a conflict of interest,

(2) Adhere to the rules and agreed upon practices and norms in order to be more effective as a leader and in debate.

- **Where to Seek Information and Legislative Assistance**: MPs cannot be experts in everything and thus should work on topics in their particular areas of interest. This will enable them to become experts on specific issues. This will also help MPs in building their reputations as serious lawmakers among colleagues and the larger citizenry. In searching for information, solicit the help of various interest groups and parliamentary staff. Also, working with legislative and commission staff of the Secretariat will be of great benefit to the MP, not only in getting information, but also in taking advantage of the research and briefings provided by parliamentary staff.

- **When and How to Speak in Public**: A big part of an MP's work involves making speeches. Well-received speeches are those that

  - Use simple language, are brief and to the point, and that do not try to speak on everything.
  - It is also best to do some research and assessment before speaking on the floor.
  - A speech should always be well balanced if an MP wants to reach as many people as possible.
  - Another important aspect of speaking is discussions with the media.
  - The media are the link between the public and their representatives in government, and are thus an important part of any democracy.
  - Maintaining a good working relationship with the media is crucial.
  - MPs should use the media to disseminate information and announce their positions on issues or activities they are

involved in. When dealing with the media, an MP needs to be professional and discreet in order to earn the respect and confidence of the public.

- **Manage Time Well**: An MP's time is a scarce resource that must be well managed.
    - Organizing, prioritizing and demonstrating commitment to issues of importance are key in the management of an MP's time.
    - The way in which MPs manage their time reflects on them as individuals.
    - The time in the legislative assembly is limited and should be used wisely in dealing with issues of importance to MPs and their constituents.
    - Every MP also has a personal life that demands time and it is equally important to attend to non-legislative responsibilities so as to maintain a balance between work and private life.
- **Develop Leadership and Diplomatic Skills**: Controversial issues will often be brought up in parliament, and some will occur in an MP's constituency.
    - MPs must always consider the consequences of whatever course of action they choose and should use their skills and position as a parliamentarian to help find solutions.
    - An MP should ask questions, conduct research and be a positive influence both on fellow parliamentarians and on the community at large.
    - Seeking solutions involves building consensus and being willing to compromise.
    - Adopting a new position as a result of new insights is a mark of strength and not weakness, and thus it helps to approach issues with an open mind rather than with a set position.

  - Leadership requires a calm and sensible approach to issues, and accepting that one may be wrong.
  - MPs should develop a reputation for being straightforward and honest, and expect to be treated as they treat those with whom they disagree.
- **Vote According to Your Conscience**: MPs should be careful about measures they choose to support.
  - Bills and motions should be analyzed in advance in order to avoid the embarrassment of having to vote against bills or motions they already agreed to.
  - After MPs have promised to vote a certain way, they may get fresh insight or information that leads them to change their mind.
  - When this happens, MPs should make their new position known to all in order to maintain credibility.
- **Maintain an Open Relationship with Constituents**: MPs should remember that they are ultimately responsible to their constituents and that voters will respect MPs for thinking through issues and consulting them before arriving at a decision.
  - Returning phone calls, answering letters, having meetings and doing whatever it takes to ensure that the constituents are aware of what an MP is doing is imperative in the maintenance of open and constructive relations with constituents.
- **Maintain Gender-Sensitivity**: MPs who seek to be effective in parliamentary work need to be gender sensitive.
  - When analyzing and implementing laws and policies, it is important to consider in which ways men and women will be affected, because more than likely this will be different.
  - It is also important to consult and engage both women and men in constituencies, and promote women as decision makers in order to instill confidence.

- Other ways in which to be a gender sensitive MP include identifying opportunities to promote gender equality, allocating adequate resources to address gender issues, monitoring commitments on achieving gender equality and using gender sensitive language.

The characteristics of a Member of Parliament encompass integrity, empathy, leadership, communication skills, adaptability, resilience, dedication to public service, global perspective, and a commitment to diversity and inclusivity. MPs that embody these characteristics are well-equipped to fulfill their responsibilities effectively, represent their constituents with integrity and compassion, and contribute positively to the governance and advancement of their nation.

"Tips for best parliamentarian"

Commitment to Public Service: Strong Knowledge Base: Effective Communication Skills: Collaboration and Consensus-Building: Analytical and Critical Thinking: Ethical Conduct and Integrity: Committee Engagement: Accessibility and Constituency Engagement: Adaptability and Resilience: Continuous Learning and Improvement:

Chapter 5
PERSONNEL MANAGEMENT

"Effective personnel management for an MP is not just about managing staff; it's about nurturing a team dedicated to serving constituents with integrity, efficiency, and compassion, ensuring that the office runs properly. It is as a beacon of public service and accountability."

Members of Parliament (MPs) play a crucial role in personnel management within their offices. Effective personnel management by MPs is essential for ensuring efficient operations, maintaining high standards of service to constituents, and upholding ethical practices in public office.

- Personnel management by MPs involves building and leading a competent team of staff who support them in their parliamentary duties and constituent service.
  - MPs typically hire parliamentary assistants, researchers, communications experts, and administrative staff to help them fulfill their responsibilities effectively.
  - It is crucial for MPs to select individuals with the necessary skills, expertise, and dedication to support their legislative work and serve the needs of constituents efficiently.
  - MPs are responsible for managing the performance and development of their staff. This includes providing clear

guidance and direction, setting expectations, and conducting regular performance evaluations to ensure accountability and productivity.

- MPs also have a duty to foster a positive work environment that promotes teamwork, professionalism, and mutual respect among staff members.
- MPs must adhere to ethical standards and transparency in personnel management.
- This involves fair and equitable treatment of staff, adherence to employment laws and regulations, and maintaining confidentiality where necessary.
- MPs should also ensure that their staff members receive adequate training and professional development opportunities to enhance their skills and knowledge.
- Effective communication is essential in personnel management by MPs. MPs should maintain open lines of communication with their staff, encouraging feedback, and addressing concerns promptly.
- Clear communication helps to clarify roles and responsibilities, align team efforts with strategic objectives, and foster a cohesive work environment where everyone feels valued and motivated.
- MPs also have a responsibility to promote diversity, equity, and inclusion within their offices.
- They should strive to create a workplace that reflects the diversity of their constituents and ensure that all individuals are treated fairly and respectfully, regardless of background or identity.
- MPs can demonstrate leadership in promoting inclusive practices and championing policies that advance equality and diversity both within their offices and in broader society.

Personnel management of a parliamentarian: Managing personnel as a parliamentarian involves overseeing a team of staff members who support various aspects of your parliamentary duties. For effective personnel management:

- **Role Clarification**: Clearly define roles and responsibilities for each staff member based on their expertise and the needs of your office. This includes administrative support, legislative research, communications, constituent services, and outreach.
- **Recruitment and Selection**: Hire staff members who are skilled, knowledgeable, and committed to public service. Conduct interviews and assess candidates based on their qualifications, experience, and alignment with your values and goals as a parliamentarian.
- **Training and Development**: Provide ongoing training and professional development opportunities to enhance the skills and knowledge of your staff. This could include workshops on parliamentary procedures, constituent relations, communication skills, and policy analysis.
- **Effective Communication**: Establish open and clear communication channels with your staff. Hold regular meetings to discuss priorities, provide updates on parliamentary activities, and solicit feedback on office operations and constituent concerns.
- **Team Collaboration**: Foster a collaborative and supportive work environment where staff members can work together cohesively to achieve common goals. Encourage teamwork, mutual respect, and recognition of individual contributions.
- **Performance Evaluation**: Conduct regular performance evaluations to assess staff members' progress, strengths, and areas for improvement. Provide constructive feedback, set goals for professional growth, and recognize outstanding performance.
- **Ethical Standards and Accountability**: Set high ethical standards for yourself and your staff in all aspects of parliamentary work.

Emphasize integrity, transparency, and accountability in handling constituent inquiries, managing office resources, and complying with parliamentary rules.

- **Constituent Engagement**: Ensure that staff members are responsive and attentive to the needs of constituents. Train them to provide courteous and timely responses to inquiries, resolve issues effectively, and maintain confidentiality when handling sensitive information.
- **Adaptability and Resilience**: Equip your staff with the skills to adapt to changing priorities, navigate complex situations, and respond flexibly to unexpected challenges in parliamentary work.
- **Work-Life Balance**: Promote a healthy work-life balance for your staff by respecting their personal time, encouraging breaks during busy periods, and fostering a supportive workplace culture that values well-being.
- By effectively managing personnel, parliamentarians can cultivate a productive and efficient office environment, enhance constituent service delivery, and ultimately fulfill their responsibilities effectively in serving the public.
- MPs can cultivate a motivated and cohesive team that supports their parliamentary work and constituency service, ultimately contributing to their effectiveness as representatives of the people.

Personnel managements of MP: Aspects of personnel management for MPs:

- **Recruitment and Hiring**: Identify staffing needs based on the workload and requirements of the parliamentary office and constituency. Recruit qualified candidates through job postings, referrals, and networking.
- **Training and Development**: Provide training and orientation for new staff members to familiarize them with their roles, responsibilities, and office procedures. Offer ongoing professional development opportunities to enhance their skills and knowledge.

- **Delegation of Responsibilities:** Delegate tasks and responsibilities effectively to ensure that workload is distributed appropriately among staff members. Clearly communicate expectations, priorities, and deadlines to facilitate efficient workflow.
- **Performance Management:** Establish performance expectations and objectives for staff members, and regularly assess their performance through feedback, evaluations, and performance reviews. Recognize and reward outstanding performance, and address any performance issues or concerns promptly and constructively.
- **Team Building and Collaboration:** Foster a positive and collaborative work environment among staff members by promoting teamwork, communication, and mutual respect. Encourage collaboration and synergy among team members to achieve common goals.
- **Conflict Resolution:** Address conflicts and interpersonal issues among staff members promptly and impartially. Act as a mediator or facilitator to resolve conflicts amicably and restore harmonious working relationships within the team.
- **Employee Well-being:** Prioritize the well-being and welfare of staff members by providing a supportive work environment, promoting work-life balance, and offering resources and support for physical and mental health.
- **Compliance and Legal Obligations:** Ensure compliance with relevant employment laws, regulations, and parliamentary rules governing personnel management. Stay informed about legal requirements and obligations related to employment, compensation, benefits, and workplace safety.
- **Communication and Feedback:** Maintain open and transparent communication channels with staff members, fostering a culture of trust, transparency, and collaboration. Encourage feedback, suggestions, and input from staff members to improve office operations and effectiveness.

- **Ethical Conduct**: Lead by example and uphold high ethical standards in all personnel management practices. Demonstrate integrity, fairness, and respect for the rights and dignity of staff members in all interactions and decisions.

- **Daily routine of a Member of Parliament:** The daily routine of a Member of Parliament (MP) can vary widely depending on factors such as parliamentary schedule, constituency commitments, and personal preferences. However, here's a generalized outline of what a typical day might look like for an MP:
    - **Morning Routine**:
        - MPs often start their day early to catch up on news and emails, and to prepare for the day ahead.
        - This may involve reading newspapers, briefing notes, and correspondence from constituents and colleagues.
    - **Constituency Work**:
        - MPs typically set aside time each day to attend to constituency matters and engage with constituents.
        - This may involve meeting with constituents, local community groups, or businesses to address their concerns, advocate for their interests, and provide assistance with various issues.
    - **Meetings and Engagements:**
        - MPs often have meetings scheduled with colleagues, party members, stakeholders, and lobbyists to discuss policy matters, legislative priorities, and political strategy.
        - They may also attend events, fundraisers, and public appearances within their constituency or elsewhere.
    - **Research and Preparation:**
        - MPs spend time researching legislative proposals, policy issues, and constituency concerns to inform their decision-making and advocacy efforts.

  - This could involve reviewing briefing materials, consulting with experts, and drafting speeches or position papers on specific topics.
- **Media and Communications:**
  - MPs may engage with the media through interviews, press conferences, and social media updates to communicate their positions, respond to inquiries, and raise awareness about important issues.
  - They may also draft press releases, newsletters, and other communication materials to keep constituents informed about their work.
- **Administrative Tasks:**
  - MPs have administrative responsibilities related to managing their office, staff, and budget.
  - This could include reviewing and signing documents, managing correspondence, and overseeing office operations.
- **Networking and Professional Development:**
  - MPs may attend networking events, seminars, and training sessions to build relationships, enhance their skills, and stay informed about developments in politics and policy.
- **Evening Routine:**
  - MPs often work late into the evening, attending evening sessions of Parliament, meetings, or events.
  - They may also use this time to catch up on administrative tasks, correspondence, and planning for the next day.
- **Personal Time:**
  - Balancing work with personal time is important for MPs to maintain their well-being and effectiveness.

- While the schedule of an MP can be demanding, finding time for relaxation, exercise, and hobbies is essential for maintaining a healthy work-life balance.

A DAY IN THE LIFE OF AN ELECTED MEMBER:

- Read and prepare for the upcoming week's meetings
- Vote in various decision-making meetings and committees
- Engage with the public to hear their views
- Attend events like public meetings, school prize giving, citizenship ceremonies, or the opening of a new park.
- Represent the council at community and cultural events like New Year, Diwali and other festivals
- Take part in community activities, like a working bee for a local stream regeneration project.
- On top of this, there will be responsibilities that relate to your specific role.

In conclusion, personnel management by Members of Parliament is a critical aspect of their role as public representatives. By building and leading effective teams, managing performance and development, upholding ethical standards, fostering communication, and promoting diversity and inclusion, MPs can ensure that their offices operate efficiently and effectively in serving the needs of constituents and contributing positively to the governance of the nation.

Chapter 6
Time Management

"Time management for MPs requires a delicate balance between legislative duties, constituency work, and personal commitments. Effective MPs prioritize tasks, delegate when necessary, and maintain a disciplined schedule to serve their constituents while fulfilling their responsibilities in parliament."

Time management encompasses various practices and techniques aimed at optimizing how you utilize your time to achieve your goals, increase productivity, and maintain a healthy work-life balance. Effective time management requires self-awareness, discipline, and adaptability. By implementing these principles and techniques, you can make the most of your time, increase productivity, and achieve your goals more efficiently Main components of effective time management are:

- **Setting Goals**: Clearly define your short-term and long-term goals, both personal and professional. Having specific objectives helps you prioritize tasks and allocate time effectively.
- **Prioritization**: Identify tasks and activities based on their importance and urgency. Prioritize high-impact tasks that contribute directly to your goals and address time-sensitive matters first.

- **Planning**: Create a structured plan for how you will use your time, whether daily, weekly, or monthly. Break down larger projects into smaller, actionable steps and allocate time for each task accordingly.
- **Scheduling**: Use calendars, planners, or digital scheduling tools to organize your time and commitments. Schedule appointments, meetings, and deadlines, and block out dedicated time for focused work, breaks, and relaxation.
- **Time Tracking**: Monitor how you spend your time to identify patterns, inefficiencies, and opportunities for improvement. Use time tracking apps or techniques to measure your productivity and assess where adjustments are needed.
- **Avoiding Procrastination**: Combat procrastination by breaking tasks into smaller, more manageable parts, setting deadlines, and eliminating distractions. Practice self-discipline and develop strategies to overcome procrastination tendencies.
- **Delegation and Outsourcing**: Delegate tasks that can be done by others or consider outsourcing non-essential activities. Focus your time and energy on tasks that align with your strengths and priorities.
- **Batching Similar Tasks**: Group similar tasks together and tackle them in batches to minimize context switching and maximize efficiency. This approach can reduce cognitive load and improve productivity.
- **Setting Boundaries**: Establish boundaries around your time and energy to prevent over commitment and burnout. Learn to say no to non-essential requests and protect time for personal activities, rest, and relaxation.
- **Continuous Improvement**: Regularly evaluate your time management practices and identify areas for improvement. Experiment with new techniques, tools, and strategies to optimize your workflow and achieve better results.

- **Manage Your Time Well**: Organizing, prioritizing and demonstrating commitment to issues of importance are key in the management of an MP's time. The way in which MPs manage their time reflects on them as individuals. The time in the legislative assembly is limited and should be used wisely in dealing with issues of importance to MPs and their constituents. Every MP also has a personal life that demands time and it is equally important to attend to non-legislative responsibilities so as to maintain a balance between work and private life. Time management is crucial for Members of Parliament (MPs) who have demanding schedules and multiple responsibilities. Here are some tips for effective time management:

  - **Prioritize Tasks**: Identify your most important tasks and priorities each day. Focus on activities that align with your goals and responsibilities as an MP, such as legislative work, constituency engagement, and policy advocacy.

  - **Use a Calendar or Planner**: Keep a detailed calendar or planner to schedule your daily, weekly, and monthly activities. Block out time for parliamentary sessions, committee meetings, constituency visits, and other commitments.

  - **Set Realistic Goals**: Set realistic goals and deadlines for completing tasks. Break down larger projects into smaller, manageable tasks and allocate time to work on them incrementally.

  - **Manage Constituency Work**: Allocate specific time slots each day or week to address constituency matters, such as meeting with constituents, attending community events, and responding to emails and phone calls.

  - **Delegate Tasks**: Delegate tasks to staff members, volunteers, or interns whenever possible. Trusting others to handle routine tasks allows you to focus on higher-priority activities that require your expertise and attention.

  - **Limit Distractions**: Minimize distractions and interruptions during focused work periods. Turn off notifications, close unnecessary tabs or applications, and create a conducive work environment to maximize productivity.

- **Batch Similar Tasks**: Group similar tasks together and complete them in batches to improve efficiency. Schedule back-to-back meetings, phone calls, or administrative tasks to minimize context switching and save time.
- **Practice Time Blocking**: Use time blocking techniques to allocate specific time blocks for different types of activities throughout the day. This helps create structure and ensures that important tasks receive dedicated attention.
- **Take Breaks and Rest**: Prioritize self-care and well-being by scheduling regular breaks and allowing time for rest and relaxation. Taking breaks helps prevent burnout, improves focus and productivity, and enhances overall mental and physical health.
- **Review and Reflect**: Regularly review your schedule and reflect on your time management practices. Identify areas where you can improve efficiency, adjust priorities as needed, and learn from your experiences to optimize your time management skills over time.

MPs can effectively balance their parliamentary duties, constituency work, and personal responsibilities, allowing them to maximize their effectiveness and make the most of their time in office

- **Time management for constituency:** Time management for constituency work is crucial for elected representatives to effectively balance their responsibilities, including legislative duties, constituent services, and personal commitments. Here's how high-tech solutions can help in managing time effectively:
- **Calendar and Scheduling Tools**:
    - Utilize digital calendar apps like Google Calendar or Microsoft Outlook to schedule and organize meetings, events, and constituency engagements.

  - Set reminders and notifications to stay on track and avoid missing important appointments or deadlines.
- **Task Management Apps:**
  - Use task management tools to create to-do lists, prioritize tasks, and track progress on constituency-related projects and initiatives.
  - Break down larger tasks into smaller, manageable steps to increase productivity and maintain focus.
- **Communication Efficiency:**
  - Employ email management software or plugins to organize and prioritize incoming emails from constituents, stakeholders, and colleagues.
  - Set up email filters and folders to categorize messages based on urgency and relevance, ensuring timely responses to critical inquiries.
- **Virtual Meetings and Teleconferencing:**
  - Conduct virtual meetings with constituents, community groups, and stakeholders using video conferencing platforms like Zoom, Microsoft Teams, or Skype.
  - Reduce travel time and logistical challenges by hosting remote meetings, particularly for constituents who may reside in remote or inaccessible areas.
- **Constituent Relationship Management (CRM):**
  - Implement CRM software to manage constituent interactions, track inquiries, and maintain a centralized database of constituent contact information and feedback.
  - Use CRM tools to categorize constituents based on their interests, concerns, and engagement levels, enabling personalized outreach and targeted communication efforts.

- **Mobile Constituent Services:**
  - Develop a mobile app or web portal where constituents can submit requests for assistance, report issues, and provide feedback on local issues and government services.
  - Enable push notifications and alerts to notify constituents of important updates, events, and announcements relevant to the constituency.
- **Social Media Management:**
  - Utilize social media management platforms like to schedule posts, monitor engagement, and respond to messages and comments across multiple social media channels.
  - Establish a content calendar to plan and coordinate social media outreach efforts, ensuring consistent and timely communication with constituents.
- **Automation and Workflow Optimization:**
  - Automate repetitive tasks and workflows using workflow automation tools, freeing up time for more high-value activities.
  - Streamline constituency-related processes such as casework management, event planning, and outreach campaigns through automation and integration with other systems.

By leveraging high-tech solutions for time management, elected representatives can optimize their workflow, increase productivity, and allocate more time and attention to serving the needs of their constituents effectively. It's essential to regularly evaluate and adjust time management strategies based on changing priorities and circumstances to ensure optimal performance and work-life balance.

- **Time management in Parliamentary responsibilities:** Time management in parliamentary responsibilities is essential for elected representatives to effectively fulfill their legislative duties, participate in debates, attend committee meetings, and engage in constituency work. Here's how high-tech solutions can aid in managing time efficiently:

- **Digital Calendars and Scheduling Tools**:
  - Use digital calendar apps or scheduling tools to organize parliamentary sessions, committee meetings, and other legislative activities.
  - Set reminders and alerts for important deadlines, debates, and voting sessions to ensure timely attendance and participation.
- **Remote Participation and Virtual Meetings:**
  - Take advantage of video conferencing platforms to participate in parliamentary sessions and committee meetings remotely, reducing travel time and logistical challenges.
  - Engage in virtual debates and discussions on legislative matters, leveraging technology to contribute to parliamentary proceedings from anywhere with an internet connection.
- **Document Management Systems:**
  - Utilize document management software to access and review legislative documents, bills, reports, and briefing materials electronically.
  - Collaborate with parliamentary colleagues and staff by sharing and annotating documents digitally, streamlining the legislative review process.
- **Speechwriting and Research Tools:**
  - Use speechwriting software or productivity tools like Microsoft OneNote to draft speeches, prepare talking points, and conduct research on parliamentary topics and policy issues.
  - Leverage online databases, research repositories, and academic journals to gather information and evidence to support parliamentary debates and positions.

- **Electronic Voting Systems:**
  - Participate in parliamentary votes using electronic voting systems, which facilitate efficient and accurate voting procedures during legislative sessions.
  - Use mobile voting apps or electronic keypads to cast votes on bills, amendments, and resolutions, eliminating the need for manual paper-based voting processes.
- **Constituency Engagement and Communication:**
  - Maintain regular communication with constituents through digital channels such as email, social media, and online forums.
  - Use constituency management software or CRM tools to track constituent inquiries, casework, and feedback, ensuring responsive and personalized outreach.
- **Workflow Automation and Integration:**
  - Automate administrative tasks and workflows related to parliamentary responsibilities, such as scheduling meetings, drafting correspondence, and managing legislative documents.
  - Integrate parliamentary management systems with other tools and platforms used for constituency work, enabling seamless coordination and information sharing between parliamentary and constituency offices.
- **Time Blocking and Prioritization:**
  - Allocate dedicated blocks of time in the parliamentary schedule for specific tasks and responsibilities, such as committee meetings, constituency surgeries, and legislative research.
  - Prioritize activities based on their urgency and importance, focusing on high-impact tasks that align with strategic objectives and legislative priorities.
- **Time management for personality:** Time management is essential for maintaining a healthy balance between work, personal

life, and self-care. Here's how high-tech solutions can aid in managing time effectively for your personal life:

- **Digital Calendar and Scheduling Apps**:
    - Use digital calendar apps like Google Calendar or Apple Calendar to schedule personal activities, appointments, and leisure time.
    - Set reminders and notifications for important events, birthdays, and personal commitments to stay organized and on track.
- **Task Management and To-Do List Apps:**
    - Utilize task management apps to create to-do lists and prioritize tasks for your personal projects and activities.
    - Break down larger tasks into smaller, actionable steps to make them more manageable and less overwhelming.
- **Self-Care and Wellness Apps:**
    - Download self-care and wellness apps that offer guided meditation, mindfulness exercises, and relaxation techniques to reduce stress and promote mental well-being.
    - Use fitness tracking apps to set exercise goals, track your workouts, and monitor your progress towards achieving a healthy lifestyle.
- **Digital Journaling and Reflection:**
    - Start a digital journal or use journaling apps like Day One or Journey to record your thoughts, experiences, and reflections on your personal life journey.
    - Schedule regular time for self-reflection and introspection to gain insights into your values, goals, and aspirations.
- **Health and Nutrition Tracking:**
    - Track your dietary habits, calorie intake, and hydration levels using nutrition tracking apps to maintain a balanced and healthy diet.

  - Set reminders for meal times, water breaks, and healthy snacks to fuel your body and maintain energy levels throughout the day.

- **Digital Detox and Screen Time Management:**
  - Use screen time management features on your devices or install apps like Freedom or Moment to limit your screen time and reduce digital distractions.
  - Schedule regular breaks from electronic devices to disconnect, recharge, and engage in offline activities that promote relaxation and well-being.
- **Financial Planning and Budgeting:**
  - Manage your finances and track your expenses using budgeting apps like Mint or YNAB to stay within your budget and achieve your financial goals.
  - Set financial goals and milestones for saving, investing, and debt repayment, and monitor your progress towards achieving them.
- **Learning and Personal Development:**
  - Dedicate time for personal growth and lifelong learning by enrolling in online courses, listening to podcasts, or reading e-books on topics of interest.
  - Use language learning apps to develop new skills and broaden your horizons.

By incorporating high-tech solutions into your personal time management strategy, you can enhance productivity, prioritize self-care, and achieve a better work-life balance. Remember to adapt your time management approach based on your individual needs, preferences, and lifestyle priorities.

- **Time management for success:** Time management is crucial for achieving success in any endeavor. Here's how high-tech solutions can help you manage your time effectively to reach your goals:

- **Digital Calendar and Scheduling Tools**:
    - Use digital calendar apps like Google Calendar or Microsoft Outlook to plan and organize your schedule.
    - Schedule your most important tasks and activities during your peak productivity hours.
    - Set reminders and notifications to keep you on track and ensure you don't miss important deadlines.
- **Task Management Apps:**
    - Utilize task management tools such as to create to-do lists and prioritize tasks.
    - Break down larger projects into smaller, actionable tasks to make them more manageable.
    - Set deadlines for each task to create a sense of urgency and accountability.
- **Time Tracking Software:**
    - Use time tracking software like to monitor how you spend your time.
    - Identify time-wasting activities and areas where you can improve efficiency.
    - Analyze your time logs to make adjustments and optimize your schedule.
- **Automation and Productivity Tools:**
    - Automate repetitive tasks using productivity tools to save time and reduce manual effort.
    - Use keyboard shortcuts and productivity extensions to streamline your workflow and minimize distractions.
    - Leverage AI-powered tools for email management, document processing, and data analysis to increase efficiency.

- **Focus and Distraction Management:**
  - Use website blockers to limit your time on distracting websites and social media platforms.
  - Practice time-blocking techniques to allocate dedicated periods for focused work and minimize interruptions.
  - Create a conducive work environment free from distractions to help you maintain focus and concentration.
- **Goal Setting and Planning:**
  - Set clear, specific goals for what you want to achieve and establish a timeline for reaching them.
  - Break down your goals into actionable steps and create a plan for how you will accomplish them.
  - Regularly review your progress and make adjustments as needed to stay on track towards achieving your objectives.
- **Self-Care and Balance:**
  - Prioritize self-care activities such as exercise, meditation, and relaxation to maintain physical and mental well-being.
  - Schedule regular breaks and downtime to recharge and prevent burnout.
  - Strive for a healthy work-life balance by setting boundaries and allocating time for personal activities and relationships.
- **Continuous Learning and Improvement:**
  - Dedicate time for ongoing learning and skill development to stay competitive and adapt to changing circumstances.
  - Invest in online courses, workshops, or certifications to enhance your knowledge and expertise in your field.
  - Seek feedback from mentors, colleagues, or peers to identify areas for improvement and refine your time management strategies.

By adopting effective time management practices, you can maximize your productivity, minimize distractions, and make the most of your time to achieve success in your personal and professional endeavors. Remember to prioritize your goals, stay disciplined, and continuously evaluate and adjust your approach to optimize your time management efforts.

- **Time management for development:** Time management is crucial for personal and professional development, allowing you to allocate time effectively to activities that foster growth and progress. Here's how high-tech solutions can aid in managing time for development:
- **Goal Setting and Planning Apps**:
  - Use goal-setting apps to define clear objectives for your development journey.
  - Break down long-term goals into smaller, achievable milestones and create action plans to work towards them systematically.
- **Learning and Skill Development Platforms:**
  - Leverage online learning platforms in learning to access a wide range of courses, tutorials, and resources.
  - Set aside dedicated time in your schedule for learning and skill development, and track your progress as you acquire new knowledge and abilities.
- **Time Tracking and Productivity Apps:**
  - Use time tracking apps like to monitor how you spend your time and identify opportunities for learning and growth.
  - Analyze your time logs to ensure that you allocate sufficient time to activities that contribute to your development goals.
- **Reading and Content Consumption Tools:**
  - Utilize e-book readers and audiobook apps like Kindle, Audible, or Apple Books to access educational and motivational content on the go.

    - Create reading lists and set reading goals to cultivate a habit of continuous learning and personal growth.
- **Journaling and Reflection Apps:**
    - Start a digital journal using apps to reflect on your experiences, insights, and lessons learned.
    - Schedule regular time for self-reflection and introspection to gain clarity on your values, aspirations, and areas for improvement.
- **Networking and Mentorship Platforms:**
    - Join professional networking platforms to connect with peers, mentors, and industry experts.
    - Participate in networking events, webinars, and workshops to expand your knowledge, build relationships, and gain valuable insights from others.
- **Project Management and Task Tracking Tools:**
    - Use project management software to plan and track development projects and initiatives.
    - Break down complex projects into manageable tasks, set deadlines, and prioritize activities based on their impact on your growth and development.
- **Feedback and Accountability Systems:**
    - Seek feedback from mentors, coaches, or peers to evaluate your progress and identify areas for improvement.
    - Establish accountability mechanisms, such as accountability partners or mastermind groups, to stay committed to your development goals and track your progress over time.

By integrating high-tech solutions into your time management strategy for development, you can optimize your learning process, stay focused on your goals, and make continuous progress towards personal and professional growth. Remember to be consistent, disciplined, and adaptable as you navigate your development journey and strive to reach your full potential.

Chapter 7
Relationship Management

"Effective relationship management for MPs involves fostering trust, understanding, and collaboration with constituents, colleagues, and stakeholders. By actively listening, empathizing, and engaging with diverse perspectives, MPs can build bridges and drive positive change for their communities and country."

Members of Parliament (MPs) are entrusted with the responsibility of representing their constituents and engaging in relationships that span from local communities to international diplomatic arenas. Effective relationship management by MPs is crucial for fostering collaboration, advocating for constituents' interests, and contributing to effective governance. MPs must cultivate strong relationships with their constituents. This involves actively listening to their concerns, maintaining open lines of communication, and being accessible and responsive to their needs. MPs often hold constituency surgeries, attend local events, and engage with community organizations to stay connected with the pulse of their electorate. By building trust and understanding with constituents, MPs can effectively represent their interests and priorities in the legislative process.

- **MPs relationship within parliamentary settings:**
    - They collaborate with fellow MPs across party lines to build consensus, negotiate policy decisions, and advance legislation that benefits the nation.

- Relationship management by MPs extends to interactions with government officials, stakeholders, and interest groups.
- MPs act as advocates for their constituents' interests in discussions with ministers, government agencies, and organizations.
- By forging constructive relationships with key stakeholders,
- MPs can influence policy outcomes, secure resources for their constituencies, and address systemic issues affecting their communities.
- MPs play a role in international relationship management.
- Through diplomatic engagements and participation in international forums, MPs represent their country's interests on the global stage.
- They contribute to discussions on global challenges such as climate change, human rights, and international security, promoting cooperation and collaboration with international partners to achieve shared goals.
- Ethical conduct and transparency are essential in relationship management by MPs. MPs must uphold integrity in their interactions, ensuring that their decisions and actions are guided by principles of accountability and public trust.
- Transparency in relationship management involves disclosing conflicts of interest, adhering to ethical standards, and maintaining honesty and fairness in all engagements.
- Effective communication is a cornerstone of relationship management by MPs.
- MPs must articulate their constituents' concerns persuasively, convey legislative priorities clearly, and engage in respectful dialogue with diverse stakeholders.
- By fostering constructive communication channels,

- MPs can build consensus, resolve conflicts, and achieve positive outcomes for their constituents and the broader community.
- By focusing on these aspects of relationship management, you can cultivate strong, meaningful connections with others, whether in personal or professional contexts.
- Building and nurturing positive relationships contributes to your overall well-being, success, and fulfillment in life.
- Relationship management involves nurturing and maintaining healthy, positive relationships with others, whether in personal or professional settings.

COMPONENTS OF RELATIONSHIP MANAGEMENT:

- **Communication**: Effective communication is essential for building and maintaining relationships. Listen actively, express yourself clearly, and show empathy and understanding towards others' perspectives.
- **Trust Building**: Establish trust and credibility by being reliable, honest, and transparent in your interactions. Keep promises, maintain confidentiality, and demonstrate integrity in your actions.
- **Empathy and Emotional Intelligence**: Cultivate empathy and emotional intelligence to understand others' feelings, needs, and concerns. Practice active listening, validate emotions, and show empathy in your interactions.
- **Conflict Resolution**: Address conflicts and disagreements constructively by seeking common ground, focusing on solutions, and maintaining respect for others' viewpoints. Use effective communication and negotiation skills to resolve conflicts peacefully.
- **Networking**: Build and maintain professional networks by connecting with colleagues, peers, mentors, and industry contacts. Attend networking events, join professional organizations, and cultivate relationships through mutual support and collaboration.

- **Client and Customer Relations**: Provide excellent customer service and client support by understanding their needs, addressing their concerns promptly, and exceeding their expectations. Build rapport and trust to foster long-term relationships with clients and customers.
- **Team Collaboration**: Foster teamwork and collaboration within teams and organizations by promoting open communication, mutual respect, and shared goals. Encourage diversity of thought and celebrate achievements together as a team.
- **Personal Boundaries**: Respect personal boundaries and establish healthy boundaries in relationships to maintain balance and prevent overextension. Communicate your needs and limitations clearly, and respect others' boundaries as well.
- **Feedback and Recognition**: Provide constructive feedback and recognition to acknowledge others' contributions and encourage their growth and development. Show appreciation for their efforts and achievements to strengthen relationships.
- **Conflict Resolution**: Address conflicts and disagreements constructively by seeking common ground, focusing on solutions, and maintaining respect for others' viewpoints. Use effective communication and negotiation skills to resolve conflicts peacefully.
- **Adaptability and Flexibility**: Be adaptable and flexible in your approach to relationships, considering others' preferences, styles, and cultural differences. Adapt your communication and behavior to build rapport and mutual understanding.
- **Relationship management with electorate:** Relationship management with the electorate is essential for elected officials to effectively represent their constituents and maintain their trust and support.
- By actively engaging with and listening to the electorate, elected officials can build trust, foster collaboration, and effectively represent the interests of their constituents.

- Strong relationships with the electorate are essential for effective governance and democratic accountability.

RELATIONSHIP MANAGEMENT WITH THE ELECTORATE:

- **Accessibility and Availability**: Be accessible and available to constituents by holding regular office hours, hosting town hall meetings, and attending community events. Make yourself approachable and responsive to constituents' concerns and inquiries.
- **Active Listening**: Listen attentively to constituents' needs, feedback, and concerns. Show empathy and understanding, and demonstrate that you value their input and perspectives.
- **Transparent Communication**: Communicate openly and transparently with constituents about your actions, decisions, and policy positions. Provide clear explanations and rationale for your stance on various issues.
- **Community Engagement**: Engage with the local community through outreach efforts, volunteer activities, and participation in civic events. Build rapport and trust by demonstrating your commitment to the well-being of the community.
- **Constituent Services**: Provide high-quality constituent services by assisting constituents with issues related to government services, benefits, and resources. Be proactive in addressing constituents' needs and resolving their concerns.
- **Feedback Mechanisms**: Establish feedback mechanisms, such as surveys, town hall meetings, and online platforms, to solicit input from constituents on legislative priorities, policy proposals, and community initiatives.
- **Accountability and Follow-up**: Hold yourself accountable to constituents by following through on promises, commitments, and campaign pledges. Keep constituents informed about your progress and actions taken on their behalf.

- **Transparency in Decision-making**: Be transparent about the decision-making process and factors influencing your policy positions and votes. Engage constituents in meaningful dialogue and debate to ensure their voices are heard and considered.
- **Adaptability and Flexibility**: Be adaptable and responsive to changing needs and priorities within the electorate. Adjust your approach and initiatives based on feedback and evolving community dynamics.
- **Building Coalitions and Partnerships**: Collaborate with community organizations, advocacy groups, and other stakeholders to address shared concerns and advance common goals. Build coalitions and partnerships to amplify your impact and effectiveness as a representative.
- **Relationship management by a politician:** Relationship management is crucial for politicians to build trust, foster collaboration, and effectively represent their constituents. By prioritizing relationship management and implementing these strategies, politicians can build strong, mutually beneficial relationships with constituents, colleagues, and stakeholders, enhancing their effectiveness and impact in the political arena. Main aspects of relationship management for politicians:
    - **Building Trust**: Trust is the foundation of effective relationships. Politicians should be honest, transparent, and reliable in their interactions with constituents, colleagues, and stakeholders. Upholding ethical standards and delivering on promises helps build and maintain trust over time.
    - **Active Listening**: Effective communication begins with active listening. Politicians should listen attentively to the concerns, needs, and perspectives of constituents, colleagues, and stakeholders. Demonstrating empathy and understanding builds rapport and fosters meaningful relationships.
    - **Engagement and Accessibility**: Politicians should be accessible and approachable to constituents, making themselves available for meetings, town hall events, and community gatherings. Regular engagement helps politicians stay connected with constituents, understand their priorities, and address their concerns effectively.

- **Networking and Relationship Building**: Politicians should actively network and build relationships with colleagues, community leaders, advocacy groups, businesses, and other stakeholders. Building a strong network of relationships helps politicians collaborate on shared goals, leverage resources, and navigate political dynamics effectively.
- **Consensus Building**: Politics often requires compromise and consensus building. Politicians should seek common ground, build bridges across divides, and work collaboratively with colleagues and stakeholders to find solutions to complex issues. Building consensus fosters cooperation and enables politicians to achieve shared objectives.
- **Conflict Resolution**: Conflicts and disagreements are inevitable in politics. Politicians should approach conflicts constructively, seeking to understand different perspectives and find mutually acceptable solutions. Effective conflict resolution skills help maintain relationships and prevent escalation of disputes.
- **Follow-Up and Accountability**: Politicians should follow up on commitments, promises, and requests made to constituents and stakeholders. Demonstrating accountability and delivering results reinforces trust and strengthens relationships over time.
- **Personal Branding**: Politicians should cultivate a positive personal brand based on authenticity, integrity, and credibility. Consistently demonstrating these qualities in their actions and communications helps politicians build a strong reputation and earn the trust of constituents and stakeholders.
- **Adaptability and Flexibility**: Political landscapes are dynamic and constantly evolving. Politicians should be adaptable and flexible in their approach to relationship management, adjusting their strategies and tactics as needed to navigate changing circumstances and priorities.

- **Long-Term Relationship Building**: Effective relationship management is not just about short-term transactions; it's about building enduring connections and partnerships over the long term. Politicians should invest time and effort in nurturing relationships, maintaining regular contact, and demonstrating ongoing commitment to constituents and stakeholders.
- **Relationship with party members:** Building and maintaining positive relationships with party members is crucial for political success and effective party leadership. By prioritizing relationship management with party members, party leaders can foster a sense of belonging, loyalty, and engagement within the party community. Strong relationships with party members are essential for organizational cohesion, grassroots mobilization, and electoral success.

STRATEGIES FOR RELATIONSHIP MANAGEMENT WITH PARTY MEMBERS:

- **Communication**: Foster open and transparent communication with party members through regular updates, newsletters, and meetings. Keep members informed about party activities, initiatives, and decisions.
- **Accessibility**: Be accessible and approachable to party members by holding regular office hours, town hall meetings, and informal gatherings. Listen to their concerns, feedback, and ideas, and demonstrate that their input is valued.
- **Inclusivity and Engagement**: Ensure inclusivity and diversity within the party by actively engaging members from different backgrounds, perspectives, and demographics. Encourage participation in party activities, committees, and decision-making processes.
- **Recognition and Appreciation**: Recognize and appreciate the contributions of party members through public acknowledgment, awards, and recognition ceremonies. Show gratitude for their efforts and commitment to the party's mission and values.

- **Empowerment and Leadership Development**: Empower party members to take on leadership roles and responsibilities within the party. Provide opportunities for skill development, training, and mentorship to nurture future leaders and activists.
- **Conflict Resolution**: Address conflicts and disagreements within the party promptly and constructively. Facilitate dialogue and mediation to resolve disputes and foster unity and cohesion among members.
- **Transparency and Accountability**: Maintain transparency in party decision-making processes and governance structures. Ensure accountability to party members by upholding ethical standards, adhering to party rules and regulations, and promoting integrity and fairness.
- **Collaboration and Teamwork**: Foster a culture of collaboration and teamwork within the party, where members work together towards common goals and shared values. Encourage cooperation and mutual support among members to maximize the party's effectiveness and impact.
- **Feedback Mechanisms**: Establish feedback mechanisms, such as surveys, suggestion boxes, or online forums, to solicit input from party members on party policies, strategies, and priorities. Act on feedback and demonstrate responsiveness to members' concerns and preferences.
- **Celebration of Successes**: Celebrate successes, milestones, and achievements within the party community. Recognize individual and collective accomplishments, and use them as opportunities to build morale and camaraderie among party members.
  - **Constituency relationship management**: Refers to the practice of building and maintaining positive relationships with constituents, particularly for elected officials or representatives. Effective constituency relationship management is crucial for ensuring that constituents feel heard, represented, and supported by their elected representatives. By prioritizing constituency relationship

management, elected officials can strengthen their connection with constituents, enhance public trust and confidence, and effectively represent the interests of the communities they serve.

- **Accessibility**: Make yourself accessible to constituents by holding regular office hours, town hall meetings, and public forums. Respond promptly to constituent inquiries, concerns, and requests for assistance.
- **Active Listening**: Listen attentively to constituents' needs, feedback, and concerns. Show empathy and understanding, and demonstrate that you value their perspectives and input.
- **Responsive Communication**: Communicate openly and transparently with constituents about your actions, decisions, and legislative priorities. Provide clear explanations and updates on issues that affect the constituency.
- **Constituent Services**: Provide high-quality constituent services by assisting constituents with issues related to government services, benefits, and resources. Advocate on behalf of constituents to address their concerns and navigate bureaucratic processes.
- **Community Engagement**: Engage with the local community through outreach efforts, volunteer activities, and participation in civic events. Build relationships with community leaders, organizations, and stakeholders to better understand the needs and priorities of the constituency.
- **Feedback Mechanisms**: Establish channels for constituents to provide feedback on legislative issues, policy proposals, and community initiatives. Use surveys, town hall meetings, and online platforms to solicit input and gauge public opinion.
- **Accountability and Transparency**: Hold yourself accountable to constituents by keeping promises, following through on commitments, and being transparent about your

actions and decisions. Be honest about the challenges and limitations you face as a representative.

- **Local Representation**: Serve as a strong advocate for the interests and priorities of the constituency at the local, regional, and national levels. Champion policies and initiatives that benefit the community and address its unique needs and concerns.
- **Relationship Building**: Build rapport and trust with constituents by demonstrating genuine care and concern for their well-being. Show appreciation for their support and engagement, and cultivate long-term relationships based on mutual respect and trust.
- **Continuous Engagement**: Maintain ongoing communication and engagement with constituents beyond election cycles. Keep constituents informed about your work as their representative and seek opportunities to involve them in the democratic process.

- **Relationship management for winning election as MP:** Winning an election as a Member of Parliament (MP) requires building strong relationships with various stakeholders, including constituents, party members, volunteers, donors, and community leaders. By prioritizing relationship management across these key stakeholder groups, you can build a strong support base, mobilize resources effectively, and increase your chances of winning an MP election. Strong relationships built during the campaign can also lay the foundation for successful governance and effective representation once elected. Mentioned below are points for winning an MP election:
  - **Constituency Engagement**:
    - Prioritize building relationships with constituents by actively engaging with them through door-to-door canvassing, town hall meetings, and community events.

  - Listen to their concerns, understand their needs, and demonstrate empathy and commitment to addressing their issues if elected.
- **Party Members and Volunteers:**
  - Cultivate strong relationships with party members and volunteers by involving them in campaign activities, organizing training sessions, and recognizing their contributions.
  - Provide opportunities for party members to participate in decision-making processes and shape campaign strategies.
- **Donors and Fundraisers:**
  - Develop relationships with donors and fundraisers who support your campaign financially. Maintain regular communication, express gratitude for their contributions, and keep them informed about the progress of the campaign.
  - Seek to build long-term partnerships with donors beyond the election cycle, demonstrating transparency and accountability in how campaign funds are utilized.
- **Community Leaders and Influencers:**
  - Build alliances with community leaders, influencers, and endorsers who can amplify your message and mobilize support within their networks.
  - Engage in dialogue with community organizations, religious leaders, and advocacy groups to understand their priorities and build coalitions around shared interests.
- **Media and Press Relations:**
  - Establish relationships with local media outlets, journalists, and reporters to generate positive coverage and visibility for your campaign.
  - Provide timely and newsworthy updates, respond promptly to media inquiries, and cultivate a professional and cooperative relationship with the press.

- **Digital Engagement and Social Media:**
    - Leverage social media platforms to connect with voters, share your message, and mobilize supporters. Engage in online conversations, respond to comments and messages, and humanize your campaign through behind-the-scenes content.
    - Build relationships with online influencers, bloggers, and social media personalities who can help amplify your campaign's reach and impact.
- **Grassroots Organizing and Canvassing:**
    - Recruit and train a dedicated team of volunteers to engage in grassroots organizing and canvassing efforts. Foster a sense of camaraderie and teamwork among volunteers, and recognize their efforts through incentives and appreciation.
- **Ethical Campaigning:**
    - Conduct your campaign with integrity, honesty, and respect for your opponents and the electoral process. Avoid negative campaigning and focus on articulating your vision and platform for the constituency.
    - Uphold ethical standards in fundraising, advertising, and voter outreach, and maintain transparency in all campaign activities.
- **Post-Election Follow-Up:**
    - After winning the election, continue to nurture and strengthen the relationships you've built with constituents, supporters, and stakeholders.
    - Fulfill your campaign promises, remain accessible to constituents, and keep them informed about your work as their elected representative.

Relationship management is a critical aspect of the role of Members of Parliament. By cultivating strong relationships with constituents, collaborating with colleagues, advocating for interests, engaging with stakeholders, representing national interests internationally, and upholding ethical standards, MPs can effectively fulfill their responsibilities as public representatives.

Chapter 8
COMMUNICATION, & SPEECH DELIVERY

"Effective communication is not just about speaking, but about connecting. It's the art of crafting words that resonate with empathy, clarity, and conviction, ensuring every message leaves a lasting impact on hearts and minds.

Communication and speech delivery are integral aspects of the role of Members of Parliament (MPs). As public representatives, MPs must master the art of communication to articulate their constituents' concerns, advocate for policies, and contribute meaningfully to legislative debates. The ability to communicate effectively enhances their influence, fosters transparency, and strengthens democratic engagement.

- MPs engage in various forms of communication to connect with their constituents.
- They use speeches, newsletters, social media, and public events to inform constituents about legislative developments, government policies, and local initiatives.
- By maintaining open lines of communication, MPs ensure that constituents are well-informed and engaged in the democratic process, fostering trust and accountability.
- MPs must possess strong speech delivery skills to effectively convey their messages in parliamentary debates and public forums.

- Speech delivery involves clarity, coherence, and persuasiveness in presenting arguments and advocating for positions on legislative matters.
- MPs use their speeches to influence opinions, build consensus, and mobilize support for policies that address pressing issues and benefit society.
- Effective speech delivery by MPs involves tailoring messages to resonate with diverse audiences
- MPs must consider the interests, values, and concerns of different demographic groups within their constituencies.
- By adapting their language and approach, MPs can effectively communicate with constituents from various backgrounds and perspectives, ensuring that their messages resonate and are understood.
- MPs participate in parliamentary debates where effective communication is essential for deliberating on legislation, scrutinizing government actions, and holding officials accountable.
- MPs engage in constructive dialogue, present evidence-based arguments, and challenge opposing viewpoints to contribute to informed decision-making and legislative outcomes.
- Ethical considerations are paramount in communication by MPs.
- They must uphold honesty, transparency, and integrity in their communications with constituents, colleagues, and the public.
- Ethical communication involves respecting diverse viewpoints, avoiding misinformation, and maintaining confidentiality where necessary to protect sensitive information.
- Experts communicate effectively by leveraging their knowledge, expertise, and experience to convey complex information in a clear, understandable manner.

- By embodying these characteristics, experts can effectively communicate their knowledge and expertise, engage their audience, and foster understanding and appreciation for complex topics and ideas.

CHARACTERISTICS FOR COMMUNICATION:

- **Clarity**: Experts communicate complex ideas and concepts clearly and succinctly, using language that is accessible to their audience. They avoid unnecessary jargon and technical terms, opting instead for plain language that can be easily understood by non-experts.
- **Contextualization**: Experts provide context and background information to help their audience understand the significance and relevance of their expertise. They frame their message in a way that relates to the audience's interests, concerns, and prior knowledge.
- **Structure**: Experts organize their communication in a logical and coherent manner, presenting information in a structured format that is easy to follow. They use headings, subheadings, and bullet points to break down complex topics into manageable sections.
- **Evidence-Based**: Experts support their arguments and assertions with evidence, data, and research findings. They cite credible sources and provide examples to illustrate key points, enhancing the credibility and persuasiveness of their communication.
- **Visual Aids**: Experts use visual aids such as graphs, charts, and diagrams to enhance their communication and illustrate complex concepts. Visuals can help clarify information, reinforce key points, and engage the audience visually.
- **Engagement**: Experts engage their audience by actively involving them in the communication process. They encourage questions, solicit feedback, and foster dialogue to promote a deeper understanding of the topic and address any misconceptions or concerns.
- **Empathy**: Experts demonstrate empathy and understanding towards their audience, recognizing that not everyone may be familiar with

the subject matter. They anticipate potential challenges or areas of confusion and adjust their communication approach accordingly to ensure clarity and comprehension.

- **Adaptability**: Experts adapt their communication style and delivery based on the needs, preferences, and level of understanding of their audience. They tailor their message to resonate with different audiences, adjusting their language, tone, and examples to effectively convey their expertise.
- **Continual Learning**: Experts remain open to learning and feedback, recognizing that effective communication is an ongoing process of refinement and improvement. They actively seek opportunities to enhance their communication skills and incorporate new knowledge and insights into their practice.
- **Authenticity**: Experts communicate authentically, conveying their passion, enthusiasm, and genuine interest in the subject matter. They are transparent about their expertise and limitations, building trust and credibility with their audience through honesty and sincerity.
    - **Good communication Characteristics:** Good communication is essential for effective interaction, understanding, and collaboration.
        - By embodying these characteristics, individuals can enhance their communication skills, build stronger relationships, and achieve greater clarity, understanding, and collaboration in their personal and professional interactions.
        - By this MPs can effectively fulfill their roles as representatives, advocates, and leaders, fostering dialogue, collaboration, and positive change within their constituencies and parliamentary settings.
        - **Clarity**: Good communication is clear and easy to understand. Messages are conveyed in a concise and straightforward manner, avoiding ambiguity or confusion.
        - **Conciseness**: Good communication is concise, conveying information efficiently without unnecessary elaboration

or repetition. It gets straight to the point, saving time and minimizing the risk of misunderstanding.

- **Active Listening**: Good communication involves active listening, where individuals pay attention to what others are saying, show empathy, and seek to understand their perspectives. This fosters mutual respect and encourages meaningful dialogue.
- **Empathy**: Good communication demonstrates empathy, showing understanding and sensitivity to others' feelings, experiences, and perspectives. Empathetic communication builds trust, strengthens relationships, and fosters collaboration.
- **Respect**: Good communication is respectful, treating others with courtesy, dignity, and consideration. It values diverse viewpoints, encourages open dialogue, and fosters a culture of inclusivity and mutual respect.
- **Feedback**: Good communication involves giving and receiving feedback constructively. It provides specific, actionable feedback that helps individuals learn, grow, and improve their communication skills.
- **Openness**: Good communication is open and transparent, encouraging honesty, authenticity, and openness. It fosters an environment where individuals feel comfortable sharing their thoughts, ideas, and concerns without fear of judgment or reprisal.
- **Flexibility**: Good communication is flexible, adapting to the needs, preferences, and communication styles of different individuals and situations. It recognizes that effective communication requires flexibility and adaptability to accommodate diverse perspectives and circumstances.
- **Clarity of Intent**: Good communication is intentional, with clear objectives, goals, and desired outcomes. It ensures that

messages are delivered with purpose and that communication efforts are aligned with organizational or personal goals.

- **Non-Verbal Communication**: Good communication encompasses both verbal and non-verbal cues, including body language, facial expressions, tone of voice, and gestures. It recognizes the importance of non-verbal communication in conveying meaning, emotion, and emphasis.
- **Timeliness**: Good communication is timely, delivering information when it is most relevant and needed. It respects deadlines, responds promptly to inquiries or requests, and keeps stakeholders informed in a timely manner.
- **Adaptability**: Good communication is adaptable, adjusting to the needs and preferences of different audiences, contexts, and communication channels. It recognizes that effective communication requires flexibility and the ability to adapt to changing circumstances.

- **Communication skills of a M.P.:** Communication skills are paramount for Members of Parliament (MPs) as they engage in various forms of communication, both within parliamentary settings and with constituents. By honing these communication skills, politicians can effectively fulfill their roles as representatives, advocates, and leaders, fostering dialogue, collaboration, and positive change within their constituencies and political arenas. Here are key communication skills crucial for an MP:
    - **Public Speaking**: MPs frequently deliver speeches in parliament, public meetings, or events. Strong public speaking skills enable them to articulate their views clearly, persuasively, and with confidence.
    - **Listening**: Effective communication involves active listening to understand constituents' concerns, feedback, and perspectives. MPs should be attentive and empathetic listeners,

demonstrating genuine interest in the needs and priorities of their constituents.

- **Debating Skills**: Parliamentary debates require MPs to engage in structured arguments, defend their positions, and respond to opposing viewpoints. MPs should possess strong debating skills, including the ability to think critically, articulate arguments persuasively, and engage in constructive dialogue.
- **Negotiation and Compromise**: MPs often negotiate with colleagues, stakeholders, and other political parties to advance legislative agendas or reach consensus on contentious issues. Strong negotiation skills, coupled with the ability to find common ground and compromise when necessary, are essential for effective governance.
- **Written Communication**: MPs communicate through various written formats, including emails, letters, press releases, and social media posts. They should be proficient in writing clearly, concisely, and persuasively to convey their messages effectively to constituents and the public.
- **Media Relations**: MPs interact with the media to communicate their views, respond to inquiries, and address issues of public interest. Effective media relations skills involve the ability to deliver key messages succinctly, handle interviews confidently, and manage media inquiries diplomatically.
- **Constituency Engagement**: MPs maintain regular communication with constituents through constituency surgeries, public meetings, and community events. Strong interpersonal skills enable MPs to build relationships, listen to constituents' concerns, and represent their interests effectively.
- **Empathy and Empathetic Communication**: MPs should demonstrate empathy and understanding when communicating with constituents, colleagues, and stakeholders. Empathetic communication involves acknowledging others' perspectives,

validating their experiences, and responding with compassion and sensitivity.

- **Crisis Communication**: In times of crisis or emergencies, MPs may need to communicate important information, provide reassurance, and coordinate responses effectively. Crisis communication skills involve staying calm under pressure, communicating transparently, and addressing concerns promptly and decisively.
- **Cross-Cultural Communication**: In multicultural societies, MPs interact with constituents from diverse cultural backgrounds. Cross-cultural communication skills enable MPs to communicate respectfully, navigate cultural differences sensitively, and build inclusive communities.

- **Communication skills of a politician:** Communication skills are critical for politicians as they are constantly engaging with constituents, fellow politicians, the media, and other stakeholders. Here are some essential communication skills for politicians:

  - **Public Speaking**: Politicians often address large audiences in rallies, town hall meetings, and public debates. Strong public speaking skills enable them to articulate their ideas clearly, persuasively, and with confidence, capturing the attention of their audience and effectively conveying their message.
  - **Debating Skills**: Political debates require politicians to engage in structured arguments, defend their positions, and respond to opposing viewpoints. Strong debating skills, including critical thinking, effective rebuttal, and persuasive rhetoric, are essential for engaging in debates and influencing public opinion.
  - **Listening**: Effective communication involves active listening to understand constituents' concerns, feedback, and perspectives. Politicians should be attentive listeners,

demonstrating empathy and genuine interest in the needs and priorities of their constituents.

- **Media Relations**: Politicians interact with the media to communicate their views, respond to inquiries, and address issues of public interest. Effective media relations skills involve the ability to deliver key messages succinctly, handle interviews confidently, and manage media inquiries diplomatically.
- **Written Communication**: Politicians communicate through various written formats, including speeches, press releases, social media posts, and policy documents. Strong written communication skills enable politicians to convey their ideas clearly, persuasively, and effectively to constituents and the public.
- **Negotiation and Compromise**: Politicians often negotiate with colleagues, stakeholders, and other political parties to advance legislative agendas or reach consensus on contentious issues. Strong negotiation skills, coupled with the ability to find common ground and compromise when necessary, are essential for effective governance.
- **Empathy and Empathetic Communication**: Politicians should demonstrate empathy and understanding when communicating with constituents, colleagues, and stakeholders. Empathetic communication involves acknowledging others' perspectives, validating their experiences, and responding with compassion and sensitivity.
- **Crisis Communication**: In times of crisis or emergencies, politicians may need to communicate important information, provide reassurance, and coordinate responses effectively. Crisis communication skills involve staying calm under pressure, communicating transparently, and addressing concerns promptly and decisively.

- **Cross-Cultural Communication**: In multicultural societies, politicians interact with constituents from diverse cultural backgrounds. Cross-cultural communication skills enable politicians to communicate respectfully, navigate cultural differences sensitively, and build inclusive communities.
- **Digital Communication**: With the rise of social media and online platforms, politicians must be adept at digital communication. This includes effectively utilizing social media channels, websites, and digital tools to engage with constituents, disseminate information, and mobilize support.

- **Do's and don'ts in communication:** Effective communication involves not only what you say but also how you say it and how you interact with others. Here are some do's and don'ts to keep in mind:

DO'S:

- **Active Listening**: Listen attentively to what others are saying without interrupting. Show empathy and understanding by acknowledging their perspective.
- **Be clear and concise**: Communicate your message in a clear and straightforward manner, avoiding unnecessary jargon or complexity.
- **Use Non-Verbal Cues**: Pay attention to your body language, facial expressions, and gestures to reinforce your message and convey sincerity.
- **Ask Questions**: Encourage dialogue by asking open-ended questions that prompt discussion and deeper understanding.
- **Show Empathy**: Demonstrate empathy and understanding towards others' feelings, experiences, and perspectives.
- **Respect Others**: Treat others with respect and courtesy, regardless of differences in opinion or background.

- **Be Open to Feedback**: Welcome feedback from others as an opportunity for growth and improvement. Listen attentively and consider constructive criticism.
- **Be Authentic**: Be genuine and authentic in your communication, expressing your thoughts and feelings honestly and transparently.
- **Adapt to Your Audience**: Tailor your communication style and approach to the needs and preferences of your audience, adjusting your language, tone, and examples accordingly.
- **Follow Up**: Follow up on communication to ensure understanding and clarity, especially in situations where action or further discussion is needed.

DON'TS:

- **Interrupting**: Avoid interrupting others while they are speaking. Wait for them to finish before responding.
- **Assuming Understanding**: Don't assume that others understand your message. Take the time to clarify and ensure mutual understanding.
- **Being Defensive**: Resist the urge to become defensive or argumentative in response to criticism or differing opinions. Instead, listen with an open mind and respond calmly and constructively.
- **Ignoring Non-Verbal Cues**: Pay attention to non-verbal cues from others, such as body language and facial expressions, as they can provide valuable insights into their thoughts and feelings.
- **Overusing Technical Jargon**: Avoid using excessive technical jargon or terminology that may be unfamiliar to your audience. Instead, use plain language that is easily understood by all.
- **Disregarding Feedback**: Don't dismiss or ignore feedback from others, even if it is critical or challenging to hear. Instead, use it as an opportunity for growth and self-improvement.
- **Losing Focus**: Stay focused on the topic at hand and avoid getting sidetracked by unrelated or tangential issues.

- **Using Negative Language**: Minimize the use of negative language or criticism, as it can be off-putting and create a defensive atmosphere.
- **Assuming One Size Fits All**: Recognize that different communication styles may be more effective with different individuals or groups. Adapt your approach accordingly.
- **Lack of Follow-Up**: Don't neglect to follow up on communication or commitments made, as it can erode trust and credibility over time.

By following these do's and don'ts, you can enhance your communication skills, build stronger relationships, and foster a more positive and productive communication environment.

- **Preparing speech:** Preparing a speech as a Member of Parliament (MP) requires careful consideration of the audience, the topic, and the desired outcome. Remember, the goal of a parliamentary speech is not just to convey information but also to persuade and inspire action. Stay authentic, confident, and passionate about your message to engage your audience effectively. Here's a structured approach:
    - **Identify the Purpose**: Determine why you're giving the speech. Is it to inform, persuade, inspire, or entertain? Understanding the purpose will guide the content and tone of your speech.
    - **Know Your Audience**: MPs often address a diverse audience, including constituents, fellow lawmakers, government officials, and the media. Consider their demographics, interests, and level of understanding on the topic. Tailor your message to resonate with them.
    - **Research the Topic**: Thoroughly research the subject matter. Gather relevant data, statistics, examples, and expert opinions to support your points. Consider different perspectives and anticipate possible counterarguments.
    - **Structure Your Speech**: Organize your speech into a clear structure with an introduction, body, and conclusion.

  - Introduction: Grab attention with a compelling opening, state the purpose of your speech, and provide an overview of what you'll cover.
  - Body: Present your main points logically and coherently. Use evidence, anecdotes, and examples to support your arguments. Consider using a chronological, problem-solution, or cause-effect structure.
  - Conclusion: Summarize the key points, restate the main message, and end with a memorable closing statement that leaves a lasting impression.
- **Consider Emotional Appeal:** Emotions can be powerful motivators. Use storytelling, personal anecdotes, or appeals to shared values to connect with your audience on an emotional level.
- **Address Potential Objections**: Anticipate and address potential objections or concerns your audience may have. Acknowledge opposing viewpoints respectfully and provide counterarguments or rebuttals.
- **Practice Delivery**: Rehearse your speech multiple times to improve fluency, pacing, and intonation. Pay attention to body language, eye contact, and vocal projection. Consider recording yourself or practicing in front of a trusted friend for feedback.
- **Adapt to the Venue**: Consider the venue, time constraints, and any cultural or contextual factors that may influence your delivery. Adjust your speech accordingly to maximize its impact.
- **Seek Feedback**: Before delivering your speech, solicit feedback from colleagues, mentors, or speech coaches. They can provide valuable insights and suggestions for improvement.
- **Be Prepared for Q&A:** Anticipate questions that may arise during the Q&A session. Prepare concise and thoughtful responses to address them effectively.

- **Speech delivered by Member of Parliament:** Delivering a speech as a Member of Parliament (MP) involves more than just reading words from a script. It's about connecting with your audience, conveying your message effectively, and influencing opinions. By following these tips and practicing your delivery, you can effectively deliver a compelling and impactful speech as a Member of Parliament. By embodying these characteristics, a speech can truly resonate with the audience and achieve its intended purpose effectively. Here's how an MP typically delivers a speech:

    - **Confidence and Presence**: Approach the lectern with confidence. Stand tall, make eye contact with your audience, and project your voice clearly. Your demeanor should convey authority and conviction.

    - **Engage the Audience**: Begin your speech with a strong opening that grabs the audience's attention. This could be a compelling anecdote, a shocking statistic, or a thought-provoking question. Engage the audience from the start to create a connection.

    - **Speak clearly and slowly**: Enunciate your words clearly and speak at a moderate pace. Avoid rushing through your speech, as this can make it difficult for the audience to follow. Pause occasionally to allow your points to sink in and to emphasize key ideas.

    - **Use Body Language**: Your body language can enhance your message and reinforce your credibility. Use gestures sparingly to emphasize key points, but avoid excessive or distracting movements. Maintain an open posture and make purposeful movements to command attention.

    - **Vary Your Tone and Pace**: Monotone delivery can bore the audience and diminish the impact of your speech. Vary your tone, pitch, and pace to maintain the audience's interest and convey emotion. Adjust your delivery according to the content of your speech—for example; use a more impassioned tone for persuasive arguments and a softer tone for empathetic messages.

- **Maintain Eye Contact**: Establishing eye contact with members of the audience can create a sense of connection and trust. Scan the room and make eye contact with different individuals throughout your speech. This shows that you're engaged with the audience and reinforces your credibility.
- **Stay Focused and Relevant**: Stick to the main points of your speech and avoid rambling or going off on tangents. Keep your language clear and concise, and use examples and anecdotes to illustrate your arguments effectively. Stays focused on the topic at hand and avoid getting sidetracked by irrelevant issues.
- **Handle Interruptions Gracefully**: During a parliamentary speech, you may encounter interruptions from other members, applause, or heckling. Stays composed and handle interruptions gracefully. Address any questions or comments respectfully, and remain focused on delivering your message.
- **Conclude Strongly**: End your speech with a powerful conclusion that reinforces your main points and leaves a lasting impression. Summarize the key takeaways, reiterate your main message, and end with a memorable closing statement or call to action.
- **Be Authentic**: Finally, be yourself. Authenticity is key to connecting with your audience and earning their trust. Speak from the heart, and let your passion for the subject shine through in your delivery.

- **Characteristics of a good speech:** A good speech possesses several key characteristics that engage the audience, effectively convey the message, and leave a lasting impact. Here are some essential qualities:

- **Clarity**: A good speech is clear and easy to understand. The message is communicated in simple language, avoiding jargon or overly complex terminology. Each point is articulated clearly, leaving no room for ambiguity.
- **Relevance**: The content of the speech is relevant to the audience and the occasion. It addresses topics that are important and meaningful to the listeners, capturing their interest and attention from the outset.
- **Structure**: A well-structured speech has a clear beginning, middle, and end. It follows a logical progression, with each point building upon the previous one. The introduction sets the stage, the body presents the main ideas, and the conclusion wraps up the speech effectively.
- **Engagement**: A good speech engages the audience from start to finish. It grabs their attention with a compelling opening, maintains their interest with interesting and relevant content, and concludes with a strong closing that leaves a lasting impression.
- **Authenticity**: Authenticity is essential in connecting with the audience. A good speech reflects the speaker's genuine beliefs, values, and emotions. It comes from the heart and resonates with sincerity, earning the trust and respect of the listeners.
- **Persuasiveness**: Whether the goal is to inform, persuade, inspire, or entertain, a good speech is persuasive in nature. It presents compelling arguments, backed by evidence and logic that persuade the audience to adopt the speaker's viewpoint or take action.
- **Memorability**: A good speech is memorable, leaving a lasting impression on the audience long after it's delivered. This may be achieved through powerful storytelling, memorable quotes, or vivid imagery that sticks in the minds of the listeners.

- **Adaptability**: A skilled speaker knows how to adapt their speech to suit the needs and preferences of the audience. They may adjust their tone, language, or delivery style based on the demographics, interests, and cultural background of the listeners.
- **Emotional Appeal**: Emotions can be a powerful tool in capturing the audience's attention and influencing their behavior. A good speech strikes an emotional chord with the listeners, evoking empathy, inspiration, or motivation to action.
- **Delivery**: Finally, the delivery of the speech is crucial. A good speaker maintains good posture, makes eye contact with the audience, and uses vocal variety and gestures to convey meaning. They speak with confidence and passion, commanding the attention of the listeners throughout the speech.

Skills in delivering a speech: Delivering a speech effectively requires a combination of skills that encompass both verbal and non-verbal communication, as well as an understanding of audience dynamics. These skills and practicing regularly, you can become a more effective and compelling speaker, capable of delivering speeches that inspire, persuade, and leave a lasting impact on your audience. Here are key skills needed for delivering a speech:

- **Public Speaking**: Develop confidence in speaking in front of an audience. Practice articulating your ideas clearly and projecting your voice to ensure everyone can hear you.
- **Voice Modulation**: Learn to vary your tone, pitch, and volume to keep your audience engaged. Use emphasis and pauses to highlight key points and add emphasis to your speech.
- **Body Language**: Master the use of body language to convey confidence and authority. Maintain good posture, make eye contact with your audience, and use gestures to emphasize key points.
- **Facial Expressions**: Your facial expressions can convey a range of emotions and add depth to your delivery. Use facial expressions to

show enthusiasm, sincerity, or empathy, depending on the content of your speech.

- **Gestures**: Use purposeful gestures to enhance your message and engage your audience. Avoid excessive or distracting movements, and ensure your gestures are aligned with your verbal content.
- **Pacing and Timing**: Pay attention to your pacing and timing when delivering your speech. Avoid speaking too quickly, which can make it difficult for your audience to follow, or too slowly, which can lose their interest.
- **Confidence**: Project confidence and authority in your delivery. Believe in yourself and your message, and let your confidence shine through in your voice, body language, and demeanor.
- **Preparation**: Thoroughly prepare your speech in advance. Practice your delivery multiple times to ensure you're comfortable with the content and confident in your ability to deliver it effectively.
- **Adaptability**: Be prepared to adapt your delivery based on the dynamics of the audience and the context of the speech. Adjust your tone, pacing, and content as needed to keep your audience engaged and responsive.
- **Empathy**: Connect with your audience by showing empathy and understanding. Tailor your message to resonate with their interests, concerns, and values, and demonstrate that you genuinely care about their needs and perspectives.
- **Resilience**: Be prepared to handle challenges or unexpected situations that may arise during your speech, such as technical difficulties or interruptions. Stay calm, composed, and focused, and maintain your confidence and poise throughout.
- **Feedback Incorporation**: Be open to feedback from others and use it to improve your delivery. Solicit feedback from trusted colleagues, mentors, or speech coaches, and incorporate their suggestions into your practice sessions.

Do's and don'ts in speech: Crafting and delivering a speech effectively requires careful consideration of various factors. By adhering to these do's and don'ts, you can deliver a speech that captivates your audience, effectively communicates your message, and leaves a lasting impression. Here are some do's and don'ts to keep in mind:

DO'S:

- **Know Your Audience**: Tailor your speech to the interests, knowledge level, and preferences of your audience.
- **Start Strong**: Grab the audience's attention from the beginning with a compelling hook, such as a captivating story, shocking statistic, or thought-provoking question.
- **Organize Your Content**: Structure your speech with a clear introduction, body, and conclusion. Organize your main points logically and use transitions to guide the audience through your speech smoothly.
- **Use Clear and Concise Language**: Communicate your message in clear, simple language that is easy for the audience to understand. Avoid jargon or overly complex terminology.
- **Engage the Audience**: Encourage audience participation through rhetorical questions, interactive activities, or opportunities for reflection. Engaged audiences are more likely to retain information and connect with your message.
- **Use Visual Aids Wisely**: If using visual aids like slides or props, ensure they enhance your message rather than distract from it. Keep visuals simple, relevant, and easy to read.
- **Tell Stories**: Stories are powerful tools for engaging the audience and conveying complex ideas. Use personal anecdotes, case studies, or examples to illustrate your points and make them more relatable.
- **Practice, Practice, Practice**: Rehearse your speech multiple times to become familiar with the content and confident in your delivery. Practice pacing, intonation, and gestures to enhance your performance.

- **Maintain Eye Contact**: Make eye contact with members of the audience to establish a connection and convey confidence. Distribute your gaze evenly across the audience to engage everyone.
- **End Strong**: Finish your speech with a memorable conclusion that reinforces your main points and leaves a lasting impression on the audience. End with a call to action, a thought-provoking question, or a powerful closing statement.

DON'TS:

- **Don't Read from a Script**: Avoid reading your speech word-for-word from a script, as it can come across as disengaged and robotic. Instead, use notes or bullet points to guide your delivery.
- **Don't Ramble or Wander Off Topic**: Stay focused on your main message and avoid going off on tangents or rambling. Stick to your key points and maintain a clear and coherent structure throughout your speech.
- **Don't Overwhelm with Information**: Avoid overwhelming the audience with too much information or technical details. Select only the most relevant and impactful points to include in your speech.
- **Don't Rush**: Speak at a comfortable pace, allowing the audience time to process your message. Avoid speaking too quickly, as it can be difficult for the audience to follow, and pause occasionally to emphasize key points.
- **Don't Use Filler Words**: Minimize the use of filler words such as "um," "uh," or "like," as they can detract from your message and undermine your credibility as a speaker.
- **Don't Ignore Non-Verbal Cues**: Pay attention to the audience's non-verbal cues, such as body language and facial expressions, to gauge their engagement and adjust your delivery accordingly.
- **Don't Monopolize the Time**: Be mindful of the time allotted for your speech and avoid going over your allotted time limit. Respect

the audience's time and ensure there is ample time for questions or discussion.

- **Don't Dismiss Questions or Feedback**: Be open to questions, feedback, and differing opinions from the audience. Respectfully address inquiries and engage in constructive dialogue to foster understanding and mutual respect.
- **Don't Lack Confidence**: Project confidence and authority in your delivery, even if you feel nervous or uncertain. Stand tall, speak clearly, and maintain eye contact to convey confidence and command attention.
- **Don't Forget to Practice Self-Care**: Prioritize self-care before your speech to ensure you're in the best possible mindset and physical condition. Get plenty of rest, stay hydrated, and practice relaxation techniques to manage nerves and anxiety.

Communication and speech delivery are critical skills that MPs must master to fulfill their responsibilities effectively. By communicating clearly, engaging constituents, delivering persuasive speeches, participating in parliamentary debates, and upholding ethical standards, MPs can contribute to transparent governance, democratic accountability, and the advancement of public interests. Effective communication strengthens the bond between MPs and their constituents, promotes informed decision-making, and enhances the democratic process as a whole.

"Tips on communication & speech delivery"

Know Audience. Clarity and Conciseness. Structuring Speech. Use of Visual Aids. Engage Your Audience. Story- telling. Adapt to the Setting. Practice and Preparation. Responding to Questions and Challenges. Seek Feedback and Continuous Improvement.

By focusing on these tips, MPs can enhance their communication skills, deliver impactful speeches, and effectively convey their message to influence public opinion, legislative debates, and policy outcomes.

Chapter 9
NURTURING THE CONSTITUENCY

"The constituency is not just a place on the map; it's a community of diverse voices, hopes, and dreams. As an MP, serving the constituency means being the voice of the people, understanding their needs, and tirelessly working to create a better future for all."

Members of Parliament (MPs) are elected to represent the interests and aspirations of their constituents in the national legislature. MPs play a crucial role in nurturing their constituencies by fostering development, promoting civic engagement, and addressing the needs of their constituents effectively. Nurturing the constituency requires MPs to advocate for resources and initiatives that promote economic growth and social well-being.

- MPs should prioritize regular and meaningful engagement with their constituents.
- This involves actively listening to their concerns, attending local events, and holding constituency surgeries to provide opportunities for direct interaction.
- By maintaining a visible and accessible presence within the community,
- MPs can build trust, establish personal connections, and gain a deeper understanding of the issues that matter most to their constituents.

- MPs can work collaboratively with local authorities, businesses, and community organizations to identify development priorities such as infrastructure projects, job creation initiatives, healthcare facilities, and educational opportunities. By championing these priorities in parliament and securing government support, MPs can contribute to the overall prosperity and quality of life in their constituencies
- MPs should actively promote civic engagement and participation among their constituents. This includes encouraging voter registration, educating citizens about their rights and responsibilities, and facilitating public forums and town hall meetings to discuss important issues.
- By empowering constituents to participate in democratic processes and decision-making,
- MPs strengthen the democratic fabric of society and ensure that community voices are heard and represented.
- MPs can nurture their constituencies by supporting local initiatives and community-driven projects.
- This may involve collaborating with grassroots organizations, volunteering for community service activities, and advocating for funding and resources to support cultural, environmental, and social initiatives that enhance community cohesion and pride.
- Ethical leadership and transparency are essential in nurturing the constituency.
- MPs should conduct themselves with integrity, honesty, and accountability in all their interactions and decisions.
- They must prioritize the public interest over personal or partisan gain, uphold ethical standards, and maintain open communication with constituents about legislative priorities, policy developments, and parliamentary proceedings.

- **Working in the electorate** Members of Parliament are the representatives of all of the constituents in their electorate. Their responsibilities are therefore often wide-ranging. The ways in which Members typically serve their constituents includes:
  - Giving assistance and advice to those in difficulty
  - Acting as a lobbyist for local interest groups
  - • Being a communicator for their party's policies and
  - Playing an active community role.
- **To meet these responsibilities**, local Members need to be active in their electorates to keep in touch with what is happening and to get to know constituents' views and problems.
  - Members must also give constituents help and advice, communicate the needs of their region to the Government, and promote their policies to the community.
  - Members provide a direct link between their constituents and the Parliament, and members
  - In large electorates can spend a lot of time travelling within their electorate.
  - Each member has an office in their electorate, and those with the largest electorates have two.
  - Constituents often bring their concerns to their local Member of Parliament.
  - Personal intervention in a constituent matter by a Member may result in priority attention from government departments.
  - If a matter is particularly urgent or serious, the Member may approach the relevant Minister directly, or may even bring the matter before the Parliament by asking a question of the responsible Minister.
  - The Member may also sponsor a petition about the issue in question.

- **Representing the public:**
    - MPs are in constant demand to give speeches, write articles for media, attend functions, and meet visitors.
    - They are regularly lobbied by interest groups and individuals who want to promote ideas.
    - They must respond to many letters and emails each year, with sense, sensitivity, and often with practical action.
    - A MPs work includes communicating with the media and the public about the issues they are involved in.
    - It is clear that constituency service is important both to citizens and politicians – indeed; it is an accepted and expected part of the job.
    - Numerous opinion polls in different regions suggest that the public believes that some form or the other of constituency service is the most important part of an MP's role,
    - MPs themselves no doubt see the benefit of meeting voters' needs for various reasons, not least to improve their chances of re-election.
- **Representation and constituency relations:**
    - Regular contact with constituents enables the MP to easily identify their needs and elicit their input on policy debates.
    - Frequent inter actions between MPs and citizens also facilitates information sharing that could make government more accountable to the people.
    - MPs can also help achieve this outcome by informing citizens about legislative actions, ensuring that citizen voices are reflected in budgets and public policy, and assisting constituents to gain access to governmental services.
    - MPs help improve constituency relations by making regular visits to constituencies, particularly while Parliament is on recess and, in some cases, establishing of offices in their constituencies.

- **Looking after his constituency:** Members of Parliament (MPs) have a range of responsibilities to their constituents, and looking after their constituency is a significant part of their role.
- By fulfilling these responsibilities, MPs demonstrate their commitment to serving the interests of their constituents and addressing their needs and concerns.
- Building strong relationships with constituents and actively engaging with the local community are essential aspects of effective constituency representation.

Here are some ways MPs typically fulfill this responsibility:

- **Representation**: MPs serve as the voice of their constituents in parliament, representing their interests, concerns, and priorities. They advocate for policies and legislation that benefit their constituency and address local issues.
- **Constituency Surgeries**: MPs hold regular constituency surgeries or office hours where constituents can meet with them to discuss their concerns, seek assistance with government services, or request help with personal matters.
- **Community Engagement**: MPs actively engage with their constituency through community events, town hall meetings, and public forums. They listen to constituents' views, participate in local initiatives, and build relationships with community leaders and organizations.
- **Assistance and Advocacy**: MPs provide assistance and advocacy to constituents facing challenges with government agencies or services. They help constituents navigate bureaucratic processes, address grievances, and access resources and support.
- **Issue Resolution**: MPs intervene on behalf of constituents to resolve issues or disputes with government agencies, local authorities, or other organizations. They liaise with relevant

stakeholders, facilitate communication, and seek solutions to constituents' concerns.

- **Communication**: MPs keep constituents informed about their work in parliament, government policies, and local developments through newsletters, social media, websites, and other communication channels. They provide updates on their activities and seek feedback from constituents.
- **Support for Local Projects**: MPs support local projects and initiatives that benefit their constituency, such as infrastructure improvements, community facilities, or economic development initiatives. They advocate for funding and resources to support these projects.
- **Accessibility**: MPs make themselves accessible to constituents by maintaining open lines of communication, responding promptly to inquiries and correspondence, and being available to meet with constituents as needed.
- **Legislative Advocacy**: MPs introduce private member's bills, table motions, and participate in debates on issues of importance to their constituency. They advocate for legislative changes that address local concerns and priorities.
- **Accountability**: MPs are accountable to their constituents for their actions and decisions. They regularly report back to constituents on their parliamentary activities, achievements, and progress on addressing local issues.
- **Relationship with his voters:** Maintaining strong relationships with voters is crucial for Members of Parliament (MPs) to effectively represent their constituents and garner support. By employing these strategies,
  - MPs can cultivate and maintain strong, positive relationships with their voters, effectively represent their interests, and build support for their leadership. By leveraging these funding sources and employing strategic approaches,

- MPs can effectively finance constituency activities, support community development initiatives, and address the needs and priorities of their constituents.
- **Regular Constituency Engagement**: MPs should regularly engage with their constituents through various channels, including town hall meetings, public forums, and community events. These interactions provide opportunities for MPs to listen to voters' concerns, share updates, and build rapport.
- **Constituency Surgeries**: Holding regular constituency surgeries or office hours allows MPs to meet one-on-one with constituents to address their individual concerns, provide assistance, and offer support. These sessions demonstrate accessibility and responsiveness to voters' needs.
- **Community Outreach**: Participating in local community events, fundraisers, and volunteer initiatives helps MPs connect with voters on a personal level and demonstrate their commitment to the community. Supporting local causes and projects fosters goodwill and strengthens relationships with constituents.
- **Door-to-Door Canvassing**: Engaging in door-to-door canvassing provides MPs with an opportunity to directly engage with voters in their homes, listen to their concerns, and solicit feedback. This personalized approach demonstrates attentiveness to individual constituents' needs and builds trust.
- **Communication Channels**: Utilizing various communication channels, such as newsletters, social media, email updates, and websites, allows MPs to keep constituents informed about their work, policy initiatives, and local developments. Regular communication fosters transparency and helps MPs stay connected with voters.
- **Listening and Responding**: Actively listening to constituents' concerns and responding promptly and effectively demonstrates

MPs' commitment to representing their interests. Addressing constituents' inquiries, requests, and grievances in a timely manner builds trust and credibility.

- **Public Advocacy**: Advocating for issues that resonate with constituents and align with their priorities demonstrates MPs' dedication to representing their interests in parliament. By championing causes that matter to voters, MPs strengthen their relationship with constituents and foster loyalty and support.
- **Accountability and Transparency**: Holding themselves accountable to constituents by regularly reporting back on their parliamentary activities, achievements, and progress on addressing local issues demonstrates transparency and builds confidence in MPs' representation.
- **Building Personal Connections**: Taking the time to build personal connections with constituents, such as remembering names, attending milestone events, and expressing genuine interest in their lives and concerns, strengthens relationships and fosters loyalty and support.
- **Seeking Feedback and Input**: Actively seeking feedback and input from constituents on legislative matters, policy initiatives, and local issues demonstrates respect for voters' opinions and empowers them to participate in the democratic process. Soliciting input from constituents helps MPs make informed decisions and better represent their interests.

- **Funding Constituency:** Funding for constituency activities typically comes from various sources, and Members of Parliament (MPs) play a role in securing and allocating these funds. Here are some ways MPs may fund their constituency:

    - **Government Funding**: MPs may access government funding allocated for constituency development projects, infrastructure improvements, or community initiatives. This funding is often distributed through government departments or local authorities and may require MPs to submit proposals or applications for specific projects.

- **Constituency Allowance**: MPs may receive a constituency allowance or budget from parliamentary authorities to cover expenses related to constituency work, such as office rent, staff salaries, travel, and communication costs. This allowance allows MPs to maintain a constituency office and provide services to constituents.
- **Political Party Support**: Political parties may provide financial support to MPs for constituency activities, such as campaign expenses, community events, or local initiatives. Parties may allocate funds to MPs based on their role, seniority, or electoral district.
- **Corporate Sponsorship**: MPs may seek corporate sponsorship or donations from businesses, organizations, or individuals to support constituency projects or events. Corporate sponsors may contribute funds or in-kind support for specific initiatives in exchange for visibility or recognition.
- **Grants and Funding Programs**: MPs may apply for grants or funding programs offered by government agencies, non-profit organizations, or philanthropic foundations to support constituency projects, social programs, or community development initiatives. These grants may be available for specific purposes, such as youth programs, environmental initiatives, or infrastructure projects.
- **Crowd funding**: MPs may use crowd funding platforms to raise funds for specific constituency projects, community events, or charitable causes. Crowd funding allows MPs to engage directly with constituents and supporters to mobilize financial support for initiatives that align with their priorities.
- **Local Government Support**: MPs may collaborate with local government authorities, municipal councils, or regional bodies

to access funding or resources for constituency projects or initiatives. Local government entities may provide funding or assistance for infrastructure projects, community services, or public events.

- **Personal Contributions**: MPs may personally contribute funds to support constituency activities or initiatives, particularly for charitable causes, community events, or projects that benefit constituents. Personal contributions demonstrate MPs' commitment to their constituency and may inspire others to support their efforts.
- **Fundraising Events**: MPs may organize fundraising events, such as galas, dinners, or charity auctions, to raise funds for constituency projects or initiatives. Fundraising events provide an opportunity for MPs to engage with constituents, supporters, and donors while generating financial support for their work.
- **Partnerships and Collaborations**: MPs may collaborate with local businesses, community organizations, educational institutions, or non-profit groups to access funding or resources for constituency projects or initiatives. Partnerships allow MPs to leverage collective resources and expertise to achieve shared objectives.

- **Utilizing MPLAD funds:** The Members of Parliament Local Area Development (MPLAD) Scheme provides MPs with funds to undertake development projects in their constituencies. By effectively utilizing MPLAD funds, MPs can address local development priorities, improve infrastructure and public services, and contribute to the socio-economic development of their constituencies. Here's how MPs typically utilize MPLAD funds:

    - **Identifying Priority Projects**: MPs consult with constituents, local authorities, and community organizations to identify priority areas for development projects. These may include infrastructure improvements, healthcare facilities, education initiatives, sanitation projects, or community welfare programs.

- **Project Proposal Submission**: MPs submit project proposals to the District Authority or District Collector, outlining the details of proposed projects, estimated costs, and expected outcomes. Proposals must comply with MPLAD guidelines and meet eligibility criteria set by the Ministry of Statistics and Programme Implementation (MoSPI`).
- **Approval and Sanction**: The District Authority or District Collector reviews and evaluates project proposals based on their feasibility, impact, and alignment with MPLAD guidelines. Once approved, funds are sanctioned for the implementation of approved projects.
- **Project Implementation**: MPs oversee the implementation of approved projects, working closely with relevant government departments, agencies, contractors, and stakeholders. They monitor project progress, ensure compliance with quality standards and timelines, and address any challenges or issues that arise during implementation.
- **Monitoring and Evaluation**: MPs conduct regular monitoring visits to project sites to assess progress, address any issues or concerns, and ensure that projects are being implemented effectively. They liaise with local authorities, project contractors, and community members to gather feedback and evaluate project outcomes.
- **Transparency and Accountability**: MPs maintain transparency and accountability in the utilization of MPLAD funds by providing regular updates to constituents, publicizing project details, and making project-related information available to the public through official channels. They ensure that MPLAD funds are utilized efficiently, effectively, and in accordance with established guidelines and regulations.

- **Public Awareness and Engagement**: MPs engage with constituents through public meetings, awareness campaigns, and stakeholder consultations to inform them about MPLAD-funded projects, gather feedback, and solicit community participation and support. They encourage community involvement in project planning, implementation, and monitoring to ensure local ownership and sustainability.
- **Coordination with Local Authorities**: MPs collaborate with local authorities, municipal bodies, district administrations, and other stakeholders to coordinate MPLAD-funded projects with existing development plans, priorities, and initiatives. They leverage partnerships and collective efforts to maximize the impact and reach of MPLAD funds and avoid duplication of efforts.
- **Innovation and Best Practices**: MPs explore innovative approaches, technologies, and best practices to enhance the effectiveness and sustainability of MPLAD-funded projects. They encourage innovation, experimentation, and knowledge sharing to achieve positive outcomes and address emerging challenges in their constituencies.
- **Documentation and Reporting**: MPs maintain comprehensive documentation of MPLAD-funded projects, including project proposals, approvals, expenditures, progress reports, and impact assessments. They submit regular reports to the District Authority, District Collector, and MoSPI, documenting the utilization of MPLAD funds and the outcomes achieved through funded projects.

Nurturing the constituency is a fundamental responsibility of Members of Parliament. By engaging actively with constituents, advocating for development and resources, promoting civic engagement, supporting local initiatives, and demonstrating ethical leadership, MPs can foster a sense of unity, progress, and well-being within their constituencies. Ultimately, constituency nurturing strengthens the bond between MPs and their constituents, promotes inclusive governance, and contributes to the overall prosperity and democratic vitality of the nation.

Chapter 10
WELL INFORMED

"An informed MP is an empowered advocate for progress. By staying curious, seeking knowledge, and engaging with diverse perspectives, they become a beacon of wisdom and insight, guiding their constituents towards a brighter tomorrow."

Members of Parliament (MPs) play a critical role in representing their constituents and shaping national policy. To fulfill their responsibilities effectively, MPs must be well-informed about a wide range of issues, including legislative matters, policy developments, constituent concerns, and national and international affairs. Being well-informed enables MPs to make informed decisions, advocate effectively for their constituents, and contribute meaningfully to parliamentary debates and discussions.

MPs should prioritize staying informed about legislative processes and procedures. This includes understanding parliamentary rules, procedures for introducing bills, and the stages of legislative scrutiny and debate. By mastering legislative processes, MPs can navigate the complexities of law-making, effectively contribute to drafting and amending legislation, and advocate for policies that align with the interests and priorities of their constituents.

MPs must stay abreast of current affairs and policy developments. This involves monitoring news sources, research reports, policy briefings, and expert analyses to understand emerging issues and trends that may impact their constituencies and the nation as a whole. By staying informed about economic developments, social trends, technological advancements, and environmental challenges, MPs can anticipate issues, propose timely interventions, and advocate for proactive policies that address evolving needs and challenges.

Besides national issues, MPs should also be knowledgeable about local concerns and priorities within their constituencies. This requires regular engagement with constituents, attending local events, conducting surveys, and meeting with community leaders and stakeholders to understand the specific challenges, opportunities, and aspirations of different communities. By maintaining a close connection with constituents, MPs can effectively represent their interests, advocate for local projects and initiatives, and address pressing concerns at the national level.

Moreover, MPs should seek to deepen their expertise in specific policy areas relevant to their legislative work and constituency interests. This may involve participating in parliamentary committees, attending specialized workshops and seminars, consulting with experts and stakeholders, and conducting independent research to develop a thorough understanding of complex issues such as healthcare, education, economic policy, environmental sustainability, and social welfare.

Ethical considerations are essential in being well-informed as an MP. MPs should prioritize integrity, transparency, and objectivity in their pursuit of knowledge. This includes critically evaluating information sources, avoiding misinformation and bias, and seeking diverse perspectives to form balanced and informed opinions on matters of public interest.

- **Member of Parliament should be well informed** being well-informed is a fundamental requirement for Members of Parliament (MPs) to effectively fulfill their responsibilities, being well-informed is essential for MPs to fulfill their roles effectively, represent their constituents' interests, and contribute to the democratic process. It empowers MPs to make informed decisions, advocate for positive change, and serve as effective leaders and representatives for their constituents. MPs can make informed decisions, effectively represent their constituents' interests, and contribute to the democratic process. They should continuously seek to expand their knowledge, engage with diverse perspectives, and remain responsive to the evolving needs and challenges facing their constituencies. By staying informed about opposition tactics, government MPs can effectively represent their constituents, advance government priorities, and contribute to constructive parliamentary discourse and decision-making. Here's why:

- **Policy Making**: MPs are involved in the process of making laws and policies that affect the lives of their constituents. To craft effective legislation, they need to be well-informed about relevant issues, research, and data.
- **Representation**: MPs represent the interests and concerns of their constituents in parliament. To do so effectively, they must understand the needs, priorities, and perspectives of the people they serve. Being well-informed allows them to advocate for their constituents' interests and address their concerns.
- **Oversight**: MPs have a responsibility to hold the government accountable for its actions and decisions. This includes scrutinizing government policies, expenditures, and actions to ensure transparency, accountability, and good governance. Being well-informed enables MPs to perform their oversight role effectively.
- **Constituency Work**: MPs engage in various constituency-related activities, such as addressing constituents' concerns, facilitating government services, and advocating for local development projects. Being well-informed about local issues, resources, and opportunities allows MPs to effectively serve their constituents and address their needs.
- **Debates and Discussions**: MPs participate in parliamentary debates, discussions, and committee meetings on a wide range of

topics. Being well-informed allows them to contribute meaningfully to these discussions, offer informed perspectives, and engage in constructive dialogue with colleagues.

- **Community Engagement**: MPs engage with constituents through public meetings, town hall discussions, and community events. Being well-informed allows them to communicate accurate information, answer questions knowledgeably, and address concerns effectively, fostering trust and confidence among constituents.
- **Global and National Issues**: MPs need to be aware of global and national issues that may impact their constituents, such as economic trends, social developments, and geopolitical events. Being well-informed about broader issues allows MPs to anticipate challenges, identify opportunities, and make informed decisions.
- **Continual Learning**: The political landscape is constantly evolving, with new challenges, opportunities, and developments emerging regularly. Being well-informed requires MPs to engage in continual learning, staying abreast of current events, research findings, and expert analyses relevant to their work.

- **What information a member of parliament needs to know:** Members of Parliament (MPs) need to be well-informed about a wide range of topics to effectively fulfill their roles and responsibilities. Here are some key areas of information that MPs typically need to know:
    - **Legislation and Parliamentary Procedures**: MPs must have a thorough understanding of parliamentary procedures, rules, and protocols to participate effectively in legislative debates, committee meetings, and other parliamentary activities.
    - **Constituency Issues**: MPs need to be familiar with the needs, priorities, and concerns of their constituents. This includes understanding local demographics, socio-economic conditions, infrastructure challenges, and community aspirations.
    - **Government Policies and Programs**: MPs should be knowledgeable about government policies, programs, and

initiatives at the national, regional, and local levels. This includes understanding the objectives, scope, and impact of government actions on constituents.

- **Current Affairs and News**: MPs need to stay informed about current events, developments, and issues at the national and international levels. This includes following news sources, staying updated on political developments, and understanding key issues affecting society.
- **Economic and Financial Matters**: MPs should have a basic understanding of economic principles, financial management, budgeting, and taxation. This enables them to assess the economic impact of policies, advocate for economic development initiatives, and address constituents' financial concerns.
- **Social and Welfare Issues**: MPs should be aware of social issues such as healthcare, education, housing, poverty, and social inequality. This includes understanding government programs and services available to address these issues and advocating for improvements where needed.
- **Environmental and Sustainability Issues**: MPs need to understand environmental challenges, conservation efforts, climate change impacts, and sustainability initiatives. This includes advocating for environmentally responsible policies and supporting initiatives to protect natural resources and mitigate climate change.
- **Legal and Justice Matters**: MPs should have a basic understanding of legal principles, the justice system, human rights, and civil liberties. This enables them to advocate for legal reforms, support access to justice initiatives, and address constituents' legal concerns.
- **Health and Public Safety**: MPs should be knowledgeable about healthcare systems, public health issues, emergency services, and crime prevention strategies. This includes advocating for improvements in healthcare infrastructure, access to healthcare services, and public safety measures.

- **International Relations and Diplomacy**: MPs should have a basic understanding of international relations, geopolitics, and diplomatic affairs. This enables them to contribute to debates on foreign policy, support international cooperation initiatives, and address global challenges affecting constituents.
- **Technology and Innovation**: MPs should be aware of technological advancements, digital trends, and innovation opportunities. This includes understanding the potential impact of technology on society, advocating for digital inclusion, and supporting innovation-driven economic growth.
- **Ethical and Professional Conduct**: MPs should be familiar with parliamentary ethics, standards of conduct, and codes of behavior. This includes adhering to principles of integrity, accountability, transparency, and public service in their interactions with constituents, colleagues, and stakeholders.

- **Well informed of opposition tactics:** Being well-informed about opposition tactics is essential for Members of Parliament (MPs) to effectively navigate parliamentary proceedings and fulfill their roles as representatives. By understanding party politics, MPs can effectively navigate the complexities of the parliamentary system, represent party interests, and contribute to informed decision-making and effective governance. By staying well-informed about current affairs and prevailing issues in the country, MPs can effectively represent their constituents, contribute to informed decision-making, and uphold their responsibilities as elected representatives in parliament. Here's why MPs should be knowledgeable about opposition tactics:

  - **Debates and Discussions**: In parliamentary debates, opposition MPs may employ various tactics to challenge government policies, critique legislation, and advocate for alternative approaches. Being aware of these tactics allows government MPs to anticipate arguments, prepare responses, and effectively defend their positions.

- **Committee Work**: Opposition MPs participate in parliamentary committees, where they scrutinize government actions, examine legislation, and hold government officials accountable. Understanding opposition tactics helps government MPs engage constructively in committee discussions, address critiques, and advance government objectives.
- **Legislative Process**: Opposition MPs may use procedural tactics, such as filibustering or delaying tactics, to obstruct the legislative process or hinder government initiatives. Government MPs need to be familiar with parliamentary rules and procedures to counteract these tactics and ensure the smooth functioning of the legislative process.
- **Question Time**: During question time in parliament, opposition MPs pose questions to government ministers, seeking clarification on policies, raising concerns, and holding the government to account. Government MPs must be prepared to respond to questions effectively, address criticisms, and articulate government positions.
- **Media and Public Perception**: Opposition parties often use media channels and public forums to criticize government policies, highlight perceived failures, and promote alternative agendas. Government MPs should be aware of opposition messaging and tactics to effectively communicate government achievements, counter misinformation, and manage public perception.
- **Constituency Relations**: Opposition MPs represent constituents who may have diverse political views and interests. Understanding opposition tactics helps government MPs anticipate constituents' concerns, address criticisms, and effectively communicate government policies and initiatives to constituents.
- **Coalition Dynamics**: In parliamentary systems with coalition governments, opposition parties may seek to exploit divisions or disagreements within the governing coalition to weaken government

support or influence policy decisions. Government MPs need to be cognizant of coalition dynamics and work collaboratively to maintain coalition unity and support.

- **Strategic Planning**: By understanding opposition tactics and strategies, government MPs can develop strategic responses, coordinate messaging, and effectively advance government priorities. This includes identifying potential vulnerabilities, preempting opposition attacks, and building consensus among coalition partners.
- **Negotiation and Compromise**: Opposition MPs may seek to negotiate with government MPs to amend legislation, address concerns, or secure concessions. Government MPs should be prepared to engage in constructive dialogue, negotiate in good faith, and seek compromises that advance the public interest while upholding government principles.
- **Democratic Accountability**: Ultimately, being informed about opposition tactics is essential for upholding democratic accountability and ensuring robust parliamentary scrutiny. By engaging thoughtfully with opposition arguments, government MPs contribute to informed debate, democratic deliberation, and effective governance.

- **Party politics:** Understanding party politics is crucial for Members of Parliament (MPs) as it shapes their roles, interactions, and decision-making within the parliamentary system. Here's why MPs must be knowledgeable about party politics:
  - **Party Discipline**: Political parties often enforce discipline among their members, including MPs, to maintain unity and cohesion. MPs are expected to support their party's positions on key issues, follow party directives, and adhere to party policies and agendas. Understanding party politics helps MPs navigate party dynamics and fulfill their party obligations.

- **Whipping System**: Parties typically employ a whipping system to ensure MPs vote in line with party positions on legislative matters. Whips, appointed by party leadership, communicate party instructions, rally support for government bills, and maintain party discipline. MPs need to understand how the whipping system operates and their role within it.
- **Party Conventions and Policies**: Political parties develop policies, platforms, and agendas that guide their legislative priorities and political strategies. MPs should be familiar with their party's conventions, policies, and core principles to effectively represent party interests and advocate for party positions in parliament.
- **Intra-Party Dynamics**: Political parties are complex organizations with diverse members, factions, and interests. MPs must navigate intra-party dynamics, build relationships with colleagues, and negotiate compromises to advance shared objectives within their party.
- **Leadership and Decision-Making**: Party leaders play a significant role in shaping party politics, setting agendas, and making strategic decisions. MPs interact with party leaders, participate in party meetings, and contribute to decision-making processes. Understanding party leadership dynamics helps MPs influence party strategies and priorities.
- **Election Campaigns**: Political parties engage in election campaigns to mobilize support, promote their platforms, and win electoral mandates. MPs actively participate in election campaigns, canvassing for votes, communicating party messages, and representing party interests to constituents. Understanding party politics helps MPs effectively contribute to election campaigns.
- **Coalition Politics**: In parliamentary systems with coalition governments, MPs may belong to different political parties or coalition partners. MPs must navigate coalition politics, negotiate agreements, and collaborate with coalition partners to advance shared policy goals while balancing party interests.

    - **Parliamentary Committees**: MPs serve on parliamentary committees where they review legislation, scrutinize government actions, and conduct inquiries. Committee memberships may be influenced by party leadership, and MPs need to align their committee work with party priorities and objectives.

    - **Communication and Messaging**: Political parties develop communication strategies, messaging, and narratives to promote their agendas, shape public opinion, and mobilize support. MPs play a role in communicating party messages, defending party positions, and engaging with constituents in accordance with party directives.

    - **Accountability and Oversight**: MPs are accountable to their constituents, political parties, and parliamentary institutions. Understanding party politics helps MPs navigate competing demands, fulfill their obligations, and uphold democratic principles of accountability and transparency.

- **Expert in current affairs and issues prevailing in the country:** Staying well-informed about current affairs and prevailing issues in the country is essential for Members of Parliament (MPs) to effectively represent their constituents and contribute to parliamentary debates and decision-making. Here's why MPs must be experts in current affairs:

    - **Legislative Process**: MPs participate in the legislative process, where they debate, amend, and vote on legislation that affects the lives of their constituents. Being knowledgeable about current affairs helps MPs understand the context, implications, and significance of proposed legislation and make informed decisions.

    - **Policy Formulation**: MPs play a role in formulating and shaping government policies and programs. Understanding current affairs allows MPs to identify emerging issues, assess public sentiment, and advocate for policy solutions that address constituents' needs and priorities.

- **Constituency Representation**: MPs represent the interests, concerns, and aspirations of their constituents in parliament. Being informed about current affairs helps MPs understand local dynamics, socio-economic trends, and community issues, enabling them to effectively advocate for constituency interests and address constituents' concerns.
- **Public Engagement**: MPs engage with constituents through public meetings, town hall discussions, and community events. Being knowledgeable about current affairs allows MPs to communicate effectively with constituents, provide informed perspectives on key issues, and respond to questions and concerns raised by constituents.
- **Media Relations**: MPs interact with the media to communicate government policies, promote legislative initiatives, and address public inquiries. Being well-informed about current affairs enables MPs to engage with the media confidently, articulate government positions, and respond to media inquiries knowledgeably.
- **Parliamentary Debates and Questions**: MPs participate in parliamentary debates, question periods, and committee hearings where they discuss current issues, scrutinize government actions, and hold government officials accountable. Being informed about current affairs equips MPs to engage in debates, ask relevant questions, and contribute constructively to parliamentary proceedings.
- **International Relations**: MPs may engage in discussions and debates on international affairs, foreign policy, and geopolitical developments. Understanding current affairs helps MPs analyze global trends, assess geopolitical risks, and contribute to discussions on international issues affecting the country's interests.
- **Crisis Management**: MPs may be called upon to respond to crises, emergencies, or national disasters. Being knowledgeable about current affairs enables MPs to understand the nature of crises,

assess their impact on constituents, and advocate for government intervention and support as needed.

- **Policy Analysis and Research**: MPs conduct policy analysis and research to develop informed positions on legislative proposals, government policies, and public issues. Being well-informed about current affairs allows MPs to access relevant information, data, and research findings to inform their policy analysis and decision-making.
- **Leadership and Advocacy**: MPs play leadership roles within their political parties, parliamentary committees, and constituencies. Being knowledgeable about current affairs enhances MPs' credibility, influence, and effectiveness as leaders and advocates for positive change and progress.

Being well-informed is fundamental to the effectiveness and credibility of Members of Parliament. By mastering legislative processes, staying abreast of current affairs, understanding local concerns, deepening expertise in policy areas, and upholding ethical standards, MPs can fulfill their responsibilities with diligence and integrity. Being well-informed empowers MPs to advocate for informed policies, represent constituents effectively, and contribute positively to the governance and development of the nation.

Chapter 11
DEALING WITH PRESS AND SOCIAL MEDIA

"Press and social media are the modern megaphones of democracy. In the hands of responsible stewards, they amplify voices, inspire change, and foster transparency. But wielded recklessly, they can sow division and misinformation. As MPs, it's our duty to harness these platforms to inform, engage, and unite our communities for the greater good."

Members of Parliament (MPs) navigate a complex media landscape where effective communication through press and social media channels is crucial for engaging with constituents, shaping public opinion, and promoting transparency in governance. How MPs manage their interactions with the press and social media platforms can significantly impact their ability to represent constituents effectively and uphold democratic principles.

- MPs should recognize the importance of engaging with the press as a means to communicate legislative activities, policy positions, and constituency achievements to the public.
- Press interactions require MPs to convey information accurately, clearly, and transparently while also respecting journalistic integrity and the role of the media in holding public officials accountable.
- MPs should be accessible to journalists, respond promptly to media inquiries, and participate in interviews and press conferences to ensure that accurate information is disseminated to the public.

- MPs must navigate social media platforms thoughtfully and responsibly.
- Social media provides MPs with direct channels to interact with constituents, share updates, gather feedback, and amplify their legislative priorities.
- MPs should use social media to engage in constructive dialogue, address public concerns, and showcase their work in parliament and within the community.
- It is essential for MPs to maintain professionalism and uphold ethical standards in their social media interactions, avoiding misinformation, divisive rhetoric, or personal attacks that undermine public trust and diminish the integrity of political discourse.
- MPs should use social media as a tool for transparency and accountability.
- They can provide insights into parliamentary proceedings, explain policy decisions, and share their voting record to demonstrate their commitment to representing constituents' interests.
- By engaging openly and authentically on social media MPs can foster greater public understanding of legislative processes and promote trust in democratic institutions.
- MPs should be prepared to handle challenges and controversies that may arise in the media or on social platforms.
- This includes addressing misinformation or false allegations promptly, correcting inaccuracies, and offering clarifications to ensure that the public receives accurate information.
- MPs should exercise caution in responding to sensitive issues, seek advice from communications professionals when necessary, and prioritize honesty and transparency in their communications.
- Ethical considerations are paramount in dealing with the press and social media.

- MPs should uphold principles of integrity, respect for privacy, and fairness in their interactions with journalists and constituents online.
- They should refrain from engaging in inflammatory or derogatory language, respect diverse viewpoints, and safeguard the confidentiality of sensitive information in accordance with legal and ethical standards.
- By effectively managing press relations, MPs can communicate their messages, engage with the public, and fulfill their responsibilities as elected representatives in parliament.
- Dealing with the press is an integral part of a Member of Parliament's (MP) role, as it allows them to communicate government policies, legislative initiatives, and constituency work to the public.

- **Ways MPs typically interact with the press:**
    - **Press Releases**: MPs issue press releases to announce important events, policy announcements, legislative proposals, or constituency initiatives. Press releases provide journalists with official statements and background information on key issues and events.
    - **Press Conferences**: MPs hold press conferences to address the media directly, answer questions, and provide detailed information on specific topics or developments. Press conferences allow MPs to communicate key messages, clarify misconceptions, and engage with journalists in real-time.
    - **Media Interviews**: MPs participate in media interviews with journalists from print, broadcast, or online media outlets. Interviews may be conducted in person, over the phone, or via video conferencing platforms. MPs use interviews to share their perspectives, provide expert analysis, and respond to journalists' inquiries on current affairs and policy matters.
    - **Opinion Articles and Columns**: MPs may write opinion articles or columns for newspapers, magazines, or online publications to

express their views on specific issues, share insights, and engage with the public. Opinion pieces allow MPs to communicate directly with readers and influence public opinion on important topics.

- **Social Media Engagement**: MPs use social media platforms such as Twitter, Facebook, and Instagram to communicate with constituents and engage with the public. They share updates, news, and announcements, respond to messages and comments, and participate in online discussions on relevant issues.
- **Media Liaison Officers**: MPs may appoint media liaison officers or communications staff to manage press relations, handles media inquiries, and coordinate media activities. Media liaison officers work closely with journalists, prepare press materials, and facilitate media coverage of MP-related events and activities.
- **Media Monitoring and Analysis**: MPs monitor media coverage of parliamentary proceedings, government policies, and constituency issues to stay informed about public perceptions and media narratives. Media monitoring helps MPs assess the impact of their communications efforts and identify opportunities to enhance their media strategies.
- **Crisis Communications**: In times of crisis or controversy, MPs may need to engage in crisis communications to address public concerns, provide reassurance, and manage media inquiries. MPs work with their communications teams to develop crisis communication plans, coordinate messaging, and respond effectively to media inquiries and public scrutiny.
- **Media Training**: MPs may undergo media training to enhance their communication skills, prepare for media interviews, and effectively engage with journalists. Media training equips MPs with techniques for delivering key messages, handling difficult questions, and managing media interactions professionally.
- **Transparency and Accountability**: MPs strive to maintain transparency and accountability in their dealings with the

press, providing accurate information, respecting journalistic independence, and adhering to ethical standards. Transparency fosters public trust and confidence in MPs' communications with the press.

- **Liaoning with press:** Liaison with the press is a crucial aspect of a Member of Parliament's (MP) communication strategy, allowing them to effectively communicate with constituents, shape public opinion, and advance their policy agenda.
    - By effectively liaising with the press, MPs can communicate their messages, engage with the public, and shape the public discourse on important issues.
    - Liaison with the press is essential for MPs to fulfill their responsibilities as elected representatives and effectively represent the interests of their constituents.

- **MPs typically liaise with the press:**
    - **Media Contacts**: MPs establish relationships with journalists, editors, and media outlets to facilitate communication and collaboration. Building a network of media contacts helps MPs ensure that their messages reach the right audiences and that they have access to accurate and timely information.
    - **Press Releases**: MPs issue press releases to announce important events, policy announcements, legislative initiatives, or constituency activities. Press releases are distributed to media outlets to provide journalists with official statements and background information on key issues and developments.
    - **Media Briefings**: MPs may hold media briefings or background briefings to provide journalists with detailed information, context, and analysis on specific topics or developments. Media briefings allow MPs to engage with journalists, answer questions, and provide insights on relevant issues.

- **Media Interviews**: MPs participate in media interviews with journalists from print, broadcast, or online media outlets. Interviews may be conducted in person, over the phone, or via video conferencing platforms. MPs use interviews to share their perspectives, provide expert analysis, and respond to journalists' inquiries on current affairs and policy matters.
- **Press Conferences**: MPs hold press conferences to address the media directly, make announcements, and answer questions on specific topics or developments. Press conferences provide an opportunity for MPs to communicate key messages, clarify misconceptions, and engage with journalists in real-time.
- **Opinion Pieces**: MPs may write opinion articles, columns, or letters to the editor for newspapers, magazines, or online publications. Opinion pieces allow MPs to express their views, share insights, and influence public opinion on important issues. MPs work with editors and journalists to publish their writings in relevant media outlets.
- **Social Media Engagement**: MPs use social media platforms such as Twitter, Facebook, and Instagram to communicate with constituents and engage with the public. They share updates, news, and announcements, respond to messages and comments, and participate in online discussions on relevant issues. MPs leverage social media to complement their traditional media outreach efforts and reach a broader audience.
- **Media Events**: MPs organize media events, such as press briefings, photo opportunities, or media tours, to generate media coverage and raise awareness of important issues or initiatives. Media events provide journalists with opportunities to interact with MPs, gather information, and produce news stories.
- **Media Liaison Officers**: MPs may appoint media liaison officers or communications staffs to manage press relations, handle media inquiries, and coordinate media activities. Media liaison officers

work closely with journalists, prepare press materials, and facilitate media coverage of MP-related events and activities.

- **Media Monitoring and Analysis**: MPs monitor media coverage of parliamentary proceedings, government policies, and constituency issues to stay informed about public perceptions and media narratives. Media monitoring helps MPs assess the impact of their communications efforts and identify opportunities to enhance their media strategies.

- **Skills of MP in dealing with press correspondents:** Dealing with press correspondents requires a specific set of skills for Members of Parliament (MPs) to effectively communicate their messages, engage with journalists, and manage media interactions. By practicing these skills, MPs can effectively engage with press correspondents, communicate their messages, and manage media interactions to advance their objectives and effectively represent their constituents. Here are some key skills MPs should possess when interacting with press correspondents:

  - **Effective Communication**: MPs should be skilled communicators, capable of articulating their ideas, positions, and messages clearly and persuasively to journalists. They should be able to convey complex information in a concise and understandable manner, adapting their communication style to suit different audiences and media formats.

  - **Media Savvy**: MPs should have a good understanding of how the media operates, including journalistic practices, deadlines, and editorial processes. Being media savvy allows MPs to navigate media interactions confidently, anticipate journalists' questions, and effectively manage media relations.

  - **Message Discipline**: MPs should demonstrate message discipline when engaging with press correspondents, staying focused on their key messages and objectives. They should be able to convey consistent and coherent messages across different media platforms and avoid being sidetracked by irrelevant or off-topic questions.

- **Active Listening**: MPs should be active listeners, paying close attention to journalists' questions, concerns, and perspectives during media interactions. By listening attentively, MPs can better understand journalists' inquiries, address their concerns, and tailor their responses accordingly.
- **Calm under Pressure**: MPs should remain calm and composed, even in high-pressure media situations such as press conferences or interviews. Maintaining composure allows MPs to handle challenging questions, defuse tense situations, and project confidence and professionalism to the media.
- **Media Training**: MPs may undergo media training to enhance their communication skills, prepare for media interviews, and effectively engage with journalists. Media training equips MPs with techniques for delivering key messages, handling difficult questions, and managing media interactions professionally.
- **Knowledgeable and Informed**: MPs should be knowledgeable and well-informed about relevant issues, policies, and developments in their areas of expertise. Being well-prepared allows MPs to provide accurate information, offer expert analysis, and respond confidently to journalists' inquiries during media interactions.
- **Flexibility and Adaptability**: MPs should be flexible and adaptable in their approach to media interactions, adjusting their communication strategies and tactics based on the nature of the media engagement, the preferences of the journalist, and the specific context of the situation.
- **Transparency and Authenticity**: MPs should demonstrate transparency and authenticity in their interactions with press correspondents, providing honest and straightforward answers to journalists' questions. Building trust and credibility with the

media requires MPs to be genuine, sincere, and open in their communications.

- **Respectful and Courteous**: MPs should treat press correspondents with respect and courtesy, regardless of differences in opinion or perspective. Maintaining positive and professional relationships with journalists helps MPs foster constructive media relations and ensure fair and balanced coverage of their activities and messages.

- **Interviews to press by MPs:** By following these steps, MPs can give effective interviews to the press, communicate their messages clearly and persuasively, and engage with constituents through the media to advance their objectives and represent their interests effectively. Giving interviews to the press is a crucial aspect of a Member of Parliament's (MP) communication strategy, as it allows them to communicate their messages, address public concerns, and engage with constituents through the media.

    - **Preparation**: Before the interview, MPs should thoroughly prepare by familiarizing themselves with the topic or issue being discussed, gathering relevant information, and anticipating potential questions from journalists. This includes reviewing background materials, data, and talking points to ensure they are well-informed and prepared to respond effectively.

    - **Know Your Audience**: MPs should consider the audience of the media outlet conducting the interview and tailor their messages accordingly. Understanding the demographics, interests, and preferences of the audience helps MPs communicate their messages more effectively and resonate with viewers or readers.

    - **Establish Key Messages**: MPs should identify key messages or talking points they want to convey during the interview and ensure they are clear, concise, and relevant to the topic at hand. Key messages should align with the MP's priorities, policy positions, and objectives, and should be communicated consistently throughout the interview.

- **Stay on Message**: During the interview, MPs should focus on delivering their key messages and avoid getting sidetracked by unrelated topics or questions. It's important to stay disciplined and steer the conversation back to the main points the MP wants to convey.
- **Be Authentic and Genuine**: MPs should be authentic and genuine in their communication, speaking honestly and sincerely about their views, experiences, and perspectives. Authenticity builds trust and credibility with the audience and helps MPs connect with viewers or readers on a personal level.
- **Listen Actively**: MPs should listen actively to the questions asked by the interviewer, paying close attention to the interviewer's concerns, interests, and perspectives. Active listening allows MPs to provide relevant and responsive answers that address the journalist's inquiries effectively.
- **Speak clearly and confidently**: MPs should speak clearly and confidently during the interview, using a calm and composed demeanor to convey professionalism and authority. Clear and confident communication helps MPs command attention and engage with the audience more effectively.
- **Stay Calm Under Pressure**: If faced with challenging or difficult questions, MPs should remain calm and composed, refraining from becoming defensive or confrontational. Instead, they should address the question directly, provide a thoughtful response, and maintain control of the conversation.
- **Bridge and Pivot**: MPs can use bridging and pivoting techniques to transition smoothly between topics or steer the conversation toward their key messages. Bridging involves acknowledging the question briefly before redirecting the conversation to the desired topic, while pivoting involves

shifting the focus of the discussion to a related but more favorable topic.

- **Follow Up**: After the interview, MPs should follow up with the journalist to express gratitude for the opportunity and provide any additional information or clarification if needed. Building positive relationships with journalists fosters continued media engagement and coverage of the MP's activities and messages.

- **Expressing opinions to press:** By utilizing these channels and formats, MPs can effectively express their opinions to the press, communicate their perspectives to constituents and the public, and influence public discourse on important issues affecting society. Members of Parliament (MPs) express their opinions to the press through various channels and formats, aiming to communicate their perspectives, advocate for their constituents, and influence public discourse. Here are some ways MPs can express their opinions to the press:

  - **Media Interviews**: MPs may participate in interviews with journalists from print, broadcast, or online media outlets. During interviews, MPs have the opportunity to express their opinions, provide expert analysis, and respond to journalists' questions on current affairs, policy issues, or legislative matters.

  - **Opinion Articles**: MPs can write opinion articles or columns for newspapers, magazines, or online publications to share their views on specific topics, policy proposals, or public concerns. Opinion pieces allow MPs to articulate their opinions in a more detailed and nuanced manner, reaching a wider audience and influencing public opinion.

  - **Press Releases**: MPs issue press releases to communicate their opinions, statements, or positions on particular issues or developments. Press releases are distributed to media outlets to provide journalists with official statements and background information on the MP's views or responses to relevant events or news.

- **Social Media**: MPs use social media platforms such as Twitter, Facebook, and Instagram to express their opinions, share insights, and engage with constituents and the public. MPs can post updates, comments, or videos expressing their opinions on various issues, interacting directly with followers and generating discussion.
- **Press Conferences**: MPs may hold press conferences or media briefings to address the press directly, make announcements, or express their opinions on specific topics or developments. Press conferences provide an opportunity for MPs to communicate their views to a broader audience and respond to journalists' inquiries in real-time.
- **Parliamentary Speeches**: MPs can express their opinions on the floor of parliament through speeches, debates, or interventions on legislative matters, policy proposals, or government actions. Parliamentary speeches allow MPs to advocate for their viewpoints, present arguments, and influence legislative outcomes.
- **Committee Proceedings**: MPs participate in parliamentary committee meetings where they discuss, debate, and scrutinize legislative proposals, government policies, or public issues. MPs can express their opinions during committee proceedings, questioning witnesses, proposing amendments, or making statements on relevant topics.
- **Constituency Engagements**: MPs engage with constituents through public meetings, town hall discussions, or community events, where they have the opportunity to express their opinions, address concerns, and listen to feedback from constituents. Constituency engagements provide MPs with a platform to communicate their views directly to the people they represent.
- **Media Events**: MPs organize media events such as press briefings, photo opportunities, or media tours to generate

media coverage and communicate their opinions on specific issues or initiatives. Media events allow MPs to engage with journalists, amplify their messages, and raise awareness of their viewpoints.

- **Letters to the Editor**: MPs can write letters to the editor of newspapers or magazines to express their opinions on published articles, editorials, or public debates. Letters to the editor provide MPs with a forum to respond to media coverage, challenge viewpoints, or highlight alternative perspectives on relevant issues.

Do's and Don'ts while giving interviews to press: When giving interviews to the press, Members of Parliament (MPs) should adhere to certain do's and don'ts to ensure effective communication, maintain professionalism, and protect their reputation. Here are some key guidelines:

DO'S:

- **Prepare Thoroughly**: Prepare for the interview by researching the topic, gathering relevant information, and identifying key messages or talking points you want to convey.
- **Stay on Message**: Focus on delivering your key messages and priorities during the interview, and steer the conversation back to these points if necessary.
- **Speak clearly and concisely**: Communicate your ideas clearly and concisely, avoiding jargon or technical language that may be difficult for the audience to understand.
- **Be Honest and Transparent**: Be honest and transparent in your responses, providing accurate information and avoiding exaggeration or misinformation.
- **Listen Actively**: Listen to the interviewer's questions attentively, and respond thoughtfully and respectfully, addressing the specific points raised.

- **Remain Calm and Composed**: Stay calm and composed, even if faced with challenging questions or criticism, and respond in a professional and respectful manner.
- **Bridge and Pivot**: Use bridging and pivoting techniques to transition smoothly between topics or redirect the conversation to your key messages if necessary.
- **Acknowledge Mistakes and Correct Misinformation**: If you make a mistake or are unsure about something, acknowledge it honestly and correct any misinformation to maintain credibility.
- **Follow Up**: Follow up with the journalist after the interview to express gratitude for the opportunity and provide any additional information or clarification if needed.
- **Review the Coverage**: Review the media coverage of the interview afterward to assess how your messages were conveyed and identify any areas for improvement in future interviews.

DON'TS:

- **Don't speculate or Guess**: Avoid speculating or guessing about uncertain or speculative topics, as this can undermine your credibility and lead to misinformation.
- **Don't Dodge Questions**: Avoid dodging questions or deflecting accountability, as this can erode trust and credibility with the audience and the press.
- **Don't Get Defensive or Argumentative**: Avoid getting defensive or argumentative in response to challenging questions or criticism, as this can escalate tensions and damage your reputation.
- **Don't Provide Confidential Information**: Avoid disclosing confidential or sensitive information that could compromise national security, violate privacy rights, or breach confidentiality agreements.
- **Don't Speak Off the Record**: Avoid speaking off the record unless you trust the journalist implicitly and understand the potential risks and consequences of doing so.

- **Don't Lose Your Temper**: Avoid losing your temper or reacting emotionally, even if the interview becomes contentious or adversarial, as this can detract from your credibility and professionalism.
- **Don't Engage in Personal Attacks**: Avoid engaging in personal attacks or disparaging remarks about individuals or organizations, as this can damage your reputation and undermine constructive dialogue.
- **Don't Overstep Your Authority**: Avoid making statements or commitments that exceed your authority or jurisdiction, as this can create confusion and lead to unintended consequences.
- **Don't Disregard Journalistic Ethics**: Avoid disregarding journalistic ethics or press standards, such as accuracy, fairness, and impartiality, as this can undermine your credibility and the integrity of the interview process.
- **Don't Forget to Follow Up**: Don't forget to follow up with the journalist after the interview to provide any additional information or clarification if needed, as this demonstrates professionalism and accountability.

By following these do's and don'ts, MPs can effectively navigate interviews with the press, communicate their messages clearly and persuasively, and maintain trust and credibility with the public and the media.

- **Using social media for benefit:** Using social media can be highly beneficial for Members of Parliament (MPs) to engage with constituents, communicate their messages, and build relationships. MPs can enhance their communication, engagement, and representation efforts, strengthening their relationships with constituents and maximizing their impact as elected representatives. Here are some ways MPs can use social media for their benefit:

  - **Connect with Constituents**: Social media platforms provide MPs with a direct and immediate way to connect with constituents. MPs can use platforms like Twitter, Facebook, and Instagram to share updates, respond to inquiries, and engage in conversations with constituents in real-time.

- **Share Information and Updates**: MPs can use social media to share information and updates about their work, including legislative initiatives, constituency activities, and public events. By keeping constituents informed, MPs demonstrate transparency and accountability in their work.
- **Amplify Messages**: Social media allows MPs to amplify their messages and reach a wider audience beyond traditional media channels. MPs can use hash tags, tagging, and sharing features to increase the visibility of their posts and engage with users interested in specific topics or issues.
- **Engage in Dialogue**: Social media provides MPs with a platform to engage in dialogue and exchange ideas with constituents. MPs can solicit feedback, answer questions, and address concerns raised by constituents, fostering a two-way conversation that promotes citizen participation and democratic engagement.
- **Humanize Representation**: Social media offers MPs an opportunity to humanize their representation by sharing personal insights, anecdotes, and behind-the-scenes glimpses into their lives and work. By showing their personality and authenticity, MPs can build trust and rapport with constituents.
- **Promote Events and Initiatives**: MPs can use social media to promote public events, town hall meetings, and constituency initiatives. Social media platforms enable MPs to reach a broader audience and attract attendees to their events, enhancing community engagement and participation.
- **Monitor Public Opinion**: Social media serves as a valuable tool for MPs to monitor public opinion, sentiment, and trends in their constituencies. By listening to conversations, tracking hash tags, and analyzing feedback, MPs can gain insights into

constituents' priorities and concerns, informing their decision-making and advocacy efforts.

- **Network and Collaborate**: Social media allows MPs to network and collaborate with colleagues, stakeholders, and community leaders. MPs can connect with other elected officials, advocacy groups, and organizations to share resources, coordinate efforts, and amplify collective voices on shared issues.
- **Educate and Inform**: MPs can use social media to educate and inform constituents about important issues, policies, and government processes. MPs can share info graphics, videos, and articles to explain complex topics in a clear and accessible manner, empowering constituents with knowledge and understanding.
- **Demonstrate Leadership**: Social media provides MPs with a platform to demonstrate leadership on key issues and showcase their commitment to serving constituents. By taking a proactive stance, advocating for solutions, and championing causes, MPs can inspire confidence and support from constituents.
- **Skills of social media:** Social media skills encompass a range of abilities that enable individuals, including Members of Parliament (MPs), to effectively use social media platforms for communication, engagement, and networking. By developing these social media skills, MPs can effectively engage with constituents, communicate their messages, and build meaningful relationships on social media platforms. Here are some skills relevant to social media:
  - **Content Creation**: The ability to create compelling and engaging content is essential for social media success. This includes writing clear and concise text, creating eye-catching graphics or visuals, and producing multimedia content such as videos or podcasts.

- **Copywriting**: Crafting engaging and persuasive copy is crucial for capturing audience attention and driving engagement on social media. Copywriting skills involve writing compelling headlines, captions, and calls to action that resonate with the target audience.
- **Visual Design**: Proficiency in visual design tools and techniques allows individuals to create visually appealing graphics, images, and videos for sharing on social media platforms. This includes skills in graphic design, photo editing, and video production.
- **Community Management**: Effective community management involves engaging with followers, responding to comments and messages, and fostering positive interactions on social media platforms. This skill requires good communication, empathy, and responsiveness.
- **Analytics and Insights**: Understanding social media analytics and insights allows individuals to track performance metrics, measure engagement, and optimize their social media strategy. This skill involves interpreting data, identifying trends, and making data-driven decisions.
- **Social Listening**: Social listening involves monitoring conversations and mentions on social media platforms to understand audience sentiment, gather feedback, and identify emerging trends or issues. This skill requires attentiveness, analytical thinking, and the ability to extract actionable insights from social media data.
- **Platform Proficiency**: Familiarity with various social media platforms, including Facebook, Twitter, Instagram, LinkedIn, and YouTube, is essential for effectively leveraging each platform's unique features and functionalities. This includes understanding platform algorithms, best practices, and etiquette.

- **Strategic Planning**: Developing a strategic approach to social media involves setting clear goals, defining target audiences, and planning content and campaigns that align with broader objectives. This skill requires strategic thinking, creativity, and the ability to adapt to changing circumstances.
- **Crisis Management**: Being prepared to handle crises or negative feedback on social media is essential for maintaining reputation and trust. Crisis management skills involve responding promptly, transparently, and empathetically to address concerns and mitigate reputational damage.
- **Continuous Learning**: Social media is constantly evolving, so individuals need to stay updated on the latest trends, features, and best practices. Continuous learning involves seeking out resources, attending training sessions, and experimenting with new strategies to stay ahead in the ever-changing social media landscape.
- **Do's and don'ts while using social media:** When using social media, including platforms like Twitter, Facebook, Instagram, and LinkedIn, there are certain do's and don'ts to keep in mind to ensure effective communication, maintain professionalism, and protect your reputation. Here are some key guidelines:

DO'S:

- **Be Authentic**: Be genuine and authentic in your interactions on social media. Show your personality, share personal insights, and engage with your audience in a sincere and relatable manner.
- **Provide Value**: Share content that provides value to your audience, such as informative articles, helpful resources, or insights into your work and interests. Aim to educate, entertain, or inspire your followers with your posts.

- **Engage with Your Audience**: Actively engage with your audience by responding to comments, messages, and mentions. Show appreciation for feedback, answer questions, and foster meaningful conversations with your followers.
- **Be Respectful**: Treat others with respect and courtesy in your interactions on social media. Avoid engaging in confrontational or disrespectful behavior, and be mindful of differing opinions and perspectives.
- **Promote Dialogue**: Encourage open dialogue and constructive discussions on social media. Welcome diverse viewpoints, foster healthy debates, and create a safe and inclusive environment for your followers to share their thoughts and opinions.
- **Use Visuals**: Incorporate visuals such as images, videos, and info graphics into your posts to make them more engaging and visually appealing. Visual content tends to attract more attention and engagement on social media platforms.
- **Stay Consistent**: Maintain a consistent presence on social media by posting regularly and at strategic times. Establish a posting schedule that works for you and your audience, and stick to it to maintain visibility and engagement.
- **Follow Social Media Etiquette**: Adhere to social media etiquette guidelines, such as respecting copyright laws, giving credit to others when sharing content, and avoiding over posting or over posting.
- **Monitor Your Reputation**: Monitor mentions, comments, and feedback about yourself or your brand on social media. Address any concerns or negative feedback promptly and professionally to manage your reputation effectively.
- **Stay Informed**: Stay informed about social media trends, updates, and best practices to keep your strategy current and effective. Continuously learn and adapt to changes in the social media landscape to maintain relevance and engagement.

DON'TS:

- **Don't Overshare Personal Information**: Avoid sharing sensitive or personal information that could compromise your privacy or security on social media. Be cautious about sharing details such as your home address, phone number, or financial information.
- **Don't Engage in Trolling or Harassment**: Refrain from engaging in trolling, harassment, or cyber bullying on social media. Treat others with respect and kindness, and report any abusive or inappropriate behavior to the platform's moderators.
- **Don't Spam**: Avoid spamming your followers with excessive or irrelevant posts. Be selective and intentional with your content, and focus on quality over quantity to maintain engagement and avoid overwhelming your audience.
- **Don't React Emotionally**: Avoid reacting emotionally to negative feedback or criticism on social media. Stay calm, composed, and professional in your responses, and address concerns or disagreements respectfully and constructively.
- **Don't Ignore Feedback**: Don't ignore feedback or comments from your audience, even if it's negative or critical. Acknowledge feedback, address concerns, and use it as an opportunity to learn and improve your social media presence.
- **Don't Violate Terms of Service**: Familiarize yourself with the terms of service and community guidelines of each social media platform you use, and avoid violating them. Respect platform rules regarding content, behavior, and usage to avoid being penalized or banned.
- **Don't Spread Misinformation**: Avoid spreading misinformation or false information on social media. Verify the accuracy of information before sharing it, and be transparent about the sources of your content to maintain credibility and trust with your audience.
- **Don't Ignore Your Audience**: Don't ignore or neglect your audience on social media. Make an effort to engage with your followers, respond

to their comments and messages, and show appreciation for their support to build a loyal and engaged community.

- **Don't over promote**: Avoid over promoting yourself, your products, or your services on social media. Strike a balance between promotional content and other types of content that provide value and engage your audience authentically.
- **Don't Burn Bridges**: Don't burn bridges or damage relationships on social media by engaging in public conflicts or arguments. Address disagreements privately and respectfully, and strive to maintain positive and professional interactions with others.

By following these do's and don'ts, you can effectively navigate social media, build meaningful connections with your audience, and enhance your personal brand or professional reputation online.

Effective management of press and social media interactions is essential for MPs to fulfill their responsibilities as public representatives. By engaging proactively, responsibly, and ethically with the press and social media platforms, MPs can enhance transparency, strengthen democratic engagement, and build trust with constituents. Ultimately, MPs should view press and social media as valuable tools for communication, accountability, and public outreach in service to their constituents and the democratic process.

"Ethics in Politics"

- **Integrity:** Politicians should demonstrate honesty, transparency, and consistency in their actions and decisions.
- **Accountability:** Politicians are accountable to the public for their decisions and actions. They should be willing to accept responsibility for mistakes.

- **Fairness and Justice**: Politicians should advocate for policies and practices that promote fairness, equality, and justice for all individuals and communities.
    - **Respect for Law**: Politicians should respect and uphold the rule of law.
    - **Respectful Conduct**: Politicians should engage in respectful and civil discourse, treating colleagues, opponents, and constituents with dignity and courtesy.
    - **Transparency**: Politicians should disclose relevant information to the public, including financial interests, campaign contributions, and decision-making processes.
    - **Public Interest**: Politicians should prioritize the public interest over personal gain or partisan interests.
    - **Promotion of Democracy**: Politicians should actively promote and defend democratic values, including free and fair elections, freedom of speech, independent media, and civic participation.
    - **Ethical Leadership**: Politicians should lead by example, inspiring trust and confidence through their ethical conduct and commitment to serving the public good.
    - **Continuous Ethics Education**: Politicians should engage in ongoing education and training on ethical standards, conflict resolution, and decision-making processes.
    - In conclusion, ethics in politics are essential for maintaining public trust, ensuring effective governance, and safeguarding democratic principles. MPs and politicians have a responsibility to uphold ethical standards, demonstrate integrity in their actions, and prioritize the well-being of their constituents and society as a whole.

Chapter 12
STRATEGIC PLANNING

"Strategic planning is the compass that guides organizations through the complexities of the future. It's the art of envisioning possibilities, setting clear objectives, and charting a course of action that transforms vision into reality."

Strategic planning is a crucial aspect of the role of Members of Parliament (MPs) as they navigate their responsibilities to represent constituents, contribute to legislative processes, and advocate for policies that address national and local issues effectively. Strategic planning enables MPs to set clear objectives, prioritize initiatives, and allocate resources strategically to achieve their goals and maximize their impact as public representatives. Strategic planning by MPs involves setting legislative priorities that align with the needs and aspirations of their constituents.

- MPs must conduct thorough research, engage with stakeholders, and analyze data to identify key issues and challenges facing their constituency.
- By prioritizing legislative initiatives that address these concerns, MPs can advocate for policies and reforms that improve the quality of life, promote economic development, and enhance social well-being within their communities.

- Strategic planning enables MPs to leverage parliamentary tools and processes effectively.
- MPs participate in committees, where they contribute expertise, scrutinize legislation, and shape policy outcomes.
- Strategic engagement in committees allows MPs to influence legislative debates, propose amendments, and collaborate with colleagues across party lines to achieve consensus on critical issues.
- Moreover, strategic planning by MPs includes proactive engagement with government officials, stakeholders, and community leaders to build coalitions and partnerships that support legislative priorities.
- MPs must cultivate relationships, negotiate effectively, and advocate persuasively for resources and support to advance their policy agenda. By leveraging networks and alliances, MPs can amplify their influence and achieve meaningful outcomes for their constituents and the nation.
- Strategic planning by MPs extends to constituency development and service delivery.
- MPs should prioritize projects and initiatives that address infrastructure needs, healthcare access, educational opportunities, and environmental sustainability within their constituencies.
- By collaborating with local authorities, businesses, and community organizations, MPs can secure funding, facilitate partnerships, and implement solutions that benefit their constituents and promote community development.
- Ethical considerations are integral to strategic planning by MPs.
- MPs must prioritize transparency, accountability, and integrity in their decision-making processes and interactions.
- Ethical strategic planning involves consulting with constituents, seeking diverse perspectives, and making decisions that prioritize the public interest over personal or partisan gain.

    - Strategic planning is essential for MPs as it enables them to set goals, allocate resources, make informed decisions, engage stakeholders, and adapt to changing contexts effectively. By engaging in strategic planning,
    - MPs can fulfill their responsibilities as elected representatives, advance their policy agenda, and make a positive impact on their constituency and society.
    - By engaging in strategic planning, MPs can effectively represent their constituents, advocate for their interests, and contribute to positive change in their communities and the broader society.
    - Strategic planning enables MPs to set clear goals, allocate resources wisely, and navigate the complex challenges of governance and representation with purpose and vision.
- **Strategic planning** is crucial for Members of Parliament (MPs) as it enables them to set clear goals, define priorities, and develop action plans to effectively represent their constituents and achieve desired outcomes. Here are several reasons why strategic planning is important for MPs:
    - **Alignment of Goals and Priorities**: Strategic planning helps MPs align their goals and priorities with the needs and interests of their constituents. By conducting a thorough analysis of their constituency and engaging with stakeholders, MPs can identify key issues, concerns, and opportunities that inform their strategic planning process.
    - **Effective Resource Allocation**: Strategic planning allows MPs to allocate resources, including time, staff, and budget, in a strategic and efficient manner. By prioritizing initiatives and activities based on their strategic objectives, MPs can optimize resource utilization and maximize their impact as elected representatives.
    - **Enhanced Decision-Making**: Strategic planning provides MPs with a framework for making informed decisions about policy

priorities, legislative initiatives, and constituency activities. By conducting thorough analysis and considering various options, MPs can make strategic decisions that advance their goals and interests.

- **Increased Accountability and Transparency**: Strategic planning promotes accountability and transparency in MPs' work by clearly defining goals, objectives, and performance indicators. MPs can track progress, measure outcomes, and report results to constituents, demonstrating their commitment to fulfilling their responsibilities effectively.
- **Stakeholder Engagement and Collaboration**: Strategic planning encourages MPs to engage with stakeholders, including constituents, community leaders, advocacy groups, and government agencies, to gather input, solicit feedback, and build partnerships. Collaboration with stakeholders enhances MPs' understanding of community needs and fosters collective action to address shared challenges.
- **Adaptation to Changing Contexts**: Strategic planning enables MPs to adapt to changing political, social, and economic contexts by anticipating future trends and adjusting their plans accordingly. MPs can proactively respond to emerging issues, challenges, and opportunities, ensuring that their strategies remain relevant and effective over time.
- **Improved Communication and Messaging**: Strategic planning helps MPs develop clear and consistent messaging that effectively communicates their goals, priorities, and achievements to constituents and stakeholders. By articulating their vision and values through strategic communication, MPs can build trust, credibility, and support among their constituents.
- **Long-Term Vision and Sustainability**: Strategic planning encourages MPs to take a long-term view of their work and set goals that contribute to sustainable development and positive

change in their constituency and society. By investing in strategic priorities and initiatives, MPs can create lasting impact and leave a meaningful legacy for future generations.

- **Efficient Use of Time and Effort**: Strategic planning enables MPs to prioritize tasks, streamline workflows, and focus their time and effort on activities that align with their strategic objectives. By avoiding distractions and maintaining a clear sense of purpose, MPs can maximize their productivity and effectiveness in serving their constituents.

- **Empowerment and Empathy**: Strategic planning empowers MPs to be proactive, visionary, and impactful in their representation of constituents. By listening to the needs and concerns of their constituents and advocating on their behalf, MPs can make a meaningful difference in the lives of the people they serve, fostering a sense of trust, empowerment, and empathy within the community.

- **Strategic planning by a member of parliament:** It involves setting long-term goals, identifying key priorities, and developing action plans to achieve them. By following this strategic planning framework, MPs can effectively prioritize their efforts, maximize their impact, and better serve the needs of their constituents. Here's a framework for strategic planning that an MP might follow:

    - **Define Objectives**: Begin by clearly defining the overarching objectives and priorities that you want to accomplish during your term in office. These objectives should reflect your values, the needs of your constituents, and the broader political context.

    - **Assess Constituency Needs**: Conduct a comprehensive assessment of the needs, concerns, and priorities of your constituents. This may involve gathering feedback through surveys, town hall meetings, and one-on-one conversations with constituents.

    - **Identify Key Issues**: Identify the key issues and challenges facing your constituency and prioritize them based on their importance and urgency. Consider both local issues that directly impact your constituents and broader national or global issues that require attention.

- **Set Goals and Targets**: Based on your assessment of constituency needs and key issues, establish specific, measurable, achievable, relevant, and time-bound (SMART) goals and targets. These goals should align with your objectives and address the most pressing issues facing your constituents.
- **Develop Strategies and Action Plans**: Develop strategies and action plans for achieving your goals and targets. This may involve identifying policy solutions, building coalitions, advocating for legislative changes, securing funding for projects, and mobilizing community support.
- **Allocate Resources**: Determine the resources, including staff, budget, and time, needed to implement your strategies and action plans effectively. Allocate resources strategically to maximize impact and achieve desired outcomes.
- **Engage Stakeholders**: Engage with stakeholders, including constituents, community organizations, businesses, government agencies, and advocacy groups, to build support for your initiatives and collaborate on shared goals.
- **Monitor Progress**: Regularly monitor and evaluate progress towards your goals and targets. Establish key performance indicators (KPIs) to track progress, identify challenges, and make adjustments as needed to stay on track.
- **Communicate and Engage**: Communicate your priorities, progress, and achievements to constituents through various channels, including newsletters, social media, town hall meetings, and media interviews. Engage with constituents regularly to solicit feedback, address concerns, and keep them informed about your work.

  - **Adapt and Evolve**: Be flexible and adaptive in your approach to strategic planning. The political landscape is dynamic, and priorities may shift over time. Continuously reassess your goals and strategies, adapt to changing circumstances, and evolve your plans as needed to remain effective in achieving your objectives.

- **What is strategic planning by MPs:** Strategic planning by Members of Parliament (MPs) involves the deliberate and systematic process of setting goals, defining objectives, and developing action plans to guide their activities and achieve desired outcomes. Strategic planning helps MPs effectively represent their constituents, advance their policy agenda, and fulfill their responsibilities as elected representatives. Here are some key components of strategic planning by MPs:

  - **Goal Setting**: MPs begin the strategic planning process by identifying overarching goals and objectives that align with their vision, values, and priorities. Goals may include legislative priorities, constituency needs, policy initiatives, or broader objectives related to governance and representation.

  - **Constituency Analysis**: MPs conduct a thorough analysis of their constituency to understand the demographic, social, economic, and political dynamics shaping the local community. This analysis helps MPs identify constituents' needs, concerns, and priorities, informing their strategic planning process.

  - **Stakeholder Engagement**: MPs engage with stakeholders, including constituents, community leaders, advocacy groups, and government agencies, to gather input, solicit feedback, and build partnerships. Stakeholder engagement ensures that MPs consider diverse perspectives and collaborate with key stakeholders in their strategic planning efforts.

  - **Policy Development**: MPs develop policies and legislative proposals that address constituents' needs and concerns, reflect their values and priorities, and contribute to positive change. Policy development involves researching issues, consulting experts, drafting legislation, and building consensus among stakeholders.

- **Communication Strategy**: MPs develop a communication strategy to effectively communicate their goals, priorities, and achievements to constituents, stakeholders, and the public. This strategy may include media engagement, social media outreach, public events, newsletters, and other communication channels.
- **Resource Allocation**: MPs allocate resources, including time, staff, and budget, to support their strategic priorities and activities. Resource allocation involves prioritizing initiatives, optimizing resource utilization, and ensuring accountability and transparency in resource management.
- **Performance Measurement**: MPs establish key performance indicators (KPIs) and metrics to evaluate the effectiveness of their strategic planning efforts and track progress toward their goals and objectives. Performance measurement allows MPs to assess outcomes, identify areas for improvement, and make data-driven decisions.
- **Flexibility and Adaptability**: MPs remain flexible and adaptable in their strategic planning process, recognizing that external factors, such as changes in the political landscape, emerging issues, or unforeseen events, may require adjustments to their plans and priorities.
- **Collaboration and Coalition Building**: MPs collaborate with colleagues, political allies, and stakeholders to build coalitions and alliances that support their strategic objectives. Collaboration enhances MPs' effectiveness in advancing their policy agenda and achieving collective goals.
- **Continuous Evaluation and Improvement**: MPs continuously evaluate their strategic planning process and outcomes, seeking feedback, learning from experience, and making adjustments as needed to improve their performance and maximize their impact as elected representatives.

- **Skills in strategic planning:** Skills in strategic planning are essential for Members of Parliament (MPs) to effectively set goals, develop action plans, and achieve desired outcomes in their roles as elected representatives. By developing and honing these skills, MPs can engage in strategic planning effectively, set clear goals, and navigate the complexities of governance and representation with purpose and vision. Skills involved in strategic planning for MPs:
    - **Analytical Skills**: MPs need strong analytical skills to assess the political, social, economic, and environmental factors influencing their constituency and the broader society. This involves collecting and analyzing data, identifying trends and patterns, and making informed decisions based on evidence and insights.
    - **Critical Thinking**: Critical thinking skills are essential for MPs to evaluate information, assess the validity of arguments, and identify potential opportunities and challenges. MPs must critically analyze policy proposals, legislative initiatives, and strategic priorities to determine their feasibility and impact.
    - **Strategic Thinking**: MPs should possess strategic thinking skills to develop long-term plans and vision for their constituency and policy agenda. Strategic thinking involves anticipating future trends, identifying strategic priorities, and aligning resources and activities to achieve overarching goals.
    - **Communication Skills**: Effective communication skills are crucial for MPs to articulate their vision, priorities, and strategies to constituents, stakeholders, and fellow lawmakers. MPs must communicate complex ideas clearly and persuasively through speeches, presentations, and written materials.
    - **Collaboration and Negotiation**: Collaboration and negotiation skills are essential for MPs to build coalitions, forge partnerships, and advance their policy agenda through consensus-building. MPs must work collaboratively with colleagues, stakeholders, and political allies to achieve common goals.

- **Leadership Skills**: Leadership skills are important for MPs to inspire confidence, mobilize support, and lead initiatives that benefit their constituents and society. MPs should demonstrate integrity, vision, and decisiveness in their leadership roles, guiding others toward shared objectives.
- **Adaptability**: MPs must be adaptable and flexible in their strategic planning efforts, as political, social, and economic conditions may change rapidly. MPs should be able to adjust their plans and strategies in response to new challenges, opportunities, and stakeholder feedback.
- **Problem-Solving**: MPs need strong problem-solving skills to address complex issues and overcome obstacles in their constituency and policy work. This involves identifying root causes, generating creative solutions, and implementing effective interventions to achieve desired outcomes.
- **Time Management**: Effective time management skills are essential for MPs to prioritize tasks, allocate resources, and meet deadlines in their strategic planning process. MPs must balance competing demands on their time and attention while ensuring that critical priorities are addressed.
- **Resilience**: Resilience is important for MPs to navigate setbacks, challenges, and setbacks that may arise in their strategic planning efforts. MPs must maintain optimism, perseverance, and determination in the face of adversity, bouncing back from setbacks and learning from experience.

- **Digital Connectivity by MPs:** Digital connectivity has become increasingly important for Members of Parliament (MPs) to effectively engage with constituents, share information, and perform their duties. By embracing digital connectivity, MPs can expand their reach, enhance communication with constituents, and foster greater transparency, accountability, and participation in the democratic process. Here's how MPs can leverage digital connectivity:

- **Social Media Presence**: Maintain active profiles on popular social media platforms such as Twitter, Facebook, and Instagram to communicate with constituents, share updates, and amplify your messages.
- **Online Constituency Office**: Establish an online presence for your constituency office, including a website or portal where constituents can access information, submit inquiries, and request assistance.
- **Virtual Town Halls**: Host virtual town hall meetings using video conferencing platforms to engage with constituents in real-time, answer questions, and discuss issues of importance.
- **Email Newsletters**: Send regular email newsletters to constituents with updates on parliamentary activities, policy initiatives, and local events. Provide opportunities for feedback and engagement.
- **Interactive Websites**: Develop interactive websites that allow constituents to explore parliamentary proceedings, track legislation, and learn about your work as an MP. Provide resources, tools, and multimedia content for education and engagement.
- **Online Surveys and Polls**: Use online survey tools to gather feedback from constituents on specific issues, policy priorities, or community needs. Conduct polls to gauge public opinion and inform decision-making.
- **Digital Content Creation**: Produce digital content such as videos, podcasts, info graphics, and blog posts to communicate complex issues, share stories, and connect with constituents in engaging ways.
- **Social Media Listening**: Monitor social media channels to listen to conversations, trends, and concerns among constituents. Use insights from social media listening to inform your outreach and engagement strategies.
- **Digital Advocacy Campaigns**: Launch digital advocacy campaigns on social media or other online platforms to raise

awareness about important issues, mobilize support, and drive action among constituents.

- **Online Constituent Services**: Offer online constituent services such as case management systems, appointment scheduling, and document submission portals to streamline interactions and improve accessibility for constituents.
- **Virtual Office Hours**: Conduct virtual office hours using video conferencing tools to provide constituents with opportunities for one-on-one consultations, assistance, and support.
- **Digital Skills Training**: Organize workshops or webinars to provide constituents with digital skills training, including internet literacy, online safety, and using digital tools for civic engagement.

- **Dos in Strategic Planning:**
    - **Define Clear Objectives:** Clearly articulate the goals and outcomes you aim to achieve through strategic planning. This ensures alignment with constituents' needs and legislative priorities.
    - **Conduct Stakeholder Analysis:** Identify and engage with key stakeholders, including constituents, community leaders, experts, and advocacy groups. Their perspectives and support are crucial for successful implementation of strategic initiatives.
    - **Gather Data and Conduct Research:** Base your strategic decisions on reliable data and thorough research. Understand the socio-economic context, demographic trends, and local issues impacting your constituency.
    - **Prioritize Initiatives:** Focus on initiatives that have the greatest impact and address critical issues facing your constituents. Prioritization ensures efficient allocation of resources and maximizes your effectiveness as an MP.
    - **Build Alliances and Coalitions:** Collaborate with colleagues across party lines, government officials, and community stakeholders to

build consensus and support for your legislative agenda. Coalitions amplify your influence and increase the likelihood of policy success.

- **Communicate Effectively:** Clearly communicate your strategic priorities, progress, and outcomes to constituents and stakeholders. Transparent communication fosters trust and accountability, enhancing support for your initiatives.
- **Monitor Progress and Adapt:** Regularly monitor the implementation of your strategic plan, evaluate progress against objectives, and be prepared to adapt strategies based on changing circumstances or new information.

- **Don'ts in Strategic Planning:**
  - **Neglect Stakeholder Engagement:** Avoid making decisions in isolation. Neglecting to engage stakeholders can lead to resistance, misunderstandings, and hindered progress on strategic initiatives.
  - **Rush the Planning Process:** Strategic planning requires careful consideration and deliberation. Rushing the process may lead to overlooking critical factors, ineffective strategies, or missed opportunities for consensus-building.
  - **Ignore Data and Evidence:** Disregarding reliable data and evidence undermines the credibility and effectiveness of strategic decisions. Base your planning on comprehensive research and factual analysis.
  - **Overextend Resources:** Avoid spreading resources too thinly across numerous initiatives. Overextension can dilute impact, compromise effectiveness, and strain your ability to deliver tangible results.
  - **Lack Adaptability:** Rigidity in strategic planning can hinder responsiveness to emerging issues or unexpected challenges. Remain flexible and open to adjusting strategies based on feedback and evolving circumstances.

- **Engage in Partisan or Divisive Tactics:** Strategic planning should prioritize the common good and collaborative solutions. Avoid partisan rhetoric, divisive tactics, or strategies that undermine unity and constructive dialogue.
- **Neglect Ethical Considerations:** Uphold ethical standards in all aspects of strategic planning. Avoid conflicts of interest, ensure transparency in decision-making, and prioritize the public interest over personal or political gain.

By adhering to these dos and don'ts, MPs can enhance the effectiveness of their strategic planning efforts, strengthen their impact on legislative outcomes, and better serve the interests of their constituents and the broader community.

Strategic planning is essential for MPs to effectively fulfill their responsibilities as public representatives. By setting clear objectives, prioritizing legislative initiatives, engaging proactively with stakeholders, and demonstrating ethical leadership, MPs can maximize their impact, achieve policy outcomes, and contribute to the advancement of their constituencies and the nation as a whole.

Chapter 13
SOCIAL AUDIT AND GRIEVANCE COMMITTEES

"Social audit and grievance committees are the guardians of accountability and justice in our communities. They stand as beacons of transparency, ensuring every voice is heard, every concern addressed, and every action taken with integrity and fairness."

Social audits play a crucial role in promoting social responsibility, sustainability, and ethical business practices by assessing organizations' social performance, engaging stakeholders, ensuring compliance with standards, and fostering continuous improvement in social impact. A social audit is a process of evaluating and assessing an organizations or entity's performance, activities, and impact on society, with a focus on social responsibility, accountability, and transparency. Social audit and grievance committees are essential mechanisms that promote accountability, transparency, and citizen participation in governance processes. These mechanisms play a crucial role in enhancing the effectiveness of public institutions, ensuring equitable service delivery, and addressing grievances and concerns of citizens.

- **Social Audit:** Social audit refers to a process where citizens and civil society organizations evaluate and assess the performance of public institutions and programs against predetermined standards and objectives. The primary objective of social audit is to promote transparency, accountability, and responsiveness in the use of public resources and implementation of government policies. Key components and objectives of a social audit:

- **Evaluation of Social Performance**: Social audits examine an organization's social performance by assessing its policies, practices, and activities in various areas such as labor relations, environmental stewardship, community development, and corporate governance. This evaluation helps identify strengths, weaknesses, and areas for improvement in the organization's social impact.
- **Stakeholder Engagement**: Social audits involve engaging with a wide range of stakeholders, including employees, customers, suppliers, local communities, NGOs, and government agencies. By soliciting feedback and input from stakeholders, social audits ensure that the perspectives and interests of all relevant parties are considered in the evaluation process.
- **Compliance with Standards and Regulations**: Social audits assess an organization's compliance with relevant standards, regulations, and guidelines related to social responsibility and sustainability. This may include international standards such as the UN Global Compact, ISO 26000, or industry-specific codes of conduct.
- **Transparency and Accountability**: Social audits promote transparency and accountability by providing stakeholders with access to information about an organization's social performance, practices, and impacts. By disclosing findings and outcomes publicly, organizations demonstrate their commitment to accountability and responsiveness to stakeholder concerns.
- **Identification of Risks and Opportunities**: Social audits help organizations identify social, environmental, and ethical risks and opportunities that may affect their long-term viability and reputation. By proactively addressing these risks and seizing opportunities for improvement, organizations can enhance their social impact and competitive advantage.

- **Continuous Improvement**: Social audits facilitate continuous improvement by establishing mechanisms for monitoring, evaluation, and feedback. By tracking progress over time and benchmarking against industry peers or best practices, organizations can identify areas for improvement and implement corrective actions to enhance their social performance.
- **Reporting and Communication**: Social audits culminate in the preparation of a social audit report, which summarizes the findings, conclusions, and recommendations of the audit process. This report is typically communicated to stakeholders through various channels, such as annual reports, websites, or stakeholder meetings, to promote transparency and accountability.
- **Importance of social audit:** Social audit holds significant importance in various contexts, especially for organizations, governments, and communities committed to social responsibility, accountability, and transparency. Overall, social audit plays a vital role in promoting social responsibility, accountability, and sustainability across various sectors and settings, ultimately contributing to positive social, environmental, and economic outcomes. Here are some key reasons why social audit is important:
    - **Enhancing Accountability**: Social audit promotes accountability by holding organizations, governments, and institutions responsible for their actions, decisions, and performance in social and environmental domains. By conducting audits, stakeholders can assess whether entities are meeting their social responsibilities and commitments.
    - **Ensuring Transparency**: Social audit promotes transparency by providing stakeholders with access to information about an organization's social and environmental performance, practices, and impacts. Transparency helps build trust, credibility, and confidence among stakeholders, fostering positive relationships and engagement.

- **Improving Governance**: Social audit contributes to improved governance by enhancing the effectiveness, efficiency, and integrity of decision-making processes within organizations and governments. By evaluating governance structures, policies, and practices, social audit helps identify areas for improvement and reform.
- **Empowering Stakeholders**: Social audit empowers stakeholders, including employees, customers, communities, and civil society organizations, by giving them a voice in assessing and influencing the social and environmental performance of organizations and governments. By engaging stakeholders in the audit process, social audit ensures that diverse perspectives and interests are considered.
- **Identifying Areas for Improvement**: Social audit helps organizations and governments identify areas for improvement in their social and environmental performance, policies, and practices. By analyzing audit findings and recommendations, entities can develop action plans to address weaknesses, mitigate risks, and capitalize on opportunities for positive change.
- **Enhancing Public Trust**: Social audit enhances public trust and confidence in organizations, governments, and institutions by demonstrating their commitment to social responsibility, accountability, and ethical behavior. Transparent and credible social audit processes reassure stakeholders that entities are acting in the public interest and delivering on their promises.
- **Driving Sustainable Development**: Social audit contributes to sustainable development by promoting responsible business practices, environmental stewardship, and social inclusion. By evaluating the social, environmental, and economic impacts of organizations and governments, social audit helps advance sustainability goals and contribute to the achievement of global development objectives.

- **Promoting Ethical Behavior**: Social audit encourages ethical behavior and integrity within organizations and governments by evaluating their adherence to ethical principles, values, and standards. By assessing compliance with codes of conduct, laws, and regulations, social audit helps prevent unethical practices and promote a culture of integrity.
- **Fostering Continuous Improvement**: Social audit fosters a culture of continuous improvement within organizations and governments by establishing mechanisms for monitoring, evaluation, and feedback. By regularly conducting audits and acting on audit findings, entities can drive positive change and strive for excellence in social and environmental performance.
- **Creating Shared Value**: Social audit creates shared value by aligning the interests of organizations, governments, and society through responsible business practices, community engagement, and sustainable development initiatives. By generating positive social and environmental impacts, entities can create value for stakeholders while contributing to the well-being of society as a whole.

- **Measuring their performance:** Only when we understand and appreciate what our Lok Sabha MPs are expected to do, can we, as common citizens understand how to measure their performance and assess how well they are playing their roles. We the citizens must come together and demand that our MPs bring out an annual report card clearly outlining their performance. They need to inform the people of their constituency on how well they performed against indicators like their attendance in the Parliament, the number of questions that they asked, their understanding and appreciation of the different policies and laws that they make, the amount of time that they spend consulting their constituents, how well they oversaw the executive and a statement disclosing their income and assets.

- A **social audit** involves systematically examining the impact of a project or service, comparing actual benefits achieved with planned benefits, and assessing unexpected impacts. Here are some key points:
    - **Purpose**: Social audits aim to build accountability and transparency between local leaders, government, and citizens regarding the use and management of public resources.
    - **Process**:
        - **Preparatory Groundwork**: Define the audit scope (e.g., specific services, programs, or projects). Form a committee to oversee the audit and involve key stakeholders.
        - **Verification**: Review official records and compare state-reported expenditures with actual spending on the ground.
        - **Public Interaction**: Social audits often include public hearings where citizens interact with officials.
        - **Impact Assessment**: Evaluate benefits achieved and unexpected outcomes.
- **Social audits help MPs:** Social audits can be valuable tools for Members of Parliament (MPs) in fulfilling their roles as elected representatives and serving the interests of their constituents.
    - Social audits can help MPs fulfill their roles as accountable, responsive, and effective representatives by providing insights into social and environmental issues, promoting transparency and integrity, fostering community engagement, and advocating for policies and initiatives that advance the interests of their constituents and society as a whole.

HERE'S HOW SOCIAL AUDITS CAN BENEFIT MPS:

- **Accountability**: Social audits help MPs hold government agencies, public institutions, and private organizations accountable for their social and environmental performance. By advocating for social audits and scrutinizing audit findings, MPs can ensure that entities responsible for delivering public services or implementing policies are transparent and accountable to the public.

- **Oversight of Government Spending**: Social audits can assist MPs in overseeing government spending and ensuring that public funds are used effectively and efficiently. By conducting audits of government programs, projects, and expenditures, MPs can identify instances of waste, fraud, or mismanagement and advocate for corrective action.
- **Community Engagement**: Social audits provide MPs with opportunities to engage with constituents and communities in assessing social and environmental issues, concerns, and priorities. By supporting community-led social audit initiatives and participating in audit processes, MPs can strengthen their connections with constituents and demonstrate their commitment to addressing local needs.
- **Policy Development and Advocacy**: Social audit findings can inform MPs' policy development and advocacy efforts by providing evidence-based insights into social and environmental challenges and opportunities. MPs can use audit findings to advocate for legislative reforms, budget allocations, or government interventions that address identified issues and improve social outcomes.
- **Promotion of Transparency and Integrity**: Social audits promote transparency, integrity, and good governance practices within government agencies and public institutions. MPs can champion social audit initiatives, advocate for legislation mandating transparency and accountability measures, and hold government officials accountable for adhering to ethical standards and codes of conduct.
- **Constituency Representation**: Social audits help MPs represent the interests and concerns of their constituents more effectively by providing insights into local social and environmental issues. By participating in social audit processes and amplifying community voices, MPs can ensure that government policies and programs are responsive to the needs of the people they represent.

- **Addressing Inequality and Social Justice**: Social audits can help MPs address inequality and promote social justice by highlighting disparities in access to public services, resources, and opportunities. MPs can use audit findings to advocate for policies and initiatives that reduce social and economic inequalities and promote inclusive development.
- **Public Awareness and Education**: Social audits raise public awareness about social and environmental issues and empower citizens to participate in governance processes. MPs can use social audit reports and findings to educate constituents about their rights, responsibilities, and opportunities for civic engagement.
- **Fostering Collaboration and Partnerships**: Social audits encourage collaboration and partnerships among government agencies, civil society organizations, and community stakeholders. MPs can facilitate dialogue and cooperation among diverse stakeholders involved in social audit initiatives, fostering collective action and shared responsibility for addressing social and environmental challenges.
- **Building Trust and Legitimacy**: Social audits help MPs build trust and legitimacy with constituents by demonstrating their commitment to transparency, accountability, and public service. By supporting social audit processes and advocating for responsive and responsible governance, MPs can enhance their credibility and effectiveness as elected representatives.
- **Work of grievance committees:** Grievance committees, also known as complaints committees or redressal committees, serve an essential function in various organizations and institutions. Their primary purpose is to address complaints, grievances, and disputes raised by individuals or groups within the organization or related to its operations. Overall, grievance committees play a crucial role in promoting transparency, fairness, and accountability within organizations by providing avenues for addressing and resolving complaints in a timely and impartial manner. Here's an overview of the work typically conducted by grievance committees:

- **Receiving Complaints:** Grievance committees are responsible for receiving complaints from employees, customers, clients, or any other stakeholders. These complaints could relate to a wide range of issues, including workplace harassment, discrimination, violation of policies, service delivery problems, or any other misconduct.
- **Investigation:** Once a complaint is received, the committee initiates an investigation process to gather relevant information and evidence regarding the matter. This may involve interviewing the parties involved, collecting documentation, and conducting site visits if necessary.
- **Mediation or Conciliation:** In some cases, grievance committees may attempt to resolve the dispute through mediation or conciliation, facilitating discussions between the parties involved to reach a mutually acceptable solution. This approach can help to address grievances swiftly and amicably, avoiding the need for formal proceedings.
- **Formal Hearings:** If the dispute cannot be resolved informally, the grievance committee may hold formal hearings to examine the evidence, hear testimony from witnesses, and allow the parties to present their cases. These hearings typically follow established procedures to ensure fairness and impartiality.
- **Decision Making:** Based on the findings of the investigation or hearings, the grievance committee makes a decision regarding the complaint. This decision may involve recommending disciplinary action, issuing directives for policy changes, or providing remedies to address the grievances raised.
- **Reporting:** Grievance committees are often required to submit reports summarizing their activities, findings, and recommendations to the relevant authorities within the organization. These reports may help identify systemic issues, trends in complaints, and areas for improvement in policies or procedures.

- **Follow-Up:** After a decision has been made, the grievance committee may monitor the implementation of its recommendations and follow up with the parties involved to ensure compliance. This helps to ensure that the resolution process is effectively concluded and that any necessary corrective actions are taken.

- **Grievance committee benefits MPs:** A grievance committee can offer several benefits to Members of Parliament (MPs) as it provides a structured mechanism for addressing complaints, concerns, and grievances raised by constituents. In summary, a grievance committee offers numerous benefits to MPs by facilitating constituent representation, accessibility, conflict resolution, problem-solving, community engagement, feedback, preventative measures, transparency, trust, capacity building, and enhanced representation. By establishing and supporting grievance committees, MPs can demonstrate their commitment to serving the public interest and upholding democratic values and principles. Here are some benefits of a grievance committee for MPs:

  - **Constituent Representation**: A grievance committee enables MPs to represent the interests and concerns of their constituents effectively. By providing a platform for constituents to voice their grievances, MPs can advocate for solutions and address issues that affect their constituents' well-being and quality of life.

  - **Accessibility and Accountability**: A grievance committee enhances MPs' accessibility and accountability to constituents by offering a formal channel for communication and engagement. Constituents can submit grievances to the committee, and MPs are responsible for addressing them promptly and transparently, thereby demonstrating their commitment to serving the public interest.

  - **Conflict Resolution**: A grievance committee facilitates conflict resolution and dispute settlement by providing a neutral forum for parties to discuss grievances, explore solutions, and reach mutually acceptable outcomes. MPs can use the committee's mediation and arbitration functions to resolve disputes and restore trust and harmony within their constituencies.

- **Problem-Solving and Advocacy**: A grievance committee empowers MPs to identify and address systemic issues and barriers that hinder constituents' access to services, resources, and opportunities. By analyzing recurring grievances and advocating for policy reforms or service improvements, MPs can address root causes and promote positive change.
- **Community Engagement**: A grievance committee fosters community engagement and participation by encouraging constituents to actively participate in the grievance resolution process. MPs can engage with constituents, community leaders, and stakeholders to gather input, solicit feedback, and collaborate on solutions to address grievances effectively.
- **Feedback and Learning**: A grievance committee provides MPs with valuable feedback and insights into constituents' needs, concerns, and experiences. By listening to constituents' grievances and addressing them proactively, MPs can learn from feedback, improve their representation, and strengthen their connection with the community.
- **Preventative Measures**: A grievance committee helps MPs identify and address grievances before they escalate into larger conflicts or crises. By proactively addressing constituents' concerns and grievances, MPs can prevent social unrest, mitigate risks, and build trust and confidence in their leadership.
- **Transparency and Trust**: A grievance committee promotes transparency and trust by ensuring that the grievance resolution process is fair, impartial, and accountable. MPs can demonstrate their commitment to transparency and ethical conduct by adhering to established procedures and standards for handling grievances.
- **Capacity Building**: A grievance committee can serve as a platform for capacity building and skill development among MPs

and their staff. By participating in grievance resolution processes, MPs can enhance their communication, negotiation, and conflict management skills, enabling them to serve constituents more effectively.

- **Enhanced Representation**: Overall, a grievance committee enhances MPs' ability to represent their constituents' interests, address their concerns, and advocate for positive change. By providing a structured mechanism for addressing grievances, MPs can strengthen democracy, promote social justice, and improve governance in their constituencies.

- **Open durbars by MPs:** Open durbars organized by Members of Parliament (MPs) are public gatherings or forums where MPs interact directly with constituents, listen to their concerns, and address issues raised by the community. These events are typically held in the constituency or district represented by the MP and provides an opportunity for constituents to engage with their elected representative in a face-to-face setting. Open durbars organized by MPs play a vital role in promoting community engagement, dialogue, problem-solving, empowerment, transparency, and accountability in governance. By hosting open durbars, MPs can strengthen their ties with constituents, address community concerns, and foster inclusive and participatory democracy at the grassroots level. Here are some key aspects and benefits of open durbars organized by MPs:

  - **Accessibility and Engagement**: Open durbars allow MPs to connect with constituents in a direct and accessible manner, fostering dialogue, engagement, and interaction between elected representatives and the community. By hosting open durbars, MPs demonstrate their commitment to listening to constituents' concerns and engaging with them on issues of importance.

  - **Community Feedback**: Open durbars provide a platform for constituents to voice their opinions, express their grievances, and provide feedback directly to their MP. Constituents can raise concerns about local development projects, government services, infrastructure needs, and other issues affecting their community, allowing MPs to understand the needs and priorities of their constituents better.

- **Problem-Solving and Resolution**: Open durbars enable MPs to address constituents' concerns and grievances, facilitate problem-solving, and advocate for solutions to address community issues. MPs can use open durbars to gather information, liaise with government officials or agencies, and advocate for policy changes or interventions to address local challenges.
- **Community Empowerment**: Open durbars empower constituents by providing them with a platform to engage directly with their elected representatives, participate in decision-making processes, and hold MPs accountable for their actions and decisions. By engaging in open dialogue with constituents, MPs can empower communities to advocate for their needs and interests effectively.
- **Transparency and Accountability**: Open durbars promote transparency and accountability in governance by providing constituents with opportunities to engage with their MP in a public and transparent manner. By hosting open durbars, MPs demonstrate transparency in their decision-making processes, listen to constituents' feedback, and remain accountable to the community they serve.
- **Community Building**: Open durbars contribute to community building and social cohesion by bringing together residents, community leaders, and stakeholders to discuss common concerns, share ideas, and collaborate on solutions. These events help build trust, foster solidarity, and strengthen social networks within the community.
- **Awareness and Education**: Open durbars raise awareness about government programs, policies, and initiatives among constituents, helping to disseminate information and educate the community about their rights, entitlements, and responsibilities. MPs can use

open durbars to provide updates on legislative developments, government services, and community projects.

- **Political Representation**: Open durbars serve as a forum for political representation, allowing MPs to advocate for the interests of their constituents and represent their concerns in the legislative process. By engaging with constituents in open durbars, MPs can ensure that their voices are heard and their needs are addressed in the policy-making arena.

- **Ensuring Accountability and Transparency in Governance:**
    - **Citizen Participation:** Social audit empowers citizens to actively participate in monitoring and evaluating public services and programs. Through public hearings, consultations, and community meetings, citizens contribute to identifying inefficiencies, irregularities, and gaps in service delivery.
    - **Transparency:** Social audit promotes openness in the management of public funds and resources. By disclosing information on expenditures, project outcomes, and performance indicators, governments enhance trust and credibility with citizens and stakeholders.
    - **Accountability:** Social audit holds public officials and institutions accountable for their actions and decisions. By identifying discrepancies or failures in service delivery, social audit encourages corrective measures and ensures responsible governance.
    - **Improvement of Services:** Insights gained from social audits help governments improve the quality, accessibility, and effectiveness of public services. Recommendations from social audit reports inform policy reforms, resource allocation decisions, and strategies for enhancing service delivery outcomes.
    - **Public Awareness and Empowerment:** Social audit increases public awareness about their rights and entitlements. It empowers citizens to demand accountability from public officials and advocate for improvements in governance processes and service delivery.

- **Grievance Committees:** Grievance committees serve as formal mechanisms for citizens to raise complaints, grievances, and issues related to public services and administrative actions. These committees provide a structured process for addressing grievances and ensuring that citizens' concerns are heard, evaluated, and resolved in a timely manner. Key aspects of grievance committees include:
  - **Accessibility and Responsiveness:** Grievance committees are accessible to citizens, providing multiple channels for submitting complaints, including online platforms, helplines, and in-person visits. Committees are tasked with responding promptly to grievances and initiating investigations as necessary.
  - **Fairness and Impartiality:** Grievance committees operate with impartiality and fairness, ensuring that all complaints are treated with seriousness and confidentiality. Committee members are trained to conduct thorough investigations and make informed decisions based on evidence and merit.
  - **Redressal and Resolution:** Grievance committees facilitate the resolution of complaints through mediation, arbitration, or recommendations for administrative action. Committees may collaborate with relevant authorities to implement corrective measures and prevent recurrence of grievances.
  - **Accountability of Public Officials:** Grievance committees hold public officials accountable for addressing citizen complaints and improving service delivery standards. By monitoring the implementation of grievance redressal mechanisms, committees ensure compliance with established procedures and timelines.
  - **Public Trust and Confidence:** Effective grievance committees contribute to building public trust and confidence in government institutions. Transparent handling of grievances and timely resolution of complaints demonstrate commitment to responsive governance and citizen-centric service delivery.

Social audit and grievance committees are indispensable tools for promoting accountability, transparency, and citizen engagement in governance. These mechanisms empower citizens to actively participate in monitoring public services, hold authorities accountable for their actions, and ensure equitable access to justice and redressal.

"Tips to look after constituency"

Regular Communication: Maintain open and frequent communication with constituents.

Constituency Visits: Conduct regular visits to their constituency.

Assistance with Issues: Assist constituents in government services and addressing individual concerns.

Advocacy and Representation: Advocate for the interests and needs of their constituency in parliament.

Community Engagement: Engage with community groups, associations, and organizations.

Policy Development: By gathering feedback from constituents, conducting consultations.

Infrastructure and Development Projects: Advocate for infrastructure projects, economic development initiatives, and public services that improve the quality of life in their constituency.

Public Outreach and Education: Engage in public outreach and education campaigns to raise awareness about government programs, policies, and rights.

Emergency Response and Support: Coordinate with local authorities and agencies to ensure timely and effective response measures.

Feedback and Accountability: Maintain accountability to their constituents by regularly seeking feedback, listening to concerns, and reporting on their activities and achievements. And adjust their priorities accordingly.

Chapter 14
To be Effective M.P.

"An effective MP is not merely a representative but a catalyst for positive change. They listen with empathy, lead with integrity, and act with purpose, tirelessly striving to empower their constituents and build a brighter future for all."

Effective Member of Parliament (MP) requires a combination of skills, knowledge, dedication, and ethical conduct. MPs play a crucial role in representing their constituents, shaping legislation, and contributing to the governance of the nation. An effective Member of Parliament requires dedication, integrity, and a deep commitment to serving constituents and advancing the common good. By prioritizing the needs of constituents, engaging in legislative excellence, advocating effectively, demonstrating ethical leadership, fostering community engagement, mastering communication skills, embracing continuous learning, and evaluating impact, MPs can make significant contributions to the democratic process and the well-being of society. To excel in their role and make a positive impact, MPs should focus on several key principles and practices:

- **Commitment to Constituents:**
  - **Engagement:** Actively engage with constituents through regular meetings, constituency surgeries, and public events. Listen attentively to their concerns, priorities, and aspirations.

  - **Accessibility:** Be accessible and approachable to constituents, both in-person and through digital platforms. Respond promptly to inquiries and requests for assistance.

- **Legislative Excellence:**

  - **Expertise:** Develop expertise in specific policy areas relevant to your constituency and national interests. Stay informed about legislative processes, parliamentary rules, and current affairs.

  - **Effective Participation:** Actively participate in parliamentary debates, committees, and discussions. Contribute constructively to policy formulation, scrutinize legislation thoroughly, and propose amendments when necessary.

- **Advocacy and Representation:**

  - **Advocacy Skills:** Advocate passionately for the interests of your constituents while considering the broader national interest. Build alliances across party lines to garner support for legislative initiatives.

  - **Visibility:** Publicly champion causes that matter to your constituents. Use your platform to raise awareness about important issues and campaign for necessary reforms.

- **Ethical Leadership:**

  - **Integrity:** Uphold high ethical standards in all aspects of your work. Demonstrate honesty, transparency, and accountability in your interactions with constituents, colleagues, and stakeholders.

  - **Conflict Resolution:** Navigate conflicts of interest responsibly and disclose potential conflicts promptly. Make decisions that prioritize the public good over personal or partisan interests.

- **Community and Stakeholder Engagement:**

  - **Building Relationships:** Build strong relationships with community leaders, businesses, non-profit organizations, and other stakeholders in your constituency.

  - **Collaboration:** Collaborate with local authorities and stakeholders to address community issues, promote development projects, and advocate for resources that benefit your constituents.

- **Communication Skills:**

  - **Clear Communication:** Communicate effectively with constituents, colleagues, and the media. Clearly articulate your positions, legislative initiatives, and policy priorities.

  - **Active Listening:** Listen actively to diverse viewpoints and perspectives. Seek feedback from constituents and stakeholders to inform your decision-making process.

- **Adaptability and Learning:**

  - **Continuous Learning:** Stay updated on emerging trends, technological advancements, and evolving policy issues. Attend workshops, seminars, and training sessions to enhance your knowledge and skills.

  - **Adaptability:** Be flexible and adaptable in responding to changing circumstances, new challenges, and opportunities for legislative action.

- **Impact Assessment and Evaluation:**

  - **Monitoring and Evaluation:** Regularly assess the impact of your legislative actions and constituency interventions. Evaluate the effectiveness of policies and projects in achieving desired outcomes.

  - **Feedback Mechanisms:** Establish feedback mechanisms to solicit input from constituents on your performance and identify areas for improvement.

PARLIAMENTARIANS CAN APPROACH WITH THE FOLLOWING ACTIONS:

- Hold public hearings

- Create committees/panels that educate, monitor, and promote awareness.
- Educate one another, parliaments, the media and constituents
- Expand risk knowledge for better decision-making
- Champion local knowledge and local expertise, emphasizing groups that are under-represented, vulnerable and/or marginalized
- Convene panels of experts.
- Involve vulnerable populations to incorporate their needs.
- Create multi-stakeholder committees – including women-led committees – to participate in policy development.
- Convene awareness-raising meetings for national and subnational sectors potentially affected by multi-hazard and systemic risk events.
- Review existing policies and legislation
    - **Consider new policies and legislation:** Success as an MP is not just about advancing your own career or agenda—it's about making a positive difference in the lives of the people you represent. Stay focused on serving your constituents with integrity and dedication, and you'll be well on your way to being a successful Member of Parliament
    - **Qualities of a Member of Parliament:** By embodying these qualities, MPs can fulfill their responsibilities as effective representatives of the people and contribute positively to the democratic process Qualities that contribute to being an effective Member of Parliament (MP):
        - **Leadership**: MPs should possess strong leadership qualities to effectively represent their constituents, advocate for their interests, and navigate the complexities of policymaking.
        - **Integrity**: Upholding high ethical standards and demonstrating honesty, transparency, and accountability in all actions is crucial for maintaining public trust.

- **Empathy**: Having empathy and understanding for the diverse needs and concerns of constituents enables MPs to effectively address issues and advocate on behalf of their communities.
- **Communication Skills**: Effective communication skills, both verbal and written, are essential for MPs to articulate their positions, engage with constituents, and collaborate with colleagues.
- **Problem-Solving Abilities**: MPs should be adept at identifying challenges, analyzing issues, and developing practical solutions to address the needs of their constituents.
- **Resilience**: The political landscape can be demanding and unpredictable. MPs should demonstrate resilience in the face of challenges, setbacks, and criticism.
- **Collaboration**: Building relationships and working collaboratively with colleagues, stakeholders, and community members is essential for achieving legislative goals and advancing the interests of constituents.
- **Adaptability**: MPs must be adaptable and responsive to changing circumstances, evolving priorities, and new challenges that arise during their tenure.
- **Commitment to Public Service**: A strong commitment to serving the public and improving the lives of constituents is fundamental for effective representation.
- **Expertise and Knowledge**: Developing expertise in key policy areas relevant to constituents' needs enables MPs to make informed decisions and effectively advocate for their communities.
- **Accessibility**: Being accessible and responsive to constituents' concerns through regular office hours, town hall meetings, and community events fosters trust and engagement.

- **Representation of Diverse Voices**: MPs should strive to represent the diverse perspectives and interests of their constituents, ensuring that all voices are heard and considered in decision-making processes.

- **Becoming a successful Member of Parliament (MP)** involves a combination of political savvy, dedication to public service, effective communication skills, and a deep understanding of your constituents' needs. Here are some steps you can take:

  - **Understand Your Constituency**: Take the time to learn about the demographics, issues, and concerns of the people you represent. Regularly engage with constituents through town hall meetings, community events, and social media to stay informed about their needs.

  - **Build Relationships**: Forge strong relationships with community leaders, local businesses, and advocacy groups. Establishing trust and credibility with these stakeholders can help you better serve your constituents and achieve your policy goals.

  - **Develop Expertise**: Focus on a few key policy areas that are important to your constituents and become an expert in those areas. Whether it's education, healthcare, or economic development, having specialized knowledge will make you a more effective advocate for your constituents.

  - **Be Accessible and Responsive**: Make yourself accessible to your constituents by maintaining regular office hours, promptly responding to emails and phone calls, and being active in the community. Being responsive to constituents' concerns demonstrates that you are committed to serving their interests.

  - **Work Collaboratively**: Success in politics often requires building coalitions and working across party lines. Collaborate with other MPs, both within your party and across parties, to advance shared goals and find solutions to common problems.

- **Communicate Effectively**: Develop strong communication skills to articulate your positions, persuade others, and effectively advocate for your constituents. This includes being able to communicate your message through speeches, media interviews, social media, and written correspondence.
- **Stay Informed**: Stay up-to-date on current events, legislative developments, and policy debates at both the national and local levels. Understanding the political landscape will help you navigate the complexities of governance and better serve your constituents.
- **Maintain Integrity**: Uphold high ethical standards and demonstrate integrity in all your actions. Building trust with your constituents is essential for long-term success as an MP.
- **Balance Priorities**: As an MP, you'll have to juggle multiple responsibilities, including legislative duties, constituency work, and party obligations. Learn to prioritize effectively and manage your time wisely to maximize your impact.
- **Seek Feedback and Adapt**: Be open to feedback from constituents, colleagues, and stakeholders, and be willing to adapt your approach based on their input. Continuous improvement is key to being a successful MP.

- **Effective MP:** Becoming an effective Member of Parliament (MP) requires a combination of skills, qualities, and strategies aimed at serving constituents, representing their interests, and contributing to the legislative process. By following these steps and demonstrating commitment, dedication, and effectiveness in your role as an MP, you can make a positive impact on your constituency, contribute to the legislative process, and serve as an effective representative of the people. Here are some key steps to being an effective MP:
    - **Engage with Constituents**: Regularly interact with constituents through open durbars, town hall meetings,

constituency visits, and other outreach activities. Listen to their concerns, understand their needs, and advocate for their interests in Parliament.

- **Stay Informed**: Stay up-to-date on local, national, and global issues, as well as legislative developments, policy debates, and current affairs. Conduct research, attend briefings, and consult experts to deepen your understanding of complex issues and make informed decisions.
- **Build Relationships**: Develop positive relationships with colleagues, stakeholders, community leaders, and government officials. Collaborate with others across party lines, forge partnerships, and build coalitions to advance shared goals and initiatives.
- **Be Accessible**: Be accessible and approachable to constituents, colleagues, and stakeholders. Respond promptly to inquiries, requests for assistance, and feedback from constituents, demonstrating responsiveness and accountability in your role as an MP.
- **Communicate Effectively**: Communicate your vision, priorities, and achievements clearly and persuasively to constituents, colleagues, and the public. Use a variety of communication channels, including social media, traditional media, speeches, and written materials, to engage with stakeholders and convey your message.
- **Advocate for Constituents**: Be a strong advocate for constituents' interests, needs, and rights in Parliament. Raise their concerns, propose solutions, and champion legislation that addresses their priorities and improves their quality of life.
- **Legislative Work**: Engage actively in the legislative process by drafting bills, participating in parliamentary debates, and serving on committees. Contribute constructively to policy discussions, offer amendments, and work collaboratively with colleagues to shape legislation.

- **Ethical Conduct**: Uphold high ethical standards and integrity in your conduct as an MP. Adhere to parliamentary rules and codes of conduct, avoid conflicts of interest, and act in the best interests of your constituents and the public good.

- **Represent Diversity**: Represent the diversity of your constituency and advocate for the interests of all communities, including marginalized and underrepresented groups. Ensure that their voices are heard and their concerns are addressed in parliamentary debates and decision-making processes.

- **Continuous Improvement**: Continuously seek opportunities for learning, growth, and self-improvement as an MP. Reflect on your performance, seek feedback from constituents and colleagues, and adapt your approach to better serve the needs of your constituents and fulfill your responsibilities as an MP.

- **Skills of MPs:** Members of Parliament (MPs) require a diverse set of skills to effectively fulfill their roles as elected representatives, legislators, and community leaders. Overall, MPs require a diverse range of skills to effectively represent their constituents, contribute to the legislative process, and address the complex challenges facing society. By continuously developing and honing these skills, MPs can fulfill their responsibilities with professionalism, competence, and dedication. Here are some key skills that are essential for MPs:

    - **Communication Skills**: MPs must possess strong verbal and written communication skills to effectively communicate with constituents, colleagues, stakeholders, and the public. This includes delivering speeches, participating in debates, writing reports, and engaging with media.

    - **Listening Skills**: MPs need to be active listeners, capable of empathizing with constituents, understanding their concerns, and effectively representing their interests in Parliament. Listening skills are essential for building trust, fostering dialogue, and resolving conflicts.

- **Analytical Skills**: MPs should have strong analytical skills to understand complex issues, evaluate evidence, and make informed decisions on legislative proposals, policy initiatives, and constituent concerns. This involves conducting research, analyzing data, and assessing the potential impact of proposed measures.
- **Problem-Solving Skills**: MPs must be adept at identifying problems, developing solutions, and addressing challenges faced by their constituents and communities. This requires creativity, critical thinking, and collaboration to find practical and effective ways to address diverse issues.
- **Negotiation and Diplomacy**: MPs need strong negotiation and diplomacy skills to navigate the political landscape, build consensus, and advocate for their constituents' interests. This involves engaging with colleagues from different political parties, forging alliances, and reaching compromise on contentious issues.
- **Leadership Skills**: MPs should demonstrate effective leadership qualities, including vision, integrity, and decisiveness. They must inspire confidence, motivate others, and mobilize support for their policy agenda and legislative priorities.
- **Interpersonal Skills**: MPs should possess strong interpersonal skills to build positive relationships with constituents, colleagues, stakeholders, and government officials. This includes empathy, tact, and the ability to work collaboratively with individuals from diverse backgrounds and perspectives.
- **Time Management**: MPs must be proficient in time management to juggle multiple responsibilities, prioritize tasks, and meet deadlines effectively. This involves balancing parliamentary duties, constituency work, committee assignments, and other commitments.

- **Adaptability and Resilience**: MPs need to be adaptable and resilient in the face of changing circumstances, competing demands, and political challenges. This requires flexibility, agility, and the ability to navigate uncertainty with composure and determination.
- **Ethical Conduct**: MPs must uphold high ethical standards and integrity in their conduct, adhering to parliamentary rules, codes of conduct, and legal obligations. This includes avoiding conflicts of interest, acting in the public interest, and maintaining trust and credibility with constituents.

- **Successful MP:** Becoming a successful Member of Parliament (MP) requires dedication, hard work, and a commitment to serving constituents, advancing legislative priorities, and contributing to the well-being of society. Here are some key steps to becoming a successful MP:
    - **Understand the Role**: Familiarize yourself with the responsibilities, duties, and expectations of an MP, including representing constituents, participating in legislative debates, and serving on parliamentary committees. Gain a clear understanding of the parliamentary process and your role within it.
    - **Connect with Constituents**: Build strong relationships with constituents by engaging with them regularly, listening to their concerns, and addressing their needs. Attend community events, host open durbars, and maintain an open line of communication to stay connected with constituents and understand their priorities.
    - **Be Informed**: Stay informed about local, national, and global issues, as well as legislative developments, policy debates, and current affairs. Conduct research, read reports, and seek expert advice to deepen your understanding of complex issues and make informed decisions.

- **Develop a Vision**: Develop a clear vision and set of priorities for your term as an MP, based on the needs and aspirations of your constituents and your own values and beliefs. Identify key issues and initiatives that you are passionate about and want to champion in Parliament.
- **Engage in Constituency Work**: Prioritize constituency work and be responsive to the needs and concerns of your constituents. Provide assistance, support, and advocacy on behalf of constituents, and ensure that their voices are heard and represented in Parliament.
- **Participate Actively in Parliament**: Engage actively in parliamentary debates, committee meetings, and legislative processes. Contribute constructively to policy discussions, propose amendments, and advocate for legislation that reflects your constituents' interests and priorities.
- **Build Alliances and Coalitions**: Forge positive relationships with colleagues from different political parties and build alliances and coalitions to advance shared goals and initiatives. Collaborate with others to build consensus, find common ground, and achieve meaningful outcomes.
- **Be Visible and Accessible**: Be visible and accessible to constituents, colleagues, stakeholders, and the public. Attend public events, meet with community groups, and maintain an active presence on social media to engage with stakeholders and communicate your message effectively.
- **Adapt and Learn**: Be adaptable and willing to learn and grow in your role as an MP. Adapt to changing circumstances, learn from experience, and continuously seek opportunities for personal and professional development.

- **Maintain Integrity and Ethics**: Uphold high ethical standards and integrity in your conduct as an MP. Act with honesty, transparency, and accountability, and avoid conflicts of interest or unethical behavior that could undermine public trust and credibility.

Chapter 15
Develop Leadership Qualities

"Effective leadership is not about titles or authority; it's about vision, integrity, and the ability to inspire others to reach their full potential. It's about listening with empathy, communicating with clarity, and fostering a culture of collaboration and accountability. At its core, effective leadership is about serving others and empowering them to succeed."

Developing leadership qualities is a journey of self-discovery, continuous learning, and deliberate practice. By cultivating self-awareness, setting a compelling vision, communication skills, mastering decision-making abilities, empowering others, embracing lifelong learning, building cohesive teams, and leading with integrity, individuals can develop into effective leaders who inspire others, drive positive change, and achieve shared goals.

Leadership is not merely a position or title; it is a set of qualities and behaviors that inspire and motivate others towards a common goal. Developing leadership qualities involves a continuous process of self-discovery, learning, and practical application of skills that enable individuals to effectively lead teams, organizations, and communities. Here are key aspects and strategies for cultivating leadership qualities:

- **Self-Awareness:**
    - **Understanding Strengths and Weaknesses:** Effective leadership begins with self-awareness. Leaders must identify their strengths, weaknesses, values, and motivations. This introspection allows leaders to leverage their strengths and work on areas needing improvement.
    - **Seeking Feedback:** Actively seek feedback from peers, mentors, and team members to gain insights into how others perceive your leadership style. Constructive feedback helps in identifying blind spots and areas for growth.
- **Vision and Goal Setting:**
    - **Setting a Clear Vision:** A strong leader articulates a compelling vision that inspires and aligns others towards a common purpose. Develop a vision that reflects your values and aspirations, and communicates it effectively to stakeholders.
    - **Goal Alignment:** Set SMART (Specific, Measurable, Achievable, Relevant, Time-bound) goals that are aligned with the vision. Break down larger goals into actionable steps to ensure progress and accountability.
- **Communication Skills:**
    - **Effective Communication:** Leaders must convey their vision, goals, and expectations clearly and persuasively. Develop skills in public speaking, writing, active listening, and non-verbal communication to connect with diverse audiences.
    - **Empathy and Emotional Intelligence:** Understand and empathize with the emotions and perspectives of others. Emotional intelligence helps leaders build trust, resolve conflicts, and foster a supportive team environment.

- **Decision Making and Problem Solving:**
    - **Analytical Thinking:** Develop critical thinking and analytical skills to assess situations, gather information, and make informed decisions. Consider risks, alternatives, and long-term implications when solving problems.
    - **Decisiveness:** Effective leaders are decisive and capable of making timely decisions, even in ambiguous or high-pressure situations. Seek consensus when appropriate but be prepared to make tough choices when necessary.
- **Delegation and Empowerment:**
    - **Delegation:** Learn to delegate tasks and responsibilities effectively based on team members' strengths and capabilities. Delegation empowers team members, fosters growth, and allows leaders to focus on strategic priorities.
    - **Empowerment:** Create a supportive environment where team members feel empowered to take initiative, innovate, and contribute to organizational goals. Encourage autonomy while providing guidance and support as needed.
- **Continuous Learning and Adaptability:**
    - **Lifelong Learning:** Commit to continuous personal and professional development. Stay updated on industry trends, best practices, and leadership theories through reading, attending workshops, and seeking mentorship.
    - **Adaptability:** Embrace change and adapt to evolving circumstances. Agile leaders anticipate challenges, pivot when necessary, and lead their teams through transitions effectively.
- **Building and Inspiring Teams:**
    - **Team Building:** Foster a cohesive and inclusive team culture based on trust, respect, and collaboration. Celebrate diversity and leverage the strengths of each team member to achieve collective success.

- **Motivation and Recognition:** Inspire and motivate others by recognizing achievements, providing constructive feedback, and offering opportunities for growth and development. Encourage a positive and supportive work environment.

- **Integrity and Ethical Leadership:**

    - **Integrity:** Uphold ethical standards, honesty, and transparency in all interactions and decisions. Demonstrate integrity by honoring commitments, taking responsibility for mistakes, and treating others with fairness and respect.

    - **Leading by Example:** Model the behaviors and values you expect from others. Act as a role model of ethical leadership and inspire trust through consistency in actions and words.

IMPROVING LEADERSHIP ABILITIES:

- **Perform an inventory of your leadership skills: It's hard to improve your leadership skills if you don't know where you're lacking. Because of this, one of the very first things you should do is take an inventory of your strengths and weaknesses in leadership.**

  Consider each quality, and ask yourself:

  - "Do I naturally possess this trait?"
  - "How do I demonstrate this trait in my work and personal life?"
  - "Do I use this trait in a leadership capacity? If so, how?"
  - "If I feel like I'm lacking in this area, is this a skill I would like to develop?"

You can also use a structured approach like the SWOT analysis (Strengths, Weaknesses, Opportunities, and Threats) to evaluate each leadership trait:

- **Strengths**: What leadership qualities do I already possess?
- **Weaknesses**: Where do I falter as a leader?

- **Opportunities**: What chances do I have to use or improve these skills?
- **Threats**: What obstacles do I face in developing these skills?
    - **Set goals:** Once you know which skills you're good at and which you need to improve, you can set tangible goals in order to become a better leader.
    - Consider following the SMART framework for your goals. Once you've identified areas for improvement, ensure your goals are Specific, Measurable, Achievable, Relevant, and Time-bound (SMART).
    - **Seek out opportunities to practice:** One of the best ways to better yourself is through practice. If you want to develop new leadership skills or utilize ones you already possess, you need to seek out leadership opportunities that will challenge you.
    - This could be volunteering to lead a team at work. It could also be mentoring someone new at your company.
    - **Workplace development:** Consider leadership training. This could be something your work offers, or you may need to seek out courses on your own. Alternatively, you could work with a coach who can help you map out a development plan and stay on track to reach your goals.
    - You should let your boss know about your intentions. They can likely help you find resources and give you opportunities to practice your leadership skills.
    - Formal education and training: Many leaders enhance their skills through formal education such as MBA programs, leadership workshops, or industry-specific training. These programs help to sharpen strategic thinking, management skills, and other important leadership qualities.
    - Mentorship and coaching: Working with mentors or coaches can provide leaders with valuable insights and feedback that

are crucial for personal and professional growth. Mentors serve as role models and guides, offering advice based on their own experiences and successes.

- Practical experience: There is no substitute for hands-on experience. Taking on leadership roles, even in small projects, helps develop crucial skills like team management, problem-solving, and decision-making. Each leadership opportunity is a learning experience that builds competence and confidence.
- Networking and industry engagement: Engaging with other leaders and professionals through platforms like LinkedIn allows for the exchange of ideas and strategies. Networking not only provides learning opportunities but also helps leaders stay abreast of industry trends and new management practices.
- **Self-study and personal development:** Reading leadership books, listening to podcasts, and engaging with thought-provoking content can help leaders gain new perspectives and ideas that can be applied in their professional lives.
- Enroll in leadership development workshops or online courses.
- **Leadership qualities in the workplace:** You don't have to be in a management position to exercise the qualities of an exceptional leader. Leaders are the ones who help and motivate the people around them. They have good ideas and set a good example.
- Employees at any level can have leadership qualities. In fact, anyone who hopes to be promoted into a leadership position in the future should work on developing the traits of a leader today.

- **Leadership qualities in the workplace:**
    - **Build strengths and overcome weaknesses**
        - Find conscious opportunities in the workplace where you can further develop your strengths or work to overcome your weaknesses.

- For example, maybe your listening skills leave something to be desired. The next time you talk to a colleague about a project, make a conscious effort to remember each point and follow up on the significant ones.

- **Be a knowledge sponge**

    - Learn everything you can about your industry and your organization. Seek out training for new skills. You can do this through self-directed learning, or you can participate in formal programs. You can also utilize learning modes such as micro learning.

    - You might have all the skills you need for your current position, but learning new things opens up future possibilities. If you're already in a management role, continuing to learn will help you have better ideas and develop a stronger strategy.

- **Develop your people skills**

    - Every day is a new opportunity to become a better leader by improving your people skills. Whether you're starting an entry-level job or taking on a major leadership role, you'll have many chances to:

    - Build relationships with your colleagues

    - Clear communication

    - Listen actively

    - Patient and Empathetic

    - Learn to negotiate and diffuse conflict

- **Do outstanding work**

    - In other words, led by example. Go above and beyond expectations, and you'll inspire others to do the same.

- **Use leadership qualities to be a better leader**

- Leadership qualities aren't mysterious attributes that some people possess and others never will. Instead, being a leader involves concrete skills that anyone, at any level of the business, can develop.
- Organizations have to develop strong leadership capabilities in all employees/workers.

- **Leadership Skills You Should Focus On**
  - As you begin to understand who you are as a leader and who you want to become, you can start to zero in on leadership skills that will transform you into the most effective leader you can be. These are some of the skills sought after in leaders across all fields and industries:
  - **Integrity**
    - Naturally, integrity is at the top of the list as one of the most critical leadership qualities.
    - A leader with integrity is honest and relies on their own moral compass and values to make decisions for the organization. An individual with a strong sense of integrity is motivated to do what is right simply because it is right. They will make that same decision whether they have an audience in public or whether they are working in private.
    - People known for having integrity are also generally considered to be respectful, approachable, fair, honest, and trustworthy, which is another reason why it is essential for truly effective leadership.
  - **Self-Awareness**
    - A self-aware individual knows that they have a distinct set of strengths and weaknesses. They can rely on their strengths to improve the organization and the team and seek assistance to compensate for their shortcomings.

- Self-awareness is essential for anyone in a leadership position because it allows the leader to know their own limitations. As a self-aware leader, you would be able to recognize when you have enough on your plate to manage, and you would subsequently delegate tasks accordingly to the rest of the team.

- **Empathy**
    - Empathy has never been more important, especially in an increasingly diverse multicultural world. An empathetic leader can recognize the feelings of others and will attempt to understand their perspective. Empathy is one of the best ways to nurture professional relationships, as it allows you to be aware of the feelings of others and to recognize how the decisions that leader make impact the team at large.
    - Corporations and businesses across all industries are finding that empathetic leaders can create a better workplace culture that is more inclusive and, as a result, more productive. Empathetic leaders allow everyone to feel like they are a valued part of the team.

- **Communication**
    - In order to become an impactful leader, you must also work to become an effective communicator. Communication skills are some of the most sought-after competencies in professionals across all industries because good communicators know how to work well with others. A good communicator is one who:
    - Listens to others and understands their needs.
    - Clearly and effectively states what needs to be completed.
    - Delegates tasks.
    - Relies on appropriate technology to deliver a message in the most effective way.

    - A leader who has effective communication skills can be clear, concise, and organized in their direction. In addition, they also have an open-door policy, making the team aware that they are available to listen at any time.

- **Active Listening**
    - Active listening is a form of listening that goes beyond simply being willing to hear what someone is saying. A leader who is also an active listener can understand what someone is saying, reflect on the points they made, and remember that information in the future.
    - To be an active listener, you must give the person speaking to you your full attention. You should be entirely present during the conversation and mentally note the points they are sharing with you. When you do this, you will be able to recall what they said in the future, and you will be able to rely on their perspective as you make decisions that will shape your group or organization.

- **Growth Mindset**
    - Leaders who have worked on developing a growth mindset are often more resilient, flexible, and adaptable. In the face of adversity, an individual with a growth mindset does not feel discouraged. Instead, they feel empowered to rise to the challenge and overcome the roadblocks they face.
    - A growth mindset is the belief that people can change and improve, even when they make a mistake or suffer a setback. An individual with a growth mindset knows they can continue to hone their skills and abilities to become a better version of them.
    - An individual with a fixed mindset believes that their abilities — and inabilities — exist and cannot be improved or changed. Noting this, it's clear why the most effective leaders in today's

world have adopted a growth mindset, and they encourage those in their teams to attempt to do the same.

- A growth mindset is the belief that people can change and improve, even when they make a mistake or suffer a setback. An individual with a growth mindset knows they can continue to hone their skills and abilities to become a better version of them.

- **Patient**
  - Patience is more than just a virtue — it's a skill that can be improved upon over time. The best leaders are patient and understanding. They are aware that they are not perfect, and neither are their team members, so they are willing to accept mistakes and encourage growth.
  - Being a patient leader does not necessarily mean being passive or accepting slow results. Instead, it means that you are willing to gently guide and nurture those around you so that they have the freedom to become the best version of themselves in a positive and uplifting environment.

- **Optimistic**
  - The most admired leaders are known for their optimistic outlook. They can stay positive in the face of adversity, and they genuinely believe that the organization will continue to improve over time.
  - While optimistic leaders can look on the bright side, it's important to note that they do not necessarily ignore negative experiences or frustrating setbacks. They acknowledge these situations, but they can look at them through a positive lens. They recognize a challenge but view it as an opportunity to grow and improve.

- As an optimistic leader, you can inspire your team to adopt a more positive outlook and focus on the best aspects of any situation.

- **Decision-Making**

    - Decision-making is a critical component of leadership and the best leaders can swiftly make clear and fair decisions. The fact of the matter is when you are in a leadership position; your team is relying on you. You are the person that they look to for guidance. As a result, they expect you to be able to make a decision that will benefit the team and allow the group to accomplish its goals in the shortest amount of time.
    - Leaders who have honed other leadership qualities, such as integrity, trust, and courage, are generally better decision-makers and feel more confident as they make choices for their organization.

- **Transparent**

    - Transparency has long been an important aspect of leadership. A transparent leader makes decisions without secrecy and is willing to explain why a specific plan has been put into place. In addition, a transparent leader is willing to accept feedback from those around them and take the actions needed to adapt accordingly.

Chapter 16
Community Engagement & Good Governance

"Community engagement by an MP isn't just a duty; it's a promise to be present, to listen, and to act on behalf of those they represent. It's about building bridges, fostering dialogue, and working together to create a stronger, more vibrant community for all."

Community engagement is integral to promoting good governance, fostering civic participation, and achieving sustainable development goals. By prioritizing transparency, inclusivity, and collaboration, governments can harness the collective wisdom and strengths of communities to build resilient, prosperous, and equitable societies. Empowered communities are not only recipients of government services but active partners in shaping the future they envision Community engagement and good governance are interconnected pillars that foster participatory democracy, accountability, and sustainable development. Effective community engagement ensures that citizens actively participate in decision-making processes, collaborate with government institutions, and contribute to shaping policies that address local needs and aspirations.

- **Importance of Community Engagement:** Community engagement is essential for fostering inclusive governance and enhancing the quality of democratic practices. It empowers citizens to:

- **Voice their Concerns:** Community engagement provides platforms for citizens to express their opinions, concerns, and priorities regarding local development projects, public policies, and service delivery.
- **Participate in Decision-Making:** By involving citizens in decision-making processes, governments can ensure that policies and programs are responsive to the diverse needs and preferences of the community.
- **Hold Governments Accountable:** Active community engagement promotes transparency and accountability in governance. Citizens can monitor the performance of public officials, demand explanations for decisions, and advocate for improved services and infrastructure.
- **Facilitate Local Development:** Engaged communities contribute local knowledge and expertise that inform effective development strategies. Collaboration between government agencies, civil society organizations, and community groups leads to sustainable solutions that address pressing social, economic, and environmental challenges.

- **Effective Community Engagement:**
  - **Communication and Information Sharing:** Governments should prioritize transparent communication channels that provide timely and accessible information to citizens. This includes public consultations, town hall meetings, online platforms, and community newsletters.
  - **Consultation and Collaboration:** Engage stakeholders early in the policy-making process to gather diverse perspectives and feedback. Collaborative decision-making ensures that policies reflect the collective interests and priorities of the community.

  - **Capacity Building:** Empower community members with knowledge, skills, and resources to actively participate in governance processes. Training programs, workshops, and civic education initiatives enhance civic literacy and strengthen grassroots leadership.
  - **Inclusivity and Diversity:** Promote inclusive participation by reaching out to marginalized groups, minorities, and vulnerable populations. Ensure that all voices are heard and represented in discussions that shape community development.
- **Benefits of Good Governance through Community Engagement:**
  - **Enhanced Civic Trust and Confidence:** Transparent and inclusive governance practices build trust between citizens and government institutions. When citizens perceive fairness and responsiveness in decision-making, they are more likely to support policies and comply with regulations.
  - **Improved Service Delivery:** Community engagement helps identify local priorities and preferences, leading to more effective allocation of resources and delivery of public services. Governments can tailor interventions to address specific community needs and achieve measurable outcomes.
  - **Social Cohesion and Resilience:** Strong community engagement fosters solidarity, social cohesion, and resilience against challenges such as natural disasters, economic downturns, and social inequalities. Collaborative efforts strengthen community bonds and empower residents to collectively address shared concerns.
  - **Sustainable Development:** By integrating community perspectives into development planning, governments can promote environmentally sustainable practices, economic growth, and equitable distribution of resources. Community-driven initiatives contribute to long-term prosperity and well-being.

- **Challenges and Considerations:** Despite its benefits, effective community engagement requires overcoming challenges such as:
    - **Resource Constraints:** Limited funding and capacity gaps may hinder governments' ability to sustain meaningful engagement over time.
    - **Power Dynamics:** Addressing power imbalances and ensuring that marginalized groups have equal voice and representation in decision-making processes.
    - **Communication Barriers:** Overcoming language barriers, digital divides, and accessibility issues to ensure that all community members can participate fully.
- **Community Engagement:** It is a vital aspect of your role as a Member of Parliament (MP), as it allows you to connect with constituents, understand their needs, and address their concerns effectively. By actively engaging with your constituents through these strategies, you can build stronger connections, gain valuable insights, and effectively represent their interests in parliament. Community engagement is not only essential for effective governance but also a cornerstone of democracy that empowers constituents and strengthens the democratic process. Here are some key strategies for community engagement:
    - **Public Meetings and Town Halls**: Organize regular public meetings and town halls in your constituency to provide constituents with an opportunity to interact with you directly, ask questions, and share their feedback and concerns.
    - **Constituency Visits**: Schedule regular visits to different areas within your constituency to meet with residents, community leaders, local businesses, and grassroots organizations. This allows you to gain firsthand knowledge of local issues and build relationships with constituents.
    - **Door-to-Door Canvassing**: Engage in door-to-door canvassing to reach out to constituents personally, listen to

their concerns, and discuss how you can address them. This approach demonstrates your accessibility and commitment to serving all constituents, regardless of their background or location.

- **Community Events**: Participate in community events, festivals, cultural celebrations, and social gatherings to connect with constituents in a more informal setting. This provides an opportunity to build rapport with diverse segments of the community and strengthen community ties.
- **Digital Outreach**: Utilize digital platforms, including social media, email newsletters, and your official website, to engage with constituents, share updates, and solicit feedback. This allows you to reach a wider audience and connect with constituents who may not attend traditional events.
- **Youth Engagement**: Engage with young people in your constituency through youth forums, school visits, and outreach programs. Encourage their participation in civic activities, listen to their perspectives, and address issues relevant to their interests and aspirations.
- **Specialized Outreach**: Tailor your outreach efforts to specific demographic groups or communities within your constituency, such as seniors, women, minorities, or people with disabilities. Ensure that their voices are heard and their needs are addressed in your policy priorities.
- **Collaborative Initiatives**: Collaborate with local government officials, community organizations, NGOs, and other stakeholders to organize joint initiatives and community projects. Working together strengthens relationships and maximizes the impact of your efforts.
- **Feedback Mechanisms**: Establish effective feedback mechanisms, such as suggestion boxes, hotlines, or online surveys, to solicit input from constituents and address their

concerns in a timely manner. Demonstrate responsiveness to constituent feedback by following up on their suggestions and taking appropriate action.

- **Transparency and Accountability**: Maintain transparency in your interactions with constituents by providing regular updates on your activities, decisions, and legislative priorities. Be accountable for your actions and decisions, and explain the rationale behind your positions to foster trust and credibility.

- **Good practices in community engagements:** Good practices in community engagement as a Member of Parliament (MP) can help foster meaningful connections, build trust, and facilitate constructive dialogue with your constituents. By incorporating these good practices into your community engagement activities, you can establish yourself as an accessible, responsive, and effective representative who prioritizes the needs and interests of your constituents. Here are some effective practices to consider:

  - **Proactive Outreach**: Initiate regular outreach efforts to engage with constituents, rather than waiting for them to come to you. Actively seek opportunities to connect with diverse segments of your constituency.

  - **Accessibility**: Ensure that your community engagement activities are accessible to all constituents, including those with disabilities, by providing accommodations such as wheelchair access, sign language interpreters, or materials in alternative formats.

  - **Inclusive Approach**: Adopt an inclusive approach that values the diversity of voices within your constituency. Create opportunities for all community members to participate, regardless of their background, identity, or affiliation.

  - **Two-Way Communication**: Foster open, two-way communication by actively listening to constituents' concerns, ideas, and feedback. Encourage dialogue and exchange of perspectives, and demonstrate responsiveness to community input.

- **Transparency**: Maintain transparency in your engagement activities by providing clear information about your objectives, processes, and outcomes. Communicate openly about your actions, decisions, and the rationale behind them.
- **Empowerment**: Empower constituents to participate meaningfully in decision-making processes and community initiatives. Provide opportunities for community members to take on leadership roles, contribute their expertise, and drive positive change in their own communities.
- **Respectful Engagement**: Conduct engagement activities with respect, empathy, and sensitivity towards community members' perspectives, experiences, and concerns. Create a safe and inclusive environment where all voices are heard and valued.
- **Collaborative Partnerships**: Foster collaborative partnerships with local organizations, community leaders, and stakeholders to leverage collective resources, expertise, and networks. Work together towards shared goals and mutual benefit.
- **Flexibility and Adaptability**: Be flexible and adaptable in your approach to community engagement, recognizing that different communities have unique needs, preferences, and priorities. Tailor your strategies to suit the specific context and dynamics of each community.
- **Feedback and Follow-Up**: Solicit feedback from constituents regularly to assess the effectiveness of your engagement efforts and identify areas for improvement. Follow up on commitments made during engagement activities and communicate outcomes back to the community.
- **Capacity Building**: Support capacity building initiatives within the community to enhance residents' skills, knowledge,

and abilities to address local challenges and opportunities. Provide access to training, resources, and support networks to empower community members to take action.

- **Long-Term Engagement**: View community engagement as a long-term commitment rather than a one-time event. Build sustained relationships with constituents over time, nurturing trust and rapport through ongoing communication and collaboration.

- **Types of community engagements:** Community engagement can take various forms, each tailored to the specific needs, preferences, and priorities of the community. By leveraging a combination of these community engagement methods, MPs can effectively connect with constituents, build trust, gather input, and work collaboratively towards addressing the needs and aspirations of the community. Here are some types of community engagement that Members of Parliament (MPs) may utilize:

  - **Public Meetings and Town Halls**: Organize public meetings or town hall events where constituents can gather to discuss issues, ask questions, and share their feedback directly with the MP.

  - **Door-to-Door Canvassing**: Engage in door-to-door outreach to connect with constituents in their homes, listen to their concerns, and provide information about parliamentary activities and services.

  - **Focus Groups**: Conduct focus group discussions with small groups of constituents to explore specific topics or issues in-depth, gather insights, and brainstorm potential solutions or initiatives.

  - **Surveys and Questionnaires**: Distribute surveys or questionnaires to gather feedback, opinions, and preferences from a broader cross-section of the community on various issues or policy matters.

- **Community Workshops and Forums**: Host workshops, forums, or roundtable discussions on specific topics or themes of interest to the community, providing opportunities for learning, dialogue, and collaboration.
- **Online Engagement**: Use digital platforms, such as social media, email newsletters, and online forums, to engage with constituents virtually, share information, and solicit feedback from a wider audience.
- **Community Events and Festivals**: Participate in community events, festivals, cultural celebrations, or local fairs to interact with constituents in a more informal setting and build relationships with diverse segments of the community.
- **Constituency Visits**: Visit different areas within the constituency to meet with residents, community leaders, businesses, schools, and organizations, and learn about local initiatives, challenges, and opportunities.
- **Stakeholder Meetings**: Hold meetings with key stakeholders, such as local government officials, community organizations, NGOs, and industry representatives, to discuss collaborative initiatives and address shared concerns.
- **Youth Engagement Programs**: Develop programs and initiatives specifically targeted at engaging youth in civic activities, such as youth councils, leadership training workshops, or student forums.
- **Civic Education Campaigns**: Launch civic education campaigns to raise awareness about democratic processes, rights and responsibilities, and the role of parliamentarians in representing and serving the community.
- **Community Service Projects**: Participate in or support community service projects, volunteer activities, or charitable initiatives that address local needs and contribute to community well-being.

- **Media Engagement**: Engage with local media outlets, including newspapers, radio stations, and television channels, to communicate with constituents, share updates, and raise awareness about key issues or initiatives.
- **Interfaith and Intercommunity Dialogues**: Facilitate dialogues and exchanges between different religious, ethnic, or cultural communities to promote understanding, tolerance, and social cohesion.
- **Advisory Councils or Committees**: Establish advisory councils or committees comprising community members, experts, and stakeholders to provide input, advice, and recommendations on specific issues or policy matters.
- **Neighborhood Associations**: Collaborate with neighborhood associations or resident welfare groups to address local concerns, coordinate community initiatives, and foster a sense of belonging and solidarity.

- **Documentation of community events:** Documenting community events as an MP is important for several reasons. It allows you to maintain a record of your activities, share updates with constituents, and demonstrate your commitment to transparency and accountability. By following these tips and approaches, you can effectively document community events as an MP, preserving valuable memories, insights, and outcomes while also engaging with constituents and demonstrating your commitment to serving their needs. Here are some tips for effectively documenting community events:
    - **Capture Moments**: Take photographs and videos during the event to document key moments, interactions, and activities. Capture images of constituents engaging with you, participating in discussions, and enjoying the event.
    - **Interview Participants**: Conduct short interviews with attendees, organizers, and volunteers to gather testimonials,

feedback, and insights about the event. Ask about their experiences, opinions, and suggestions for future events.

- **Collect Data**: Gather data and statistics related to the event, such as attendance numbers, demographics of participants, and any outcomes or achievements resulting from the event.
- **Create Written Reports**: Prepare written reports summarizing the event, including its objectives, agenda, activities, and outcomes. Provide an overview of discussions, key points raised, and any decisions or action items identified during the event.
- **Compile Testimonials**: Compile testimonials and quotes from attendees, community leaders, and stakeholders expressing their thoughts, appreciation, and feedback about the event. Use these testimonials in your documentation and communications.
- **Use Social Media**: Share real-time updates and highlights from the event on social media platforms such as Twitter, Facebook, and Instagram. Post photos, videos, and short updates to engage with constituents who couldn't attend in person.
- **Write Blog Posts or Newsletters**: Write blog posts, newsletters, or articles about the event, detailing its purpose, significance, and impact. Include anecdotes, insights, and reflections on your experiences and interactions during the event.
- **Publish Press Releases**: Issue press releases to local media outlets highlighting the event, its objectives, and any notable outcomes or achievements. Provide quotes, photos, and contact information for media inquiries.
- **Share Videos or Live streams**: If feasible, record videos or live stream the event to reach a broader audience and allow

constituents to participate virtually. Upload recordings to your website or social media channels for later viewing.

- **Engage Volunteers**: Involve volunteers in documenting the event by assigning them specific tasks such as photography, videography, note-taking, or conducting interviews. Delegate responsibilities to ensure comprehensive coverage of the event.
- **Evaluate and Reflect**: After the event, take time to evaluate its effectiveness, identify lessons learned, and reflect on areas for improvement. Use feedback from participants and organizers to inform planning for future events.
- **Archive Documentation**: Maintain a centralized archive of documentation for all community events, organized by date, location, and theme. Store digital files securely and keep physical copies of important documents for reference.

- **Do's and Don'ts of community engagements:** By adhering to these do's and don'ts, you can conduct community engagement activities effectively, build trust and rapport with constituents, and foster meaningful dialogue and collaboration for the benefit of your constituency and community. Here are some do's and don'ts for community engagement as a Member of Parliament:

DO'S:

- **Listen Actively**: Listen attentively to the concerns, needs, and perspectives of community members without interrupting or dismissing their opinions.
- **Empathize**: Show empathy and understanding towards community members, acknowledging their experiences and emotions, even if you may not agree with them entirely.
- **Be Accessible**: Make yourself accessible and approachable to community members by attending events, holding regular office hours, and responding promptly to inquiries and concerns.

- **Communicate Clearly**: Communicate information effectively using clear, jargon-free language, and provide concise explanations of complex issues or policies.
- **Engage Diverse Voices**: Ensure that your community engagement efforts are inclusive and represent the diversity of voices within your constituency, including marginalized or underrepresented groups.
- **Build Relationships**: Focus on building genuine relationships with community members based on trust, respect, and mutual understanding. Foster long-term connections rather than solely seeking short-term gains.
- **Follow Up**: Follow up on community concerns and commitments made during engagement activities by taking concrete actions and providing feedback on progress or outcomes.
- **Collaborate**: Collaborate with community organizations, local leaders, and stakeholders to address shared challenges and leverage collective resources and expertise.
- **Educate and Inform**: Provide accurate information and educational resources to community members to help them make informed decisions and participate meaningfully in civic life.
- **Respect Boundaries**: Respect personal boundaries and cultural sensitivities during engagement activities, and be mindful of privacy concerns when discussing sensitive issues.

DON'TS:

- **Dominate Discussions**: Avoid dominating discussions or monopolizing the conversation during community engagements. Allow others to express their views and opinions freely.
- **Dismiss Concerns**: Refrain from dismissing or trivializing community concerns, even if you may disagree with them. Respect differing perspectives and validate community members' experiences.

- **Make False Promises**: Avoid making unrealistic promises or commitments that you cannot fulfill. Be honest about what you can realistically achieve and communicate any limitations or challenges openly.
- **Ignore Feedback**: Don't ignore or disregard feedback from community members, even if it is critical or challenging. Acknowledge feedback respectfully and address concerns constructively.
- **Engage Selectively**: Avoid engaging only with certain segments of the community or prioritizing the interests of specific groups over others. Ensure that engagement efforts are inclusive and equitable.
- **Underestimate Community Knowledge**: Don't underestimate the knowledge and expertise of community members. Value their insights and contributions to the discussion, even if they may not align with your own perspectives.
- **Violate Trust**: Uphold the trust placed in you by community members by maintaining confidentiality, respecting confidentiality, and safeguarding sensitive information shared during engagement activities.
- **Be Patronizing**: Avoid speaking down to community members or adopting a patronizing attitude. Treat everyone with respect and dignity, regardless of their background or status.
- **Focus Solely on Politics**: Refrain from focusing solely on political agendas or partisan interests during engagement activities. Prioritize community needs and concerns above political considerations.
- **Disregard Local Customs**: Respect local customs, traditions, and cultural practices during engagement activities. Be sensitive to cultural differences and avoid actions or statements that may cause offense or misunderstanding.
    - **Good governance:** Good governance is essential for effective and accountable leadership that serves the best interests of the people. By adhering to these principles and practices of good governance,

leaders and institutions can build trust, promote stability, and create an enabling environment for sustainable development, prosperity, and social justice. Here are some key principles and practices that contribute to good governance:

- **Rule of Law**: Uphold the supremacy of the law and ensure that all individuals, including government officials, are subject to and accountable under the law.
- **Transparency**: Foster transparency in decision-making processes, public administration, and the use of public resources. Provide access to information, data, and government proceedings to promote accountability and public trust.
- **Accountability**: Hold government officials accountable for their actions, decisions, and use of public resources. Establish mechanisms for oversight, scrutiny, and redressal of grievances to ensure accountability to the public.
- **Participation**: Promote citizen engagement and participation in democratic processes, policymaking, and governance. Create opportunities for meaningful civic engagement, dialogue, and collaboration between government and civil society.
- **Responsive Institutions**: Develop responsive, inclusive, and efficient institutions that are capable of addressing the needs and concerns of the people. Ensure that government institutions are accessible, responsive, and accountable to citizens.
- **Fairness and Equity**: Ensure fairness, equity, and non-discrimination in the delivery of public services, allocation of resources, and distribution of benefits. Uphold the rights and dignity of all individuals, regardless of their background or status.
- **Efficiency and Effectiveness**: Promote efficiency, effectiveness, and professionalism in government operations,

service delivery, and resource management. Streamline processes, eliminate waste, and optimize the use of resources to achieve desired outcomes.

- **Ethical Leadership**: Lead by example and uphold high ethical standards in public service. Demonstrate integrity, honesty, and accountability in all actions and decisions, and reject corruption, nepotism, and abuse of power.
- **Inclusivity**: Embrace diversity and inclusivity in governance processes, policies, and decision-making bodies. Ensure representation and participation of all segments of society, including marginalized groups, women, minorities, and vulnerable populations.
- **Long-Term Perspective**: Adopt a long-term perspective in policymaking and planning, considering the interests and well-being of future generations. Invest in sustainable development, environmental conservation, and resilience-building measures.
- **Collaboration and Partnership**: Foster collaboration, partnership, and cooperation between government, civil society, private sector, and other stakeholders. Harness collective efforts and expertise to address complex challenges and achieve common goals.
- **Adaptability and Innovation**: Remain adaptable and open to innovation in governance practices, technologies, and approaches. Embrace new ideas, technologies, and methodologies to improve governance effectiveness and responsiveness.

- **Good governance shown by MP:** Members of Parliament (MPs) can demonstrate good governance through various actions and behaviors that uphold democratic values, promote transparency, accountability, and responsiveness to the needs of constituents. By exemplifying these principles and practices, Members of Parliament can contribute to the promotion of good governance, strengthen democratic institutions, and build trust and confidence among citizens in their representatives and government. Here are some ways in which MPs can exhibit good governance:

- **Legislative Responsibilities**: MPs fulfill their legislative responsibilities by actively participating in parliamentary debates, scrutinizing legislation, proposing amendments, and advocating for laws that serve the public interest.
- **Constituency Representation**: MPs represent the interests and concerns of their constituents in parliament by raising their voices on issues that affect their communities, advocating for policy changes, and addressing grievances through appropriate channels.
- **Transparency and Accountability**: MPs maintain transparency in their activities, including their voting record, parliamentary expenses, and interactions with lobbyists. They are accountable to their constituents for their actions and decisions, providing regular updates and explanations for their work.
- **Community Engagement**: MPs engage with their constituents through regular interactions, public meetings, town hall events, and online platforms. They listen to the needs of their constituents, gather feedback, and work collaboratively with local communities to address their concerns.
- **Ethical Conduct**: MPs adhere to high ethical standards in their conduct, refraining from conflicts of interest, corruption, or unethical behavior. They uphold the principles of integrity, honesty, and accountability in all aspects of their work.
- **Representation of Marginalized Groups**: MPs advocate for the rights and interests of marginalized groups within their constituencies, including women, minorities, indigenous communities, persons with disabilities, and other vulnerable populations.

- **Oversight and Scrutiny**: MPs exercise their oversight role by holding the government accountable for its actions, scrutinizing government policies and expenditures, and investigating cases of maladministration or corruption.
- **Policy Advocacy**: MPs advocate for policies and initiatives that promote social justice, economic development, environmental sustainability, and human rights. They work across party lines to build consensus and advance the common good.
- **Collaboration with Stakeholders**: MPs collaborate with stakeholders, including government agencies, civil society organizations, businesses, and academia, to address complex challenges and achieve shared objectives.
- **Education and Outreach**: MPs educate their constituents about democratic processes, civic rights and responsibilities, and government programs. They empower citizens to participate in governance and advocate for their interests effectively.
- **Promotion of Democratic Values**: MPs promote democratic values such as freedom of expression, rule of law, pluralism, and tolerance within their constituencies and beyond. They defend democratic institutions and processes against threats to their integrity and independence.
- **Commitment to Public Service**: MPs demonstrate a commitment to public service by prioritizing the interests of the public over personal or partisan interests. They serve as role models for ethical leadership and responsible governance.

Chapter 17
Winning Indian Parliament Elections

"Parliamentary elections are the heartbeat of democracy, where every vote is a voice, and every voice shapes the future. It's a time for reflection, debate, and ultimately, a collective decision on the direction of our nation. Let us cherish this privilege, honor the process, and participate with the gravity it deserves."

Winning Indian parliamentary elections is a multifaceted endeavor that involves strategic planning, effective campaigning, understanding local dynamics, and connecting with voters across diverse demographics. Winning Indian parliamentary elections requires a combination of strategic planning, effective communication, grassroots mobilization, coalition building, and a strong organizational structure. Candidates, who connect authentically with voters, understand local dynamics, and effectively leverage resources stand a better chance of winning and serving as effective representatives in the Indian parliament.

HERE ARE KEY ELEMENTS FOR WINNING ELECTIONS:

- **Constituency Understanding and Engagement:**
    - **Local Issues:** Understanding local issues, sentiments, and priorities of the constituency is crucial. MPs must address these effectively through their campaigns and policies.

  - **Door-to-Door Campaigns:** Personal interactions with voters through door-to-door campaigns help build rapport and understand their concerns firsthand.
- **Strong Political Party Affiliation:**
  - **Party Endorsement:** Having the backing of a major political party with a strong grassroots network and established voter base provides credibility and resources for campaigning.
  - **Party Machinery:** Leveraging the party's organizational structure for voter outreach, mobilization, and ensuring high voter turnout on Election Day.
- **Effective Campaign Strategy:**
  - **Message Clarity:** Articulating a clear and compelling message that resonates with voters, addressing their aspirations and concerns.
  - **Media Presence:** Utilizing both traditional media (TV, newspapers) and social media platforms to reach a wide audience, especially younger voters.
  - **Public Meetings and Rallies:** Holding public meetings, rallies, and town hall events to connect directly with voters and garner support.
- **Strategic Alliances and Coalitions:**
  - **Coalition Building:** Forming alliances with other political parties or community leaders to broaden support base and strengthen electoral prospects.
  - **Caste and Community Dynamics:** Understanding caste equations and community affiliations in the constituency, and forming alliances accordingly.
- **Personal Integrity and Track Record:**
  - **Clean Image:** Maintaining a clean image with integrity, honesty, and a record of effective service or activism in the community.

- **Track Record:** Showcasing achievements and initiatives undertaken for the constituency's development during previous terms in office.

- **Financial Resources:**
  - **Fundraising:** Securing adequate funds for campaign expenses, including advertising, rallies, and logistical support.
  - **Compliance:** Adhering to election expenditure limits and ensuring transparency in financial transactions.

- **Voter Mobilization and Turnout:**
  - **Ground Mobilization:** Deploying volunteers and party workers for voter identification, persuasion, and ensuring voter turnout on Election Day.
  - **Incentives:** Offering incentives such as promises of development projects, welfare schemes, or employment opportunities to mobilize voters.

- **Election Day Management:**
  - **Polling Booth Management:** Ensuring smooth conduct of polling, maintaining law and order, and addressing any issues or disputes that may arise.
  - **Monitoring:** Monitoring voter turnout and ensuring supporters cast their votes, and addressing any irregularities promptly.

- **Post-Election Engagement:**
  - **Gratitude and Continuity:** Expressing gratitude to voters and maintaining regular communication with constituents post-election.
  - **Fulfilling Promises:** Fulfilling campaign promises, continuing engagement with local issues, and representing the constituency effectively in parliament.

FACTORS THAT COULD INFLUENCE ELECTIONS:

- **Political Landscape**: The political landscape in India is dynamic, with several national and regional parties vying for power. The Bharatiya Janata Party (BJP) and the Indian National Congress (INC) are the two largest national parties, but regional parties also play significant roles, particularly in certain states.
    - **Campaign Issues**: Electoral campaigns typically revolve around a range of issues, including economic development, social welfare, national security, corruption, and identity politics. Parties often tailor their campaigns to appeal to specific voter demographics and regional concerns.
    - **Leadership**: Leadership and the appeal of individual leaders can have a significant impact on election outcomes. Prime Minister Narendra Modi, as the leader of the BJP, has been a dominant figure in Indian politics, but the popularity of regional leaders in key states also shapes electoral dynamics.
    - **Alliances**: Pre-election alliances and coalitions between parties can influence electoral outcomes, particularly in states where regional parties hold sway. Strategic alliances can help parties maximize their electoral prospects and secure a majority in parliament.
    - **Social Media and Technology**: The use of social media and technology in election campaigning has grown significantly in recent years, allowing parties to reach out to voters more effectively and mobilize support. Digital campaigning strategies are likely to play an increasingly important role in future elections.
    - **Demographics**: India's diverse demographic landscape, including factors such as caste, religion, language, and socio-economic status, often shapes electoral outcomes. Parties often engage in targeted outreach to specific demographic groups to secure their support.
    - **Voter Turnout**: Voter turnout is a crucial factor in determining election results. Efforts to mobilize voters and ensure high turnout,

particularly among key demographics, can have a significant impact on the outcome of parliamentary elections.

- **Winning elections in India:**
    - **Party Nomination**: MPs are usually nominated by political parties to contest elections in specific constituencies. Parties select candidates based on various factors, including their popularity, political influence, loyalty to the party, and electability.
    - **Campaigning**: Candidates engage in extensive campaigning to reach out to voters and garner support. Campaign strategies may include public rallies, door-to-door canvassing, social media outreach, and advertising through traditional and digital media platforms.
    - **Local Issues**: MPs often focus on addressing local issues and concerns relevant to their constituencies during their campaign. They may promise to address issues such as infrastructure development, healthcare, education, employment, and public services.
    - **Party Affiliation**: In India's parliamentary system, party affiliation plays a significant role in determining electoral success. Voters often consider the party's overall platform, leadership, and performance when deciding whom to vote for elections.
    - **Personal Appeal**: Some MPs may rely on their personal appeal, charisma, or public image to attract voters. Candidates with a strong personal following or a positive reputation in their constituencies may have an advantage in winning elections.
    - **Mobilizing Support**: Winning MPs typically mobilize support from various sections of society, including political party workers, local leaders, community groups, religious organizations, and influential individuals. Building a broad coalition of support is crucial for electoral success.

- **Election Day Turnout**: Voter turnout on Election Day also plays a crucial role in determining the outcome of elections. MPs and their respective parties often make efforts to ensure high voter turnout among their supporters through effective voter mobilization strategies.

It's important to note that electoral dynamics can vary significantly from one constituency to another, and there are no universal formulas for winning elections. Factors such as caste and religious demographics, incumbency, alliances between political parties, and regional issues can all influence election outcomes

- **Reason for loosing elections:** However, there are several common factors that could contribute to a candidate's loss in parliamentary elections:

    - **Anti-Incumbency**: If the candidate is an incumbent MP, voter dissatisfaction with their performance or policies during their term in office could lead to anti-incumbent sentiment, resulting in their defeat.

    - **Weak Campaigning**: Ineffective or poorly executed election campaigns, including insufficient outreach to voters, weak messaging, or inadequate mobilization efforts, could contribute to a candidate's loss.

    - **Internal Party Issues**: Factionalism or internal divisions within a political party could weaken support for the party's candidates and lead to electoral losses.

    - **Strong Opponent**: Facing a formidable opponent with a strong campaign, widespread support, or a compelling message could pose a significant challenge to a candidate's re-election prospects.

    - **Controversies or Scandals**: Involvement in controversies, scandals, or allegations of corruption could damage a candidate's reputation and erode voter confidence, leading to electoral defeat.

- **Shift in Demographics**: Changes in demographic patterns, such as shifts in voter demographics or the emergence of new voting blocs, could alter the electoral calculus and contribute to a candidate's loss.
- **Regional Factors**: Regional dynamics, including the influence of regional parties, local issues, or regional sentiment, could impact electoral outcomes in specific constituencies.
- **National Trends**: National-level factors, such as the performance of political parties at the national level, overarching political trends, or broader socio-economic conditions, could influence voter behavior and contribute to electoral losses for individual candidates.
- **Campaign Finance**: Lack of adequate campaign funding or resources could hinder a candidate's ability to effectively reach out to voters and compete against well-funded opponents.
- **Unforeseen Events**: Unforeseen events, such as natural disasters, public health crises, or geopolitical developments, could shift voter priorities or perceptions, affecting electoral outcomes unpredictably.

These are just some potential reasons why an MP may lose elections in 2024 or any other year. Actual outcomes are influenced by a complex interplay of factors specific to each constituency and election cycle.

Winning elections requires careful planning, effective strategies, and adherence to ethical practices. Here are some dos and don'ts for candidates aiming to win elections:

DOS:

- **Understand Your Constituency:** Conduct thorough research to understand the demographics, issues, and concerns of the constituency. Tailor your campaign messages and strategies accordingly.

- **Build a Strong Campaign Team:** Surround yourself with competent and dedicated individuals who can manage different aspects of the campaign, from communications to ground mobilization.
- **Develop a Clear Message:** Articulate a compelling vision and set of policies that resonate with voters. Focus on addressing their needs and aspirations.
- **Engage with Voters:** Personally engage with voters through door-to-door canvassing, public meetings, and community events. Listen actively to their concerns and communicate your plans effectively.
- **Utilize Media Effectively:** Use both traditional media (TV, radio, newspapers) and digital platforms (social media, websites) to reach a wider audience. Ensure your message is consistent across all channels.
- **Build Alliances and Coalitions:** Form alliances with other political parties, community leaders, and influential individuals who can support your campaign and broaden your voter base.
- **Be Transparent and Accountable:** Maintain transparency in campaign finances and adhere to legal and ethical standards. Build trust with voters by being open about your background, intentions, and policies.
- **Mobilize Supporters on Election Day:** Ensure your supporters are aware of polling locations and encourage them to vote. Monitor voter turnout and address any issues or challenges promptly.
- **Follow Election Rules and Regulations:** Familiarize yourself with electoral laws and regulations. Ensure all campaign activities comply with legal requirements to avoid penalties or disqualification.

DON'TS:

- **Avoid Negative Campaigning:** Refrain from personal attacks, mudslinging, or spreading false information about opponents. Focus on promoting your own strengths and policies instead.

- **Don't Ignore Local Issues:** Understand and prioritize local issues that matter to voters. Ignoring or neglecting community concerns can alienate potential supporters.
- **Don't Promise Unrealistic Goals:** Be realistic about what you can achieve if elected. Avoid making exaggerated promises or commitments that cannot be fulfilled.
- **Avoid Corruption or Unethical Practices:** Maintain integrity throughout your campaign. Do not engage in bribery, vote-buying, or any form of corruption that undermines the electoral process.
- **Don't Neglect Voter Registration:** Ensure your supporters are registered to vote before Election Day. Ignoring voter registration efforts can lead to lower turnout among your supporters.
- **Don't Underestimate the Importance of Ground Campaigning:** While media and digital outreach are important, personal connections and grassroots campaigning are crucial for winning over undecided voters.
- **Avoid Complacency:** Stay focused and driven throughout the campaign period. Complacency can lead to missed opportunities and a decline in voter support.
- **Don't Disregard Feedback:** Listen to feedback from voters, party members, and campaign advisors. Adapt your strategies based on insights and lessons learned during the campaign.
- **Don't Violate Election Code of Conduct:** Respect the election code of conduct set by electoral authorities. Violations can result in legal repercussions and damage your reputation.

By following these dos and don'ts, candidates can enhance their chances of winning elections while maintaining ethical standards, fostering voter trust, and contributing positively to democratic processes.

- **Voters often look for in a contestant:**
    - **Integrity and Trustworthiness:**

  - Voters prioritize candidates who demonstrate honesty, transparency, and ethical conduct. They look for individuals with a track record of integrity and who uphold moral values.

- **Leadership Qualities:**
  - Effective leadership skills are crucial. Voters assess candidates based on their ability to inspire, make tough decisions, and lead by example. They look for individuals who exhibit competence, confidence, and a clear vision for the future.

- **Understanding of Issues:**
  - Competence in understanding and addressing key issues affecting the constituency or nation is essential. Voters expect candidates to have a grasp of local, national, and sometimes international matters relevant to their roles.

- **Track Record and Experience:**
  - Past accomplishments and experience play a significant role. Voters look for candidates with a proven track record of delivering on promises, contributing positively to their community or profession, and demonstrating capability in relevant fields.

- **Commitment to Public Service:**
  - Voters value candidates who genuinely prioritize public service over personal gain. They look for individuals who are dedicated to improving the lives of constituents, advocating for their interests, and representing them effectively.

- **Accessibility and Responsiveness:**
  - Accessibility and responsiveness to constituents' concerns are important. Voters appreciate candidates who are approachable, actively engage with the community, and are accessible through various communication channels.

- **Empathy and Understanding of Diversity:**
    - Sensitivity to the needs and concerns of diverse communities within the constituency is critical. Voters seek candidates who demonstrate empathy, inclusivity, and a commitment to representing all segments of society fairly.
- **Communication Skills:**
    - Effective communication is key to connecting with voters. Candidates who can articulate their ideas clearly, engage in meaningful dialogue, and listen actively to constituents' feedback tend to resonate more with voters.
- **Stance on Critical Issues:**
    - Voters evaluate candidates based on their stance on critical issues such as healthcare, education, economy, environment, social justice, and national security. Consistency in positions and the ability to offer viable solutions are valued.
- **Political Affiliation and Alignment:**
    - Political party affiliation and alignment with voters' ideological preferences can influence decisions. Voters may support candidates who represent parties or movements that resonate with their beliefs and values.
- **Campaign Conduct and Ethical Standards:**
    - The conduct of the campaign itself reflects on the candidate. Voters prefer candidates who run ethical campaigns, avoid negative tactics, and adhere to electoral laws and regulations.

In conclusion, voters evaluate candidates based on a combination of personal qualities, professional experience, understanding of issues, commitment to public service, and alignment with their values and priorities. Successful candidates often demonstrate a blend of leadership skills, integrity, empathy, and a genuine dedication to serving the interests of their constituents.

Chapter 18
10 Commandments of Parliamentarians

"Parliamentarians uphold the commandments of democracy: to serve with integrity, to legislate with wisdom, and to advocate with compassion. They are entrusted with the sacred duty to represent, to protect, and to advance the interests of their constituents and their nation, guided by the principles of justice, equality, and the common good."

"TEN COMMANDMENTS OF PARLIAMENTARIANS"

We can create a list of guiding principles inspired by the values and responsibilities inherent to parliamentary roles. Here are "10 Commandments of Parliamentarians":

- **Serve the Public**: Remember that your foremost duty is to serve the best interests of the public and your constituents.
- **Uphold Integrity**: Act with honesty, transparency, and integrity in all your dealings as a parliamentarian.
- **Respect Democracy**: Respect the democratic process, including the rule of law, freedom of speech, and the rights of minorities.
- **Listen Actively**: Listen attentively to the voices and concerns of your constituents, representing their interests faithfully.

- **Promote Accountability**: Hold yourself and others accountable for your actions, decisions, and use of public resources.
- **Strive for Unity**: Work towards unity and consensus-building, recognizing that collaboration across party lines is essential for effective governance.
- **Be Informed**: Stay informed about key issues, legislation, and developments relevant to your role as a parliamentarian.
- **Engage with Civility**: Engage in debates and discussions with civility and respect, fostering an atmosphere of constructive dialogue.
- **Exercise Empathy**: Exercise empathy and compassion in your interactions with colleagues, constituents, and stakeholders.
- **Commit to Progress**: Commit to advancing policies and initiatives that promote progress, justice, and the well-being of society as a whole.

These "commandments" encapsulate the core values and principles that guide parliamentarians in fulfilling their responsibilities to their constituents and to the democratic process. By adhering to these principles, parliamentarians can uphold the trust placed in them by the public and contribute to the betterment of their communities and nations.

- **Skills of Narendra Modi:** Narendra Modi, the Prime Minister of India, is known for several skills and attributes that have contributed to his success in politics. These skills and attributes have contributed to his popularity and success as a political leader in India. However, opinions about his leadership vary among different segments of the population, and his tenure as Prime Minister has been subject to both praise and criticism. **Key skills include:**
    - **Oratory Skills**: He is an accomplished public speaker known for his ability to captivate audiences with his speeches. He effectively communicates his vision, ideas, and policies, often using persuasive language and rhetorical techniques to connect with the masses.

- **Strategic Thinking**: He demonstrates strategic thinking and planning in his approach to governance and policy-making. He formulates long-term strategies to address key challenges facing the country and leverages data-driven decision-making to achieve desired outcomes.
- **Political Acumen**: He possesses strong political acumen and understands the dynamics of Indian politics. He has successfully navigated complex political landscapes, built alliances, and managed coalition governments to advance his agenda and maintain electoral support.
- **Leadership Skills**: As a leader, he exhibits decisiveness, resilience, and determination. He inspires confidence and loyalty among his supporters and has the ability to rally people behind his vision and goals.
- **Visionary Leadership**: He is known for his visionary leadership, with a focus on economic development, infrastructure, and social welfare initiatives. He has articulated ambitious goals such as "Make in India," "Digital India," and "Clean India," and has taken steps to realize these visions.
- **Effective Communication**: He communicates directly with the public through social media platforms, including Twitter and Facebook, to share updates, engage with citizens, and address their concerns. His digital communication strategy has helped him connect with a broader audience and shape public opinion.
- **Global Diplomacy**: He has played an active role in shaping India's foreign policy and engaging with the international community. He has pursued a proactive approach to diplomacy, strengthening India's relations with key allies and promoting its interests on the global stage.
- **Crisis Management**: His crisis management skills during times of national emergencies, such as natural disasters and

public health crises. He has mobilized resources, coordinated relief efforts, and provided leadership during challenging situations.

- **Innovative Thinking**: He encourages innovation and entrepreneurship as drivers of economic growth and development. He has launched initiatives such as Startup India and Skill India to foster a culture of innovation and empower the youth.
- **Personal Branding**: He has built a strong personal brand characterized by his humble origins, strong work ethic, and dedication to public service. His image as a decisive leader with a hands-on approach to governance resonates with many voters.

GLOBAL SKILLS OF MODI:

Shri. Narendra Modi, as the Prime Minister of India, has several global skills that have influenced his leadership on the international stage:

- **Diplomacy and International Relations**: He has shown adeptness in diplomacy, engaging with world leaders and representing India's interests effectively in various international forums such as G20, BRICS, and the United Nations.
- **Economic Diplomacy and Trade Relations**: Under his leadership, India has pursued an economic diplomacy strategy, foreign investment, promote trade agreements, and strengthen economic ties with countries. His initiatives like 'Make in India' and 'Digital India' to boost India's economic growth and integration into global supply chains.
- **Global Leadership on Climate Change**: His advocacy for global action on climate change. India under his leadership has committed to ambitious renewable energy targets, spearheaded the International Solar Alliance (ISA), and actively participated in global climate negotiations, promoting sustainable development practices globally.

- **Soft Power and Cultural Diplomacy**: He has promoted India's rich cultural heritage and soft power to enhance bilateral relations and India's image abroad. Initiatives such as International Day of Yoga, India's cultural diplomacy through festivals and exhibitions, and promoting Indian languages and literature have contributed to strengthening people-to-people ties globally.
- **Security and Counter-terrorism Cooperation**: Modi has prioritized enhancing India's security cooperation with various countries and international organizations to combat terrorism, promote maritime security, and safeguard regional stability. He has advocated for collective action against terrorism at global platforms and strengthened defense partnerships.
- **Digital Diplomacy and Innovation**: He has utilized digital platforms effectively to engage with global audiences, promote India's interests, and connect with the Indian diaspora worldwide. Initiatives like 'Digital India', 'Startup India', and 'Skill India' have showcased India's technological capabilities and innovation potential on the global stage.
- **Humanitarian Diplomacy**: His compassion and leadership in humanitarian efforts, including disaster relief, humanitarian assistance to countries in need, and evacuation operations during crises. India's proactive response to global health emergencies and humanitarian disasters has earned international recognition.
- **Strategic Partnerships and Multilateral Engagement**: He has focused on strengthening strategic partnerships with key countries and engaging in multilateral forums to advance India's strategic interests, security cooperation, and global influence. He has emphasized the importance of a multipolar world order and reform of international institutions to reflect contemporary realities.

MODI ON POVERTY:

Narendra Modi, as Prime Minister of India, has initiated policies and programs aimed at alleviating poverty and promoting economic development. These initiatives reflect his commitment to poverty alleviation, inclusive development, and improving the quality of life for disadvantaged communities in India. Initiatives focused on poverty alleviation under his leadership:

- **Jan Dhan Yojana**: Launched in 2014, the Pradhan Mantri Jan Dhan Yojana (PMJDY) aimed to provide financial inclusion to all households in India by ensuring access to financial services such as bank accounts, insurance, and pension schemes. This initiative aimed to empower the poor by promoting savings, access to credit, and facilitating direct benefit transfers.
- **Pradhan Mantri Awas Yojana (PMAY)**: PMAY, launched in 2015, aims to provide affordable housing for all urban and rural households by 2022. It offers financial assistance to eligible beneficiaries for constructing new homes, purchasing or renovating existing homes, and aims to reduce homelessness and improve living conditions for the poor.
- **Skill India Mission**: Launched as part of the Make in India initiative, Skill India aims to enhance the employability and entrepreneurial skills of India's youth. It provides vocational training and certification programs across various sectors to equip individuals with skills needed for better job opportunities and entrepreneurship.
- **Ayushman Bharat - Pradhan Mantri Jan Arogya Yojana (PMJAY)**: PMJAY, launched in 2018, is the world's largest health insurance scheme aimed at providing health coverage to over 500 million vulnerable Indians. It provides cashless access to medical treatment and hospitalization for beneficiaries, focusing on reducing out-of-pocket healthcare expenses for the poor.
- **Swachh Bharat Mission**: Launched in 2014, the Swachh Bharat Mission aims to achieve universal sanitation coverage and eliminate open defecation in India. It focuses on constructing toilets, promoting cleanliness and hygiene practices, and improving

sanitation infrastructure, thereby improving health outcomes and quality of life for the poor.

- **Digital India**: Launched to transform India into a digitally empowered society and knowledge economy, Digital India aims to bridge the digital divide by providing digital infrastructure, digital literacy, and access to digital services to all citizens, including those in rural and remote areas.
- **Rural Electrification**: The Deen Dayal Upadhyaya Gram Jyoti Yojana (DDUGJY) and the Saubhagya scheme aim to achieve 100% rural electrification by providing electricity connections to households, promoting energy efficiency, and enhancing productivity and quality of life in rural areas.
- **Doubling Farmers' Income**: The government has launched various initiatives and reforms in the agriculture sector, such as PM-KISAN (providing direct income support to farmers), crop insurance schemes, agricultural marketing reforms, and promoting sustainable farming practices to enhance farmers' income and livelihoods.

- **Modi on peace and war:** Narendra Modi's approach to peace and war reflects a commitment to diplomacy, regional stability, counter-terrorism, and strategic defense preparedness, while advocating for peaceful coexistence, respect for sovereignty, and international cooperation to address global challenges effectively. His approaches regarding peace and war, both domestically and internationally:
  - **Commitment to Peaceful Coexistence**: He has emphasized India's commitment to peaceful coexistence with its neighbors and the global community. He has advocated for resolving disputes through dialogue, diplomacy, and peaceful negotiations, while promoting mutual respect and understanding among nations.
  - **Diplomatic Engagement**: His active diplomatic engagement to strengthen India's bilateral and multilateral relationships, promotes regional stability, and contributes to global peacekeeping efforts.

- **Non-interference in Internal Affairs**: He has advocated for respecting national sovereignty, promoting democracy, and supporting inclusive development within countries through bilateral partnerships and international cooperation.
- **Counter-terrorism**: He has taken a strong stance against terrorism, advocating for global cooperation to combat terrorism in all its forms and manifestations. He has called for decisive action against terrorist groups, their sponsors, and safe havens, emphasizing the need for collective efforts to address terrorism as a global threat.
- **Strategic Defense Preparedness**: He has prioritized strengthening India's defense capabilities and modernizing its armed forces to ensure national security and deterrence. He has supported indigenous defense manufacturing, technological advancements, and strategic partnerships to enhance India's defense preparedness in a volatile global security environment.
- **Regional Stability and Cooperation**: He has promoted initiatives for regional connectivity, economic integration, and people-to-people exchanges to foster peaceful relations and address common challenges such as poverty, climate change, and natural disasters.
- **Promotion of International Law and Order**: He has shown the importance of upholding international law, respecting maritime rights, and promoting a rules-based international order and has advocated for reforming global institutions to reflect contemporary realities and ensure equitable representation and decision-making processes.
- **Humanitarian Assistance and Disaster Relief**: His commitment to humanitarian assistance and disaster relief efforts globally. India has provided assistance to countries affected by natural disasters, conflicts, and humanitarian crises, demonstrating solidarity and support for vulnerable populations.

LEARNING FROM NARENDRA MODI:

- **Vision and Goal Setting**: He is known for setting ambitious goals and articulating a clear vision for India's development. Learning to define clear objectives and communicate a compelling vision can inspire action and mobilize support towards achieving long-term goals.
- **Effective Communication**: His communication skills are noteworthy, characterized by clarity, conviction, and the ability to connect with diverse audiences. Learning to communicate effectively, using language that resonates with people's aspirations and concerns, is crucial for building trust and fostering engagement.
- **Innovation and Technology**: He has stressed on innovation, digital transformation, and leveraging technology to drive economic growth and governance reforms. Learning to embrace innovation, adopt new technologies, and use data-driven insights can enhance efficiency and effectiveness in decision-making.
- **Bold Reforms and Policy Implementation**: He has pursued bold reforms across various sectors, such as GST (Goods and Services Tax), bankruptcy code, and agricultural reforms.
- **Focus on Infrastructure and Connectivity**: He has prioritized infrastructure development, including roads, railways, and digital connectivity, to enhance economic opportunities and improve quality of life.
- **Empowerment and Skill Development**: Initiatives like Skill India and Make in India underscore his emphasis on empowering youth, promoting entrepreneurship, and enhancing employability. Learning to invest in human capital development, vocational training, and creating opportunities for economic participation can foster inclusive growth.
- **Global Diplomacy and Strategic Alliances**: He has strengthened India's diplomatic engagements globally, fostering strategic alliances and partnerships. Learning to engage diplomatically, build alliances

based on shared interests, and contribute positively to global issues can enhance a country's influence and credibility.

- **Resilience and Adaptability**: His leadership during crises, such as the COVID-19 pandemic, has highlighted resilience, adaptability, and the ability to mobilize resources swiftly.
- **Community Engagement and Grassroots Connect**: His approach includes actively engaging with communities, listening to grassroots concerns, and implementing policies that address local needs. Learning to connect with diverse communities, understand their perspectives, and involve them in decision-making can strengthen governance and promote inclusivity.
- **Decisive Leadership**: He is known for his decisive leadership style, characterized by making bold decisions and taking decisive actions. He has initiated several reforms across various sectors, including economic, agricultural, and governance reforms.
- **Digital Savvy and Communication**: He effectively utilizes digital platforms and social media to communicate directly with the public. He uses these platforms to share his vision, policies, achievements, and engage with citizens on various issues.
- **Policy Innovation and Implementation**: He emphasizes innovation in policymaking and focuses on effective implementation. He has launched initiatives such as Make in India, Digital India, Swachh Bharat Mission, and Ayushman Bharat, among others, aimed at transforming key sectors of the economy and improving quality of life.
- **International Diplomacy**: He has been active in international diplomacy, forging strategic partnerships with various countries and engaging in multilateral forums.
- **Focus on Development and Welfare**: His governance agenda prioritizes development and welfare initiatives aimed at inclusive growth. He has focused on providing basic amenities, enhancing healthcare facilities, promoting education, and improving infrastructure in rural and urban areas.

- **Efficiency and Accountability**: He emphasizes efficiency in governance and accountability in public administration. He has promoted transparency, digital governance, and measures to curb corruption through initiatives like Direct Benefit Transfer (DBT) and digital payments.
- **Public Engagement and Feedback**: His engagements with the public through various channels, including public addresses, town hall meetings, social media interactions, and the Mann Ki Baat radio program. He seeks feedback from citizens and incorporates public opinion into policy formulation.
- **Crisis Management**: His strong leadership during crises, such as the COVID-19 pandemic, by implementing nationwide measures to curb the spread of the virus, mobilizing resources for healthcare infrastructure, and initiating economic stimulus packages to mitigate the impact on the economy.
- **Personal Work Ethic**: He is known for his disciplined work ethic, often working long hours and maintaining a rigorous schedule. He prioritizes productivity, efficiency, and attention to detail in his approach to governance

DAILY ROUTINE OF NARENDRA MODI:

While specific details of his routine are not publicly disclosed in great detail, an overview based on available information and general practices of political leaders:

- **Early Morning Schedule**: He typically starts his day early, often waking up before dawn. This allows him to begin his day with meditation or yoga, which he practices regularly. He has been an advocate for yoga and its health benefits.
- **Physical Fitness**: His emphasizes on physical fitness and he often engages in exercise routines, including brisk walking or yoga, to maintain his health and stamina. His commitment to fitness is well-known, and he encourages citizens to adopt healthy lifestyles.

- **Reading and Information Gathering**: Like many leaders, he likely spends time in the morning reviewing newspapers, reports, and briefing notes to stay updated on national and international developments. This helps him prepare for daily engagements and decision-making.
- **Official Engagements**: As Prime Minister, his schedule is packed with official engagements, including meetings with government officials, cabinet ministers, and foreign dignitaries. He oversees policy discussions, reviews progress on key initiatives, and makes strategic decisions on various matters.
- **Public Addresses and Events**: He participates in public events, addresses the nation through televised speeches or radio programs like Mann Ki Baat, and interacts with citizens through social media platforms. These engagements help him communicate policies, address public concerns, and garner support for government initiatives.
- **Travel and Diplomatic Engagements**: He undertakes domestic and international travel for official visits, diplomatic engagements, and attending summits or conferences. These trips are crucial for fostering bilateral relations, promoting India's interests globally, and participating in international forums.
- **Late Evening Work**: He often works late into the evening, attending to pending matters, reviewing reports, and preparing for the next day's agenda. **Digital Engagement**: He maintains an active presence on social media platforms, where he shares updates, interacts with citizens, and receives feedback.
- **Personal Time**: While his schedule is demanding, He carves out personal time for relaxation, reflection, and spending time with family. Balancing personal life with the demands of high office is crucial for maintaining mental well-being and sustained productivity.

Chapter 19
Good Practices by Parliamentarians

"Good practices by parliamentarians embody the principles of accountability, transparency, and inclusivity. They engage with constituents openly, listen attentively, and make decisions thoughtfully, always mindful of the impact on those they serve. By upholding ethical standards, fostering collaboration, and championing the public interest, they earn the trust and respect of their communities, strengthening democracy at its core."

Parliamentarians play a pivotal role in representing the interests of their constituents, shaping legislative agendas, and promoting effective governance. Adopting good practices enhances their effectiveness, fosters public trust, and strengthens democratic institutions. Adopting good practices is essential for parliamentarians to uphold democratic values, promote effective governance, and serve the interests of their constituents diligently. By embodying commitment to constituents, legislative excellence, transparency, stakeholder engagement, public service, continuous learning, and accountability, parliamentarians contribute to building resilient democratic institutions and fostering trust in representative democracy. Good practices that parliamentarians should embody to fulfill their responsibilities conscientiously and ethically.

- **Commitment to Constituents:**
  - **Accessibility and Engagement:** Good parliamentarians prioritize regular engagement with constituents through town hall meetings, public forums, constituency offices, and digital platforms. They actively listen to concerns, respond to inquiries promptly, and advocate for local interests in parliament.
  - **Advocacy and Representation:** Effective parliamentarians advocate passionately for the needs and aspirations of their constituents. They articulate clear positions on legislative issues, collaborate with stakeholders, and champion policies that benefit their communities.
- **Legislative Excellence:**
  - **Preparation and Participation:** Good parliamentarians thoroughly research legislative proposals, attend parliamentary sessions regularly, and actively participate in debates and committee work. They contribute constructively to policy discussions, propose amendments based on evidence, and uphold parliamentary standards.
  - **Cross-Party Collaboration:** Effective parliamentarians build relationships across party lines to find common ground, negotiate compromises, and advance bipartisan solutions to complex challenges. They prioritize national interest over partisan politics.
- **Transparency and Accountability:**
  - **Ethical Conduct:** Good parliamentarians adhere to high ethical standards, including integrity, honesty, and transparency. They disclose conflicts of interest, uphold parliamentary codes of conduct, and prioritize public service over personal gain.
  - **Financial Disclosure:** Transparent financial practices, including timely reporting of assets, income, and expenses, ensure accountability to constituents and prevent corruption or undue influence.

- **Engagement with Stakeholders:**
  - **Consultation and Dialogue:** Effective parliamentarians engage with diverse stakeholders, including civil society organizations, business leaders, academics, and advocacy groups. They seek input on legislative proposals, solicit feedback on policy impacts, and foster inclusive decision-making processes.
  - **Representation of Diverse Views:** Good parliamentarians represent diverse perspectives within their constituencies, ensuring that marginalized voices, minorities, and underrepresented groups are heard and considered in policymaking.
- **Commitment to Public Service:**
  - **Public Education and Awareness:** Parliamentarians educate constituents about legislative processes, government policies, and civic rights and responsibilities. They communicate effectively through public speeches, newsletters, social media, and community outreach activities.
  - **Service Delivery:** Good parliamentarians advocate for improved public services, infrastructure development, healthcare, education, and social welfare programs that benefit their constituents and promote equitable development.
- **Professional Development:**
  - **Continuous Learning:** Effective parliamentarians stay informed about evolving issues, research new policy solutions, and attend professional development opportunities, such as seminars, workshops, and academic courses.
  - **Adaptability:** They adapt to changing political landscapes, technological advancements, and societal trends, remaining responsive to the evolving needs and priorities of their constituencies.

- **Building Trust and Confidence:**
  - **Accountability Mechanisms:** Good parliamentarians establish mechanisms for accountability, including public reporting on legislative activities, responsiveness to constituent inquiries, and regular feedback from stakeholders.
  - **Openness to Feedback:** They welcome constructive criticism, engage in dialogue with critics, and demonstrate a willingness to learn and improve their performance as elected representatives.

The subjects covered by Members of Parliament (MPs) can vary widely depending on their interests, expertise, constituents' needs, and national priorities. These are just some of the subjects that MPs may cover in their roles as elected representatives, lawmakers, advocates, and community leaders. The specific issues addressed by MPs can vary depending on the priorities of their constituents, the political context, and the challenges facing their country or region.

- **Common subjects that MPs often address:**
  - **Legislation**: MPs are responsible for debating, amending, and voting on legislation in parliament. They may introduce bills or propose amendments to existing laws to address various issues, ranging from healthcare and education to infrastructure and economic policy.
  - **Constituent Services**: MPs often assist their constituents with a wide range of issues, including accessing government services, resolving disputes with government agencies, securing funding for local projects, and advocating for policy changes to address local concerns.
  - **Policy Advocacy**: MPs advocate for specific policy positions or changes to government policies on behalf of their constituents or interest groups. They may raise awareness about social, economic, or environmental issues and push for legislative or administrative action to address them.

- **Oversight and Accountability**: MPs play a crucial role in holding the government accountable for its actions. They participate in parliamentary committees, question government ministers, and scrutinize government policies and expenditures to ensure transparency, accountability, and good governance.
- **Public Engagement**: MPs engage with the public through public meetings, town halls, social media, and other platforms to gather input, share information, and build support for their policy priorities. They may also communicate government policies and decisions to their constituents.
- **International Relations**: MPs may participate in parliamentary diplomacy, representing their country in international forums, engaging with foreign counterparts, and contributing to discussions on global issues such as peace and security, trade, and human rights.
- **Community Development**: MPs often work to promote community development and empowerment by supporting local initiatives, organizations, and projects aimed at improving education, healthcare, infrastructure, and economic opportunities in their constituencies.
- **Emergency Response**: In times of crisis or emergencies, MPs play a vital role in coordinating relief efforts, providing support to affected communities, and advocating for government assistance and resources to address the crisis effectively.
- **Public Health and Safety**: MPs may advocate for policies and initiatives to promote public health and safety, including measures to address healthcare access, disease prevention, disaster preparedness, and public safety concerns such as crime and violence.
- **Environmental Protection**: MPs may advocate for environmental conservation, sustainability, and climate action by supporting legislation, raising awareness about

environmental issues, and promoting policies to mitigate the impact of climate change and protect natural resources.

- **Good practices by parliamentarians:** Good practices among parliamentarians help uphold democratic values, ensure effective governance, and foster trust between representatives and the public. By adhering to these good practices, parliamentarians can contribute to a healthy democratic system that serves the interests of all citizens. Here are some key practices:
    - **Transparency:** Parliamentarians should strive to be transparent in their actions, including disclosing conflicts of interest, financial disclosures, and decision-making processes. Transparency builds trust and accountability.
    - **Accountability:** Elected representatives should be accountable to their constituents by regularly communicating with them, listening to their concerns, and explaining their actions and decisions.
    - **Ethical Conduct:** Parliamentarians should adhere to high ethical standards, including honesty, integrity, and respect for the rule of law. They should avoid engaging in corrupt practices or unethical behavior.
    - **Commitment to Public Service:** Serving the public interest should be paramount for parliamentarians. They should prioritize the needs of their constituents over personal or party interests.
    - **Respect for Diversity:** Parliamentarians should respect the diversity of their constituents, including differences in opinion, background, and identity. They should work to represent and advocate for the interests of all members of society, regardless of their affiliations.
    - **Constructive Debate:** Healthy parliamentary debate involves respectful dialogue, active listening, and a willingness to

consider different perspectives. Parliamentarians should engage in constructive debate to address issues effectively and find common ground.

- **Legislative Oversight:** Parliamentarians play a crucial role in overseeing the executive branch and holding it accountable. They should exercise robust legislative oversight to ensure that government actions are lawful, transparent, and in the public interest.
- **Collaboration:** Effective governance often requires collaboration across party lines and branches of government. Parliamentarians should be willing to work together with colleagues from different political backgrounds to achieve common goals and serve the public interest.
- **Continual Learning:** The legislative landscape is constantly evolving, and parliamentarians should commit to ongoing learning and professional development to stay informed about relevant issues, policies, and best practices.
- **Accessibility:** Parliamentarians should be accessible and responsive to their constituents, making themselves available for communication and actively seeking feedback from the public.

- **Successful Parliamentarians:** Successful parliamentarians often possess a combination of qualities and practices that enable them to effectively represent their constituents and contribute to the legislative process. By embodying these qualities and practices, successful parliamentarians can make significant contributions to the legislative process and effectively represent the interests of their constituents.

CHARACTERISTICS IN SUCCESSFUL PARLIAMENTARIANS:

- **Strong Communication Skills:** Successful parliamentarians are adept communicators who can articulate their ideas clearly, engage in persuasive debates, and effectively convey the concerns and interests of their constituents.

- **Integrity:** Integrity is essential for earning the trust of constituents and colleagues alike. Successful parliamentarians demonstrate honesty, ethical conduct, and a commitment to serving the public interest above personal gain.
- **Political Savvy:** Understanding the political landscape and dynamics is crucial for navigating the complexities of parliamentary processes and building coalitions to advance legislative agendas.
- **Empathy and Compassion:** Successful parliamentarians demonstrate empathy and compassion towards their constituents, understanding their needs and concerns, and advocating on their behalf.
- **Leadership:** Leadership qualities, such as vision, decisiveness, and the ability to inspire and motivate others, are important for effective parliamentary leadership and for driving positive change.
- **Commitment to Public Service:** Successful parliamentarians are driven by a genuine commitment to public service and a desire to make a positive impact on their communities and society as a whole.
- **Collaboration:** Collaboration is key for achieving legislative goals and addressing complex challenges. Successful parliamentarians are skilled collaborators who can work across party lines and build consensus to achieve common objectives.
- **Knowledge and Expertise:** In-depth knowledge of relevant policy areas, legislative processes, and governance mechanisms is essential for effective lawmaking and oversight.
- **Accessibility:** Successful parliamentarians are accessible to their constituents, actively engaging with them, listening to their concerns, and providing assistance and support as needed.
- **Adaptability:** The political landscape is constantly evolving, and successful parliamentarians demonstrate adaptability and resilience in

responding to changing circumstances and effectively addressing new challenges.

- **Skills of parliamentarians:** Parliamentarians can effectively represent the interests of their constituents, contribute to the legislative process, and promote good governance and democracy. Parliamentarians require a diverse set of skills to effectively fulfill their roles and responsibilities. Here are some key skills:
  - **Communication Skills:** Parliamentarians must be skilled communicators, able to articulate their ideas clearly and persuasively in debates, speeches, and discussions. They also need strong listening skills to understand the concerns of their constituents and colleagues.
  - **Negotiation and Diplomacy:** The ability to negotiate and engage in diplomatic dialogue is crucial for building consensus, resolving conflicts, and advancing legislative agendas in a collaborative manner.
  - **Analytical Skills:** Parliamentarians need strong analytical skills to assess complex policy issues, evaluate evidence, and make informed decisions on legislation and public policy.
  - **Critical Thinking:** Critical thinking skills are essential for evaluating the merits of different arguments, identifying flaws in reasoning, and making well-informed judgments on legislative matters.
  - **Political Acumen:** Understanding the political landscape, including the dynamics within parliament and among political parties, is essential for navigating the legislative process and achieving legislative goals.
  - **Strategic Planning:** Parliamentarians must be able to develop strategic plans to achieve their policy objectives, including identifying key stakeholders, building coalitions, and mobilizing support for their initiatives.

  - **Problem-Solving Skills:** Parliamentarians encounter various challenges in their work, from addressing constituent concerns to resolving legislative disputes. Strong problem-solving skills are essential for effectively addressing these challenges and finding workable solutions.
  - **Interpersonal Skills:** Building positive relationships with colleagues, constituents, and stakeholders is crucial for effective parliamentary work. Parliamentarians must demonstrate empathy, respect, and the ability to collaborate with others.
  - **Ethical Leadership:** Upholding high ethical standards and demonstrating integrity in their actions is essential for earning the trust and respect of the public and colleagues.
  - **Adaptability:** The political landscape is constantly evolving, and parliamentarians must be adaptable and resilient in responding to changing circumstances, emerging issues, and new challenges.
- **Who are/were great parliamentarians:** Throughout history, there have been numerous parliamentarians who have made significant contributions to their respective countries and the advancement of democratic principles. Here are a few notable examples:
  - **Winston Churchill:** A towering figure in British politics, Churchill served as Prime Minister of the United Kingdom during World War II and again in the 1950s. His leadership, oratory skills, and resolve played a pivotal role in guiding Britain through one of its darkest periods and ultimately to victory.
  - **Nelson Mandela:** While perhaps best known for his role in ending apartheid and becoming the first black president of South Africa, Mandela's early political career included serving as a parliamentarian. His commitment to reconciliation and justice left an indelible mark on South African politics and society.

- **Abraham Lincoln:** Before becoming the 16th President of the United States, Lincoln served in the Illinois State Legislature and the U.S. House of Representatives. His leadership during the American Civil War and his efforts to abolish slavery reshaped the nation's political landscape.
- **Margaret Thatcher:** As the first female Prime Minister of the United Kingdom, Thatcher implemented sweeping economic and social reforms that had a profound impact on British politics and society. Her leadership style and policies continue to shape political discourse in Britain and beyond.
- **Benjamin Disraeli:** A Victorian-era British statesman, Disraeli served as Prime Minister of the United Kingdom on two occasions. He is remembered for his political agility, eloquence, and contributions to the Conservative Party's ideology.
- **Barbara Jordan:** An American lawyer, educator, and politician, Barbara Jordan was the first African American woman to serve in the Texas Senate and the first Southern African-American woman to be elected to the United States House of Representatives. Known for her powerful oratory and advocacy for civil rights and social justice, Jordan left a lasting legacy in American politics.
- **Lee Kuan Yew:** As the first Prime Minister of Singapore, Lee Kuan Yew played a central role in transforming Singapore from a small colonial trading post into a prosperous modern nation-state. His pragmatic approach to governance and emphasis on meritocracy and economic development helped establish Singapore as a global economic powerhouse.

These parliamentarians, among others, demonstrated exceptional leadership, vision, and dedication to public service, leaving a lasting impact on their countries and the world.

- **Winston Churchill as a parliamentarian**

Winston Churchill's legacy as a parliamentarian is marked by his eloquence, resilience, and leadership during some of the most tumultuous times in British history. His career spanned over half a century, during which he served as both a Member of Parliament (MP) and as Prime Minister.

One of Churchill's defining moments as a parliamentarian came during World War II. Appointed Prime Minister in 1940, he rallied the British people with his stirring speeches and resolute leadership, famously declaring, **"We shall fight on the beaches, we shall fight on the landing grounds, we shall fight in the fields and in the streets, we shall fight in the hills; we shall never surrender."** His ability to inspire the nation during its darkest hour solidified his reputation as a great leader.

Despite his success during the war, Churchill faced criticism and electoral defeat shortly after its conclusion. However, he remained active in politics, returning as Prime Minister in 1951 until 1955, leading the country through the early years of the Cold War. Overall, Winston Churchill's tenure as a parliamentarian left an indelible mark on British politics and history, shaping the course of the nation during some of its most challenging moments. Churchill's parliamentary career was characterized by his wit, intellect, and oratorical skills. He was a fierce debater known for his quick retorts and sharp comebacks. Beyond his political achievements, he was also a prolific writer, winning the Nobel Prize in Literature in 1953 for his historical writings.

- **Skills of Barack Obama: as a parliamentarian**

Overall, Barack Obama's skills as a parliamentarian were characterized by his oratory prowess, negotiation abilities, intellectual depth, charismatic leadership, and strategic thinking. These qualities contributed to his effectiveness as a senator and laid the groundwork for his successful presidency. Barack Obama's skills as a parliamentarian were evident during his time as a senator representing Illinois from 2005 to 2008 before his presidency. Here are some of the skills he demonstrated:

- **Oratory skills**: Obama's greatest strength as a parliamentarian was his ability to communicate effectively. He was known for his eloquent speeches and powerful rhetoric, which captivated audiences and inspired supporters. His speeches often appealed to both reason and emotion, helping him build consensus and persuade colleagues to support his initiatives.
- **Negotiation and compromise**: Obama was adept at building coalitions and finding common ground with colleagues across the political spectrum. He understood the importance of compromise in a divided political environment and was willing to work with Republicans to advance bipartisan legislation. His skillful negotiation helped him navigate complex legislative processes and achieve policy objectives.
- **Intellectual acumen**: Obama's background as a constitutional law professor provided him with a deep understanding of legal and political principles. He was known for his thoughtful analysis and grasp of complex issues, which earned him respect among his peers. His intellectual prowess enabled him to effectively debate policy matters and craft well-reasoned arguments in support of his positions.
- **Charisma and leadership**: Obama possessed a natural charisma and leadership ability that commanded attention and respect. He had a knack for connecting with people on a personal level and inspiring them to action. His leadership style emphasized inclusivity, empathy, and integrity, qualities that helped him foster cooperation and unity within the Senate.
- **Strategic thinking**: Obama was a strategic thinker who approached legislative challenges with a long-term perspective. He understood the importance of setting priorities, building consensus, and seizing opportunities for progress. His strategic approach to policymaking

enabled him to achieve significant legislative victories during his time in the Senate, including landmark legislation on issues like healthcare and ethics reform.

WEAK PARLIAMENTARIANS:

- They may struggle to fulfill their responsibilities effectively due to deficiencies in communication, leadership, experience, integrity, flexibility, or judgment. Weak parliamentarians may exhibit certain characteristics or behaviors that hinder their effectiveness in legislative roles. Here are some traits that might be associated with weak parliamentarians:
    - **Lack of communication skills**: Weak parliamentarians may struggle to articulate their ideas effectively or communicate with their colleagues and constituents. This can hinder their ability to build consensus, negotiate effectively, and advance their policy agenda.
    - **Poor leadership abilities**: Weak parliamentarians may lack the leadership qualities necessary to inspire confidence and rally support for their initiatives. They may struggle to motivate their colleagues, set strategic priorities, and navigate the complexities of the legislative process.
    - **Inexperience or lack of knowledge**: Weak parliamentarians may lack the experience or expertise needed to effectively fulfill their legislative responsibilities. They may be unfamiliar with parliamentary procedures, unaware of key issues, or ill-equipped to engage in informed debate and decision-making.
    - **Lack of integrity or ethical lapses**: Weak parliamentarians may engage in unethical or inappropriate behavior that undermines public trust and confidence in the legislative institution. This can include conflicts of interest, corruption, or misconduct that tarnishes their reputation and credibility.

- **Inflexibility or unwillingness to compromise**: Weak parliamentarians may be rigid in their positions and unwilling to engage in constructive dialogue or compromise with their colleagues. This can lead to gridlock and dysfunction within the legislative body, impeding progress on important issues.
- **Poor judgment or decision-making**: Weak parliamentarians may demonstrate poor judgment in their actions or decisions, leading to ineffective or detrimental outcomes. This can erode their credibility and diminish their ability to influence policy outcomes.

DO'S AND DON'TS OF PARLIAMENTARIANS:

DO'S:

- **Listen to constituents**: Actively listen to the concerns and needs of your constituents. Understanding their perspectives is crucial for effective representation.
- **Engage in respectful debate**: Engage in civil and respectful debate with colleagues, even when there are disagreements. Constructive dialogue fosters collaboration and helps find common ground.
- **Stay informed**: Keep yourself informed about key issues, legislation, and developments in your field. Knowledge empowers you to make informed decisions and contribute meaningfully to debates.
- **Build relationships**: Build positive relationships with colleagues across party lines. Collaboration and cooperation are essential for achieving legislative goals and serving the public interest.
- **Be transparent**: Be transparent in your actions and decisions. Communicate openly with constituents about your priorities, positions, and the reasons behind your votes.
- **Uphold ethical standards**: Adhere to high ethical standards and integrity in your conduct as a parliamentarian. Act in the best interests of the public and avoid conflicts of interest or unethical behavior.

DON'TS:

- **Disregard constituents**: Don't ignore the concerns or needs of your constituents. Your primary responsibility is to represent their interests and advocate on their behalf.
- **Resort to personal attacks**: Avoid resorting to personal attacks or disrespectful behavior towards colleagues. Such conduct undermines the integrity of the legislative process and impedes productive discourse.
- **Misuse power or privilege**: Don't misuse your power or privilege as a parliamentarian for personal gain or political advantage. Uphold the trust placed in you by the public and act with integrity at all times.
- **Neglect preparation**: Don't neglect preparation for debates, hearings, or legislative sessions. Thorough preparation enables you to make informed contributions and effectively advocate for your positions.
- **Act unilaterally**: Avoid acting unilaterally without consulting stakeholders or considering diverse perspectives. Collaboration and consensus-building are essential for effective governance and policy-making.
- **Violate rules or norms**: Don't violate parliamentary rules or norms, such as parliamentary etiquette or procedural guidelines. Respect for these rules is essential for maintaining order and fairness in the legislative process.
- By adhering to these do's and don'ts, parliamentarians can fulfill their responsibilities effectively, serve the interests of their constituents, and contribute to the functioning of a healthy democracy.

TIPS FOR PARLIAMENTARIANS:

- **Track Record:** If a candidate is defeated, is the candidate still walking the ground and understanding the constituency's needs and people? Even if the candidate may be shifted due to party requirements for the next elections, a candidate who is defeated and genuinely wants to serve the people should continue finding ways and means to stay on in the constituency and understand the ground

- **Belief and Commitment to the Party Cause:** Any member of a political party should have a strong belief to why he or she exists in said political party. He believes in opposition unity. Even though he may not be the best candidate, he is still determined to fight elections
- **Political parties** are not vehicles just to send people into Parliament; they represent a group of people with common fundamentals. If one has a strong belief for a certain way nation should be run, stay put even through the party's bad moments.
- **Evaluation of Policy:** Anyone who wants to enter Parliament should have a fair idea of policy fundamentals. One could be more well-versed on various segments of government, and have a broad-based view on policy from a whole-of-government approach. Often, public policy traverses across different ministries. Parliament is a law-making body. It passes bills and amends laws through rigorous debate. This can only happen if these are discussed from multiple broad perspectives.
- **Interest for Nation:** No matter opposition or incumbent, everyone should be working together for the good of Nation. There is always a place within government, NGOs or otherwise to help improve the country. Someone who scandalizes his or her own country clearly has some other agenda up his or her sleeve.
- **Relationship builder:** Never underestimate the value of building relationships with each other, with staff, and with the greater community. The investment of time and energy on the front end will save you emotional angst on the back end. Disrespect, contempt, and personal attacks create unhealthy relationships that undermine sound governance. If one wishes another to fail, then everyone fails. Good relationships and sound policy serve your community; spite or pandering seldom does.
- **A team player**: A healthy governing body knows that each person was elected by the public as individuals, but that they must work together

as a team. Being an effective team player means being able to advocate for one's position while remaining curious and open minded about the position of others. It also means they work constructively with others without dominating the flow of information or ideas. Their role is to debate and vote as individuals but then respect and support the decision of the majority. They are able to set aside personal interests and influences for the common good.

- **Emotionally mature**: Local leaders need to be in tune with their own emotional state and know how it affects them. Given that they are required to make decisions in the best interests of the community – despite opposition – they must be able to withstand criticism. Being emotionally mature means staying engaged, welcoming dissent, and not over-reacting to it. At times, it may mean coping with the intense emotions of others.
- **Approachable**: Leadership means listening carefully to others with a desire to understand concerns, ideas, and perspectives. Elected officials are expected to be accessible to the community through meetings and events, and by phone and email.
- **Critical thinker**: Today's problems often come from yesterday's solutions. Elected officials should consider how to best limit shifting a problem into the future by maintaining a long-term perspective and considering the potential impact of decisions.
- **Prepared**: Never underestimate the mental preparation required to make decisions about the long-term sustainability of a community. *Effective* elected officials are committed to doing their homework. They come prepared to participate in discussions by researching and reading background materials prior to attending meetings, sessions, committees, etc.
- **Financial acumen**: Policy makers need to understand basic financial information and be able to evaluate budgets and financial statements. If they do not, then they should be willing to seek training to improve their skills. They need to comprehend the long-term taxation and budget consequences of financial proposals and decisions.

Chapter 20
DEALING ANTI-INCUMBENCY

"Anti-incumbency is not merely a rejection of the present but a call for renewal and accountability in governance. It underscores the electorate's demand for change, transparency, and effectiveness in leadership. It serves as a reminder to politicians that power is entrusted, not owned, and must be wielded responsibly for the betterment of society."

In democratic systems worldwide, anti-incumbency has emerged as a notable phenomenon where voters express dissatisfaction or disillusionment with incumbent politicians or parties in power. While anti-incumbency reflects democratic accountability and the electorate's right to demand change, it also poses challenges for governance stability and policy continuity. Incumbents must listen to voter concerns, address grievances, and demonstrate a sincere commitment to serving the public interest to mitigate anti-incumbency sentiments. By fostering transparency, integrity, responsive governance, and effective communication, incumbents can navigate the complexities of anti-incumbency and strengthen democratic institutions for the benefit of all citizens.

CAUSES OF ANTI-INCUMBENCY:

- **Unfulfilled Promises:** Voters often hold incumbents accountable for unmet promises or failure to deliver on campaign commitments, such as economic growth, job creation, infrastructure development, or social welfare programs.

- **Perceived Corruption:** Allegations or instances of corruption, nepotism, cronyism, or ethical misconduct among incumbent officials erode public trust and confidence in their ability to govern transparently and ethically.
- **Policy Failures:** Incumbents may face criticism for ineffective policy responses to pressing issues, including healthcare, education, poverty alleviation, environmental protection, and public safety.
- **Economic Downturn:** During periods of economic recession, inflation, or unemployment, incumbents often bear the brunt of public frustration over perceived mismanagement of the economy or inadequate fiscal policies.
- **Public Perception of Arrogance or Disconnect:** Incumbents perceived as detached from the concerns and priorities of ordinary citizens, displaying arrogance or elitism, may alienate voters seeking genuine representation and responsiveness.

IMPLICATIONS OF ANTI-INCUMBENCY:

- **Electoral Outcomes:** Anti-incumbency sentiments can influence electoral outcomes, leading to the defeat of incumbent candidates or parties in favor of new political alternatives or opposition candidates promising change.
- **Political Instability:** Frequent turnover of elected officials due to anti-incumbency can contribute to political instability, impacting policy continuity, governance effectiveness, and long-term planning.
- **Challenges for Governance:** Incumbents facing anti-incumbency may struggle to implement their agenda, pass legislation, or build consensus, hindering their ability to govern effectively and address pressing national issues.
- **Democratic Accountability:** Anti-incumbency serves as a mechanism for holding elected officials accountable for their performance and responsiveness to public concerns, reinforcing democratic accountability and transparency.

ADDRESSING ANTI-INCUMBENCY:

- **Responsive Governance:** Incumbents can mitigate anti-incumbency by prioritizing responsive governance, actively engaging with constituents, and addressing legitimate grievances through policy reforms and inclusive decision-making processes.
- **Transparency and Integrity:** Upholding high ethical standards, transparency in decision-making and accountability for actions can help rebuild public trust and credibility among disillusioned voters.
- **Effective Communication:** Incumbents should effectively communicate their achievements, initiatives, and policy impacts to educate voters about their contributions and efforts to address public concerns.
- **Policy Innovation:** By innovating policies, delivering tangible results, and demonstrating a commitment to improving the quality of life for all citizens, incumbents can differentiate themselves from their predecessors and competitors.

Reasons for anti- incumbency: Anti-incumbency sentiment can stem from various reasons, reflecting dissatisfaction or disillusionment with current elected officials or parties. Anti-incumbency reflects the dynamic nature of democratic politics, where incumbents must continuously earn and maintain public trust through effective governance, responsiveness to constituent needs, and ethical leadership. Understanding these reasons helps incumbents and political parties strategize to address concerns and strengthen their electoral prospects. Some key reasons for anti-incumbency include:

- **Failure to Deliver Promises**: Voters often hold incumbents accountable for unfulfilled promises made during election campaigns. If key pledges such as economic growth, job creation, or infrastructure development remain unmet, it can lead to frustration and disillusionment.

- **Corruption and Scandals**: Instances of corruption, unethical behavior, or scandals involving incumbents can erode public trust and credibility. Such incidents highlight a perceived lack of integrity and accountability, contributing significantly to anti-incumbency sentiments.
- **Economic Performance**: Poor economic conditions, including high unemployment rates, inflation, or stagnating wages, can lead voters to blame incumbents for failing to manage the economy effectively. Economic hardships often fuel anti-incumbency sentiment, as voters seek change in hopes of better economic prospects.
- **Perceived Arrogance or Disconnect**: Over time, incumbents may become disconnected from ordinary citizens or appear arrogant in their approach to governance. This can alienate voters who feel their concerns are not being heard or addressed by those in power.
- **Policy Failures or Controversies**: Specific policy failures, controversial decisions, or unpopular legislative actions can trigger anti-incumbency sentiment. Voters may disagree with the direction taken by incumbents on critical issues such as healthcare, education, environment, or social welfare.
- **Lack of Transparency and Accountability**: When incumbents fail to maintain transparency in decision-making processes or are perceived as avoiding accountability for their actions, it undermines public trust. Voters may view such behavior as evidence of a broader governance failure.
- **Longevity and Stagnation**: Simply being in power for an extended period can breed anti-incumbency sentiment. Some voters may believe that new leadership is necessary to bring fresh ideas, perspectives, and solutions to address evolving challenges effectively.
- **Political Polarization**: In polarized political environments, incumbents may face opposition simply due to ideological

differences or partisan loyalty among voters. This can contribute to entrenched anti-incumbency sentiment, where loyalty to a party or ideology outweighs support for individual incumbents.

- **Media Influence**: Negative or critical media coverage can amplify existing grievances against incumbents, shaping public opinion and contributing to anti-incumbency sentiment.
- **Demographic and Societal Changes**: Shifting demographics, evolving social norms or generational differences can influence voter preferences and contribute to anti-incumbency sentiment as new generations of voters seek representation that aligns with their values and priorities.
- By implementing these strategies, MPs can effectively tackle anti-incumbency sentiment, strengthen their relationship with constituents, and improve their chances of re-election. It requires a proactive and sincere commitment to serving the public interest and addressing the concerns of those they represent.

- **Anti-incumbency** is often a complex and multifaceted phenomenon influenced by a variety of factors, and there are no guaranteed solutions. Fighting anti-incumbency, which is the tendency of voters to vote against the party or candidate currently in power, can be challenging but not impossible. By implementing some strategies, politicians and parties can effectively counteract anti-incumbency sentiments and improve their electoral prospects. Strategies that politicians can employ to mitigate the effects of anti-incumbency:
  - **Effective Governance**: Focus on delivering tangible results and fulfilling campaign promises during your term in office. Demonstrate effective governance by addressing key issues, improving public services, and implementing policies that benefit constituents.
  - **Transparency and Accountability**: Maintain transparency in government operations and decision-making processes. Be accountable for your actions and decisions, and communicate

openly with constituents about your achievements, challenges, and plans for the future.

- **Regular Constituency Engagement**: Stay connected with your constituents throughout your term by holding regular meetings, town halls, and public forums. Listen to their concerns, address their grievances, and solicit their feedback on important issues.
- **Visibility and Accessibility**: Be visible and accessible to your constituents, both in person and through various communication channels. Attend community events, visit local businesses, and engage with residents on social media to demonstrate your commitment to serving them.
- **Responsive Representation**: Actively represent the interests of your constituents in parliament or legislative bodies. Advocate for their needs, champion their causes, and work to address their concerns through legislative action and policy initiatives.
- **Focus on Local Issues**: Prioritize local issues and concerns that directly affect your constituents' daily lives. Invest in infrastructure projects, healthcare facilities, education programs, and economic development initiatives that benefit your constituency.
- **Effective Communication**: Develop clear and compelling messaging that highlights your achievements, vision, and plans for the future. Communicate your accomplishments effectively through traditional media, social media, and direct outreach to constituents.
- **Building Alliances**: Forge alliances with other political parties, community leaders, and interest groups to broaden your support base and counter the effects of anti-incumbency. Collaborate with like-minded individuals and organizations to strengthen your electoral prospects.
- **Campaign Innovation**: Adopt innovative campaign strategies and tactics to reach voters and mobilize support. Utilize data analytics,

digital marketing, and grassroots organizing techniques to identify and target key demographics effectively.

- **Addressing Public Dissatisfaction**: Acknowledge public dissatisfaction with the status quo and demonstrate a willingness to address legitimate concerns. Offer concrete solutions and reforms to address issues such as corruption, unemployment, inequality, and social injustice.
- **Effective Leadership**: Lead by example and demonstrate strong leadership qualities such as integrity, empathy, and decisiveness. Inspire confidence and trust among voters by demonstrating your ability to lead effectively and navigate challenging circumstances.
- **Adapting to Changing Dynamics**: Stay attuned to changing political dynamics, public sentiment, and emerging issues. Be flexible and adaptive in your approach, adjusting your strategies and priorities as needed to effectively respond to evolving circumstances.

- **Issues in anti –incumbency:** Anti-incumbency refers to the sentiment among voters where they express dissatisfaction or disappointment with the performance of the current elected representatives or political incumbents. This sentiment often manifests in election results where incumbents lose their positions. Anti-incumbency reflects the democratic principle of accountability, where voters hold their elected officials responsible for their actions and decisions. It is a complex phenomenon influenced by various factors, and its impact can vary widely depending on the political and social context of a region or country. Here are some key issues associated with anti-incumbency:
    - **Performance and Accountability**: Incumbents are often judged based on their performance in office. If they fail to deliver on promises, address public concerns effectively, or are involved in scandals or corruption, voters may choose to vote them out.
    - **Disconnect with Voters**: Over time, incumbents may become disconnected from the electorate they represent. This could be due

to spending too much time in office, losing touch with local issues, or being perceived as aloof from the concerns of ordinary citizens.

- **Desire for Change**: Voters may simply desire change after a prolonged period of the same representatives holding office. There is often a sentiment that new faces or parties may bring fresh perspectives and solutions to longstanding problems.
- **Economic and Social Factors**: Economic downturns, rising unemployment, inflation, or other economic factors can contribute to anti-incumbency. If people perceive that their economic situation has worsened under current leadership, they may express their dissatisfaction at the polls.
- **Trust and Integrity**: Trust is crucial in politics. If incumbents are seen as dishonest, untrustworthy, or lacking integrity, voters are likely to seek alternatives who they perceive as more honest and reliable.
- **Party Loyalty Shifts**: Changes in political party dynamics can also contribute to anti-incumbency. If a particular party has been in power for a long time, voters may grow weary of its policies and seek change by voting for a different party.
- **Media Influence**: Negative coverage or scrutiny from media outlets can significantly impact public perception of incumbents, influencing anti-incumbency sentiments.
- **Local and Regional Issues**: Sometimes, specific local or regional issues may lead to anti-incumbency. If voters feel their concerns have been ignored or mishandled by their representatives, they may vote against them in the next election.

Tackling anti –incumbency: Members of Parliament (MPs) facing anti-incumbency sentiment can take several strategic approaches to address and mitigate its impact. Here are some effective strategies for MPs to tackle anti-incumbency:

- **Performance and Delivery**: Focus on delivering tangible results and fulfilling promises made to constituents. MPs should prioritize addressing local issues, advocating for infrastructure development, improving public services, and supporting economic growth initiatives that directly benefit their constituents.

- **Regular Constituency Engagement**: Maintain regular communication and engagement with constituents. This includes holding town hall meetings, attending community events, conducting surveys or feedback sessions, and actively listening to the concerns and priorities of local residents.
- **Transparency and Accountability**: Demonstrate transparency in decision-making processes and financial matters. MPs should be open about their actions, voting records, and use of public funds; ensuring constituents understand and trust their leadership.
- **Accessibility and Responsiveness**: Be accessible to constituents by maintaining open lines of communication through various channels, such as social media, email, and local office hours. MPs should promptly respond to inquiries, complaints, and requests for assistance from constituents.
- **Focus on Local Issues**: Prioritize addressing local issues and concerns that matter most to constituents. This may include advocating for improvements in healthcare, education, transportation, housing, environmental protection, and other relevant issues impacting the community.
- **Building Strong Relationships**: Develop strong relationships with community leaders, local organizations, and stakeholders. Collaborate with them on initiatives that benefit the community and demonstrate effective leadership and collaboration skills.
- **Effective Use of Resources**: Use parliamentary resources effectively and efficiently to support local initiatives and projects. MPs should allocate funds and resources to projects that have a direct positive impact on constituents, demonstrating their commitment to improving local conditions.

- **Campaigning and Messaging**: During election cycles, address anti-incumbency sentiments directly by highlighting achievements, ongoing initiatives, and future plans. MPs should communicate their vision for the constituency and how they intend to address remaining challenges effectively.
- **Personal Integrity and Ethics:** Uphold high ethical standards and integrity in their personal conduct and public office. MPs should avoid involvement in scandals, corruption, or unethical behavior that could damage their reputation and contribute to anti-incumbency sentiments.
- **Adaptation and Flexibility**: Be willing to adapt to changing circumstances and listen to feedback from constituents. MPs should be responsive to evolving needs and priorities within their constituency, demonstrating flexibility in their approach to governance.

Dealing with anti-incumbency: Dealing with anti-incumbency requires a proactive and strategic approach from political incumbents and their parties. By adopting these strategies, political incumbents can effectively address anti-incumbency sentiments, improve their chances of re-election, and maintain strong public support over the long term. It requires a commitment to accountability, transparency, and responsiveness to the needs and aspirations of the electorate. Strategies to address the effects of anti-incumbency:

- **Performance and Delivery**: Focus on delivering on campaign promises and effectively addressing the needs of constituents. This includes improving governance, implementing policies that benefit the public, and ensuring transparency in decision-making processes.
- **Communication and Engagement**: Maintain regular and transparent communication with the electorate. This involves actively listening to concerns, holding town hall meetings, utilizing social media and other platforms to inform and engage voters, and responding promptly to queries and criticisms.

- **Accountability and Transparency**: Demonstrate a commitment to accountability and ethical governance. This includes taking responsibility for mistakes, addressing corruption or misconduct promptly, and maintaining high standards of integrity in public office.
- **Local Outreach and Representation**: Stay connected with local communities and grassroots organizations. Understand and respond to local issues promptly and effectively, ensuring that constituents feel represented and their concerns are taken seriously.
- **Policy Innovation and Adaptation**: Continuously innovate and adapt policies to meet evolving challenges and address new priorities. Show flexibility and responsiveness to changing circumstances, demonstrating the ability to lead effectively in dynamic environments.
- **Campaign Strategy**: During election cycles, acknowledge and address anti-incumbency sentiments directly. Campaign on a platform that highlights achievements, future plans, and a vision for addressing ongoing challenges. Engage in positive campaigning that emphasizes strengths and solutions.
- **Public Perception Management**: Proactively manage public perception through effective media relations and communication strategies. Address negative narratives promptly and truthfully, while highlighting positive achievements and initiatives.
- **Building Coalitions and Alliances**: Foster alliances and partnerships with other political actors, community leaders, and stakeholders. This can help broaden support bases, mitigate opposition, and demonstrate a collaborative approach to governance.
- **Long-Term Vision and Leadership**: Present a compelling long-term vision for the future that resonates with voters. Demonstrate strong leadership qualities, including decisiveness, empathy, and a clear sense of direction that inspires confidence and trust.

- **Continuous Feedback and Improvement:** Establish mechanisms for continuous feedback from constituents and stakeholders. Use this feedback to inform policy decisions and improve service delivery, demonstrating responsiveness to public input.

Dos & Don'ts

"A perfect MP embodies integrity, empathy, and dedication. They listen earnestly, act decisively, and advocate tirelessly for the welfare of their constituents. They bridge divides, champion justice, and inspire unity, transcending political lines to serve the greater good. Their leadership is defined not by perfection, but by their unwavering commitment to uphold the values of democracy and represent the voice of the people with honesty and humility."

Political leaders are vital – they determine the allocation of power and money through governmental policies, establish partnerships with other stakeholders, and make decisions that can have a major effect on a nation's well-being and its citizens. **Political leadership** requires a leader to focus on a country's long-term betterment, above and beyond any short-term personal gains. Strong **political leadership** requires a mixture of charm and honesty, and the capacity to evaluate a circumstance and make a judgment based on what will be better for the majority.

Do's for politicians: By following these "do's," politicians can enhance their effectiveness, build strong relationships, and make a positive impact on their communities and society as a whole.

- **Do Listen Actively**: Actively listen to the concerns, needs, and perspectives of your constituents, colleagues, and stakeholders. Listening attentively helps build trust, understanding, and rapport.
- **Do Communicate Effectively**: Communicate your positions, priorities, and policies clearly and transparently. Use language that is accessible and relatable to your audience, and be open to feedback and questions.
- **Do Uphold Ethical Standards**: Adhere to high ethical standards in all aspects of your work. Demonstrate honesty, integrity, and accountability in your actions, and avoid conflicts of interest or the appearance of impropriety.
- **Do Prioritize Constituents**: Prioritize the needs and interests of your constituents above personal or political gain. Make decisions that reflect their best interests and advocate on their behalf effectively.
- **Do Collaborate and Build Coalitions**: Work collaboratively with colleagues, community leaders, advocacy groups, and other stakeholders to achieve common goals. Building coalitions and finding common ground fosters cooperation and enables you to achieve greater impact.
- **Do Stay Informed and Educated**: Stay informed about current events, policy issues, and developments in your constituency and beyond. Continuously educate yourself on relevant topics and seek expert advice when needed to make informed decisions.
- **Do Engage with Constituents**: Engage regularly with constituents through town hall meetings, community events, social media, and other channels. Be accessible, responsive, and visible in your constituency to connect with constituents and address their concerns.
- **Do Empower Others**: Empower constituents, colleagues, and stakeholders to participate in the democratic process and contribute

to decision-making. Foster an inclusive environment where diverse voices are heard and respected.

- **Do adapt and innovate**: Be adaptable and innovative in your approach to governance and problem-solving. Embrace change, experiment with new ideas, and learn from both successes and failures to improve your effectiveness as a politician.
- **Do Lead by Example**: Lead by example and demonstrate the values and qualities you wish to see in others. Inspire trust, confidence, and respect through your actions, and be a positive role model for your constituents and colleagues.

Don'ts for a politician to keep in mind: By avoiding these "don'ts," politicians can maintain integrity, build trust, and effectively serve the interests of their constituents and society as a whole.

- **Don't Ignore Constituents**: Avoid neglecting the needs and concerns of your constituents. Ignoring or dismissing their voices can erode trust and undermine your effectiveness as a representative.
- **Don't Compromise Ethics**: Refrain from engaging in unethical behavior or actions that compromise your integrity. Uphold high ethical standards in all aspects of your work to maintain public trust and credibility.
- **Don't Abuse Power**: Avoid abusing your position of power or authority for personal gain or political advantage. Use your influence responsibly and ethically to serve the public interest.
- **Don't Engage in Partisan Politics**: Resist the temptation to prioritize party loyalty over the interests of your constituents. Strive to represent all constituents, regardless of political affiliation, and work across party lines to find common ground and achieve shared goals.
- **Don't Disregard Feedback**: Don't dismiss or ignore feedback from constituents, colleagues, or stakeholders, even if it's critical or challenging. Embrace constructive criticism as an opportunity for growth and improvement.

- **Don't Make False Promises**: Avoid making unrealistic promises or commitments that you cannot fulfill. Be honest and transparent with constituents about what you can realistically achieve, and work diligently to deliver on your commitments.
- **Don't Ignore Diversity**: Don't ignore the diverse perspectives and needs of your constituents. Embrace diversity and inclusivity, and ensure that all voices are heard and considered in decision-making processes.
- **Don't Avoid Accountability**: Refrain from shirking accountability or responsibility for your actions. Take ownership of your decisions, admit mistakes when necessary, and strive to learn from them to improve your performance as a politician.
- **Don't Burn Bridges**: Avoid burning bridges or alienating colleagues, constituents, or stakeholders through divisive or confrontational behavior. Foster constructive dialogue, seek common ground, and build relationships based on mutual respect and cooperation.
- **Don't Lose Sight of Values:** Don't lose sight of your values, principles, and the reasons why you entered public service. Stay true to your convictions and ideals, and let them guide your decisions and actions as a politician.

- **Qualities We Should Look for in Our Political Leaders**
  - **Wisdom:** That wisdom is considered a key—or perhaps, the key—quality in a good ruler. When a political leader is wise, he hates pride, arrogance, and perverted speech.
  - **Understanding:** A good ruler has a moral compass. He understands right from wrong and is eager to know the proper ethical course of action. The political leader who possesses knowledge and understanding has learned to conduct him with honor and integrity.
  - A good king will delight in the truth and love those who speak what is right.

- People flourish under an honorable ruler and suffer under a morally deformed ruler. "
- The governing authorities ought to be people of sound moral judgment.

- **Justice:** A good ruler builds up the land by justice In particular, this means two things.
  - First, our political leaders should not give favorable treatment to the rich and powerful. "He should judge righteously and defend the rights of the poor and needy.
  - Second, when political leaders rule by justice, they punish wrongdoers. Justice is about fairly applying the law and consistently enforcing the law.
- **Humility:** In short, we need political leaders who are humble enough to learn, to grow, to listen to others, and to change course when they have acted in the wrong way or have set out on the wrong path.
- **Self-control**

Political leadership skills will prove to be a successful leader who can easily distinguish between success and failure. A successful leader has a visionary dream and understands how to turn his visions into success stories in the modern world.

- **Good communicator**: **Communicate your vision** clearly to your team and tell them the strategy to accomplish the goal, you'll find it very difficult to get the results you want. If you can't effectively communicate your message to your team, you can never be a good leader. Words can get people motivated and make them do the unimaginable.
- **Honesty and Integrity**: **A**re two main elements that make for a strong leader. How do you demand integrity from your supporters if you neglect such qualities? Leaders excel because they hold to their basic principles and convictions, and that won't be possible without ethics.

- **Decision maker**: A leader should be capable of making the **right decision at the right time**. Leaders take actions that have a huge effect on people. A leader should think long and hard before taking a decision but stand by it once the decision is made.
- **Must be able to inspire others:** Perhaps the toughest thing a leader to do is convince **people to follow them**. This will only be done by providing a clear example and encouraging your followers. As a leader, you should think optimistically, and your positive attitude should be evident from your actions. A leader should keep cool under strain and retain a degree of encouragement. If you excel in inspiring your colleagues, you will comfortably resolve every obstacle now and in the future.
- **Must delegate tasks effectively:** Focusing on core duties is vital for effective leadership while leaving the rest to others. Empowering and delegating tasks to your followers. When you try to micromanage your employees, lack of trust can grow, and, most significantly, you won't be willing to work on critical things as you should. Different duties should be delegated among the subordinates and see how they perform. Provide them with all the tools and help they need to attain the target and allow them to bear responsibilities.
- **Man with a vision and purpose:** Influential leaders have intent and vision. Not only can they imagine the future, but they also express their dreams with their supporters. A strong leader discusses why they are going towards the path that they are heading and reveals the approach and course of action to accomplish the purpose.
  - A political leader's first goal should be
  - Representing one's government, not just oneself.
  - Given the reality that politics may be complicated and often messy; a strong leader should balance their actions with what is right for a nation and living by the maxim," **the nation before self.**"

- Consequently, a **political leader** will be able to take severe actions in the interest of the country if required.
- A leader should be able to recognize unique sector specialists who are confident.
- More critically, a leader should realize when it is best to believe in authority.
- Leaders will have the correct expertise to take prompt and reasonable actions based on sound judgment.
- A democratic leader should also recognize the benefits and most importantly, the disadvantages of democracy,
- Guide, honor, and listen to his supporters while encouraging mutual accountability and team-work.
- Lastly, a **political leader** should travel widely,
- Attending important gatherings within the country and outside. This is imperative as the leader will establish valuable networks and expertise with other internationally renowned leaders.

- **Qualities of a poor leader:** Sometimes the qualities of an excellent leader and a terrible one are surprisingly similar. If you want to evolve into a better leader yourself or help develop one on your team, you'll need to pay close attention to certain traits. Here are the most common character traits:
  - **Lack of vision:** Inadequate leaders can do a lot of the same things good leaders do. But the leader's decisions need to have a purpose, such as driving the team closer to the business's strategic goals.
  - **Inability to produce results**: It's simple. No leader succeeds at everything all the time, but the excellent ones will have something to show for their efforts.
  - **Uninspiring:** If an individual can't uplift, motivate, or inspire others, they'll need to learn how before they can be a good

leader. That's because leadership isn't something you do by yourself — it's about the people you lead.

- **Overconfidence:** A good leader is dauntless — they can confidently take on challenges.
- **Apathy:** Too many people come to their jobs without feeling a sense of investment or ownership in their work. This can cause them to produce sloppy work and even have negative relationships with coworkers.

Glossary for Members of Parliament (MPs)

- **Constituency**: The geographic area represented by an MP and its residents.
- **Legislation**: Laws proposed, debated, and enacted by parliament.
- **Bill**: A proposed law presented for debate and approval by parliament.
- **Debate**: Formal discussion of a bill or issue in parliament.
- **Committee**: A group of MPs assigned to examine bills, policies, or issues in detail.
- **Speaker**: Presiding officer in parliament who maintains order and oversees proceedings.
- **Whip**: MP responsible for ensuring party discipline and attendance for votes.
- **Constituency Surgery**: Regular meetings where MPs meet constituents to address concerns.
- **Policy**: Plan or course of action adopted by government to achieve goals.
- **Budget**: Financial plan outlining government revenue and spending.
- **Constituency Development**: Projects and initiatives to improve the constituency.
- **Motion**: Proposal put forward for debate and decision in parliament.

- **Opposition**: MPs not in governments who scrutinize and challenge policies.
- **Cross-party**: Cooperation or agreement between MPs from different parties.
- **Cabinet**: Group of senior ministers chosen by the Prime Minister to lead government departments.
- **Question Time**: Session where MPs question government ministers on policies.
- **Public Accounts Committee (PAC)**: Committee overseeing government expenditure and financial management.
- **Public Bill**: Legislation affecting the general public, introduced by government or private members.
- **Private Member's Bill**: Legislation introduced by an MP who is not a government minister.
- **White Paper**: Government document proposing policy options for consultation.
- **Green Paper**: Preliminary government document inviting public discussion on policy proposals.
- **Prorogation**: Formal end of a parliamentary session.
- **Adjournment**: Temporary suspension of parliamentary proceedings.
- **Hansard**: Official report of parliamentary debates.
- **Select Committee**: Committee appointed to inquire into specific matters and report findings to parliament.
- **Dissolution**: Formal termination of a parliament before a general election.
- **Backbencher**: MP who is not a minister or party leader.
- **Royal Assent**: Formal approval by the monarch for a bill to become law.

- **Standing Orders**: Rules governing proceedings in parliament.
- **Government Whip**: MP responsible for ensuring government members attend and vote.

(A)

"Act (of Parliament)" - In India, a Bill passed by the two Houses of Parliament and assented to by the President.

"Address (President's/Presidential)" - A prepared speech delivered by the President of India to both Houses of Parliament assembled together at the commencement of the first session of each year informing Parliament of the causes of its summons which is later laid before and discussed on a formal Motion of Thanks in each House of Parliament.

"Adjournment of the House" - Suspend (proceedings) for the day; to put off until a future day. The word 'Adjourn' applies to the action of a deliberative body etc. in bringing a sitting to a close, with the intention of resuming on the next working day or a specified later date. In Lok Sabha, the Speaker determines when sitting of House is to adjourn sine die or to a particular day or to an hour or part of same day.

"Adjournment Motion" - A Motion for discussing 'a specific and important matter that should have urgent consideration'. It can be moved by any member of the House and is in the nature of emergency motion of censure upon the Government. The object is to draw the attention of the Government to a matter of urgent public importance so as to criticize the decision of Government in an urgent matter in regard to which a motion or resolution with proper notice will be too late.

"Admonition" - A punishment administered by the Presiding Officer of a legislature to an offender for breach of privilege or contempt of the House in case of an offence which is not so grave as to warrant his committal; it is the mildest form of punishment.

"Affirmation" - A positive declaration; a solemn declaration without oath; a solemn declaration made by a member of a legislature in lieu of oath before he takes his seat in the House. "I, A.B., having been elected a Member of the House of the People do solemnly affirm that I will bear true faith and allegiance to the Constitution of India as by law established, that I will uphold the sovereignty and integrity of India and that I will faithfully discharge the duty upon which I am about to enter."

"Allocation of Time" - In India, the practice is that all items of business to be transacted by the House during the Government time including those, to which the Speaker is empowered to allot time himself, are normally placed before the Business Advisory Committee for allocation of time. The report of the Business Advisory Committee is presented to House for approval after which the allocation of time in respect of Bills and other business becomes an order of the House.

"Amendment(s)" - A device to alter a motion moved or question under discussion in the Legislature; includes omission, substitution, addition and insertion of certain words, figures or marks to the clause of a bill, a resolution or a motion or to an amendment made thereof.

"Annual Financial Statement" - A statement made by the Minister in charge of Finance in the legislature containing the probable income and expenditure of the Government for any year; familiarly known as Budget.

"Answers (to questions)" - In the Indian Parliament, oral answers are given to Questions distinguished by an asterisk while those not distinguished by an asterisk are listed for written answers; supplementary questions are asked for further elucidating any matter of fact regarding which an answer has been given, if permitted by the Speaker. Normally the first hour of every sitting is allotted for answering questions.

(B)

"Bill(s)" - A draft of a legislative proposal put in the proper form which when passed by both the Houses of Parliament and assented to by the President becomes an Act.

"Breach of Privilege" - Disregard of any of the privileges, rights and immunities either of the Members of Parliament individually or of either House of Parliament in its collective capacity or of its committees; also includes actions which obstruct the House in the performance of its functions and thereby lower its dignity and authority such as disobedience of its legitimate orders or libel upon itself, or its member or officers which are called contempt of the House (for details see 'Privileges').

"Business, list of" - In the Indian Parliament, it is known as List of Business, prepared under the authority of the Speaker by the Secretary-General and a copy thereof is supplied to every member; contains the items of business, Govt. and Private members', scheduled to be taken up on a particular day; the first item generally is Questions; Oath or affirmation and obituary reference, whenever listed, precede Questions; List of Questions though part of List of Business, is issued separately; List of Business, the List of Questions, the List of Amendments, cut-motions and the Bills, all combined form the Order Paper for the day.

"Business of the House" - The relative order of all the items of business in the House of a Legislature to be taken up on a particular day. Government Business for a whole week is announced in advance in the House by the Minister for Parliamentary Affairs.

(C)

"Calling Attention" - The act of requiring somebody to give his attention to; to point out; a parliamentary procedure to call the attention of the Government to a matter of urgent public importance.

"Censure Motion" - A motion moved against the Government censuring its policy in some direction or an individual minister or ministers of the Government.

"Commonwealth Parliamentary Association" - The Commonwealth Parliamentary Association is an organization composed of Branches formed in the legislatures of various Commonwealth countries. It consists of main Branches formed in the National Parliaments of Commonwealth, State and Provincial branches formed in State or Provincial Legislatures within member countries of the Commonwealth and territorial Parliaments.

"Concurrent List" - A list of subjects appended to a federal Constitution in respect of which the federal legislature and the State or regional legislatures have power to make laws, federal law prevailing in case of conflict.

"Constitution" - The system of fundamental laws and principles of a government written or unwritten; system of laws and customs established by sovereign power of a State for its own guidance.

"Contempt of the House" - Any act or omission which obstructs or impedes either House of Parliament in the performance of its functions, or which obstructs or impedes any member or officer of such House in the discharge of his duty, or which has a tendency, directly or indirectly, to produce such results is treated as a contempt even though there is no precedent of the offence.

"Cut Motions" - During the discussion on the demands for grants, motion can be moved to reduce the amount of a demand; such a motion is called cut motion.

(D)

"Delegated Legislation" - "Delegated legislation" and "delegation of legislative power" is the conferring of authority upon a subordinate authority to frame rules, regulations etc. Each regulation, rule, sub-rule, bye-law etc. framed in pursuance of the provisions of the Constitution or Act of Parliament under the power delegated thereunder to a subordinate authority is required to be laid on the Table of Lok Sabha within a period of fifteen days after publication in the Gazette.

"Deputy Speaker" - Deputy Speaker is elected from amongst its members; he is not subordinate to the Speaker and holds an independent position; he is answerable to the House alone. In the absence of the Speaker, the Deputy Speaker is required to perform the duties of the Office of the Speaker and preside over the sitting of the House and also the joint sitting of the Houses of Parliament and exercises the powers of the Speaker.

"Directive Principles of State Policy" - Constitutional directions and principles fundamental in the governance of the country.

"Dissolution" - The President of India dissolves the Lok Sabha on the advice of the Prime Minister. At the end of its term of five years, the House stands automatically dissolved even if no formal order of dissolution is issued by the President. With dissolution, the life of the House comes to an end and it cannot again assemble until after a general election.

"Disqualifications for" - Constitutional or statutory rules which make a person unfit or unqualified to be chosen as member of a Legislature; also those which make a member unfit for being its member subsequent to his election.

"Division" - Division is ordered by the Chair when his opinion on the question just decided by voice vote is challenged by members who demand a division.

(E)

"Election Commission" - A constitutional body in India created for the purpose of holding elections to Parliament, State Legislatures and offices of President and Vice-President.

"Electoral College" - An intermediary body chosen by electors to choose the representatives in an indirect election.

"Enacting Formula" - The section of a Bill or statute which establishes the whole document as a law.

(G)

"Government" - A Parliamentary government consists of cabinet which is responsible to the legislature for its actions. Government carries on general administration and Parliament exercises general control of governmental acts.

"Government Assurances" - Assurances, promises, undertakings given by Ministers from time to time on the Floor of the House; for ensuring their implementation in reasonable time.

(H)

"Houses of Parliament" - The two Houses of Indian Parliament are: the Rajya Sabha (Council of States) and the Lok Sabha (House of the People).

"Hung Parliament" - Parliament wherein no party has won a working majority

(L)

"Leader of the House" - In Lok Sabha, the Prime Minister usually functions as the Leader of the House; if he is not a member of this House, a Minister, who is a member of the Lok Sabha and is nominated by the Prime Minister, functions as such. Leader of the House is an important Parliamentary functionary.

"Leader of Opposition" - Leader of the largest minority party in a legislature; an office recognized under the Rules of the House.

"Leave of Absence" - The formal granting of leave of absence to a Member of Parliament.

"Leave of the House" - The formal approval given by the House of a Legislature to a member to move a motion or withdraw the same. The member can seek the leave of the House only after he has been permitted to do so by the Speaker; he then rises in his place and asks for leave. After the leave is granted, the member cannot withdraw his motion without the permission of the House.

"Legislation (Subordinate)" - Making of statutory instruments or orders by a body subordinate to the legislature in exercise of the power within specific limits conferred by the legislature; also covers statutory instruments themselves.

(M)

"Maiden Speech" - M.P.'s first speech in Parliament; one's first or earliest speech, especially in Parliament.

(O)

"Office of Profit" - An employment with fees and emoluments attached to it; it also carries some power of patronage; the holder of it is entitled to exercise executive, financial or judicial powers.

"Ordinance" - The President of the Union and the Governors of the States have legislative power to promulgate Ordinances, such power is co-extensive with the legislative competence of Parliament.

(P)

"Panel of Chairmen" - The body of members whom the Speaker nominates from among the members to preside over the sittings of the House in the absence of the Speaker and the Deputy Speaker.

"Papers laid on the Table" - Laying of Parliamentary papers or documents on the Table of both Houses of Parliament for bringing them on the record of the House.

"Parliament—Jurisdiction and Powers of" - Parliament consists of the President and the two Houses; each of its branches has peculiar powers in connection with their joint legislative function.

"Parliamentary Papers" - The papers connected with the proceedings of the House as well as those presented to the House; the copies of these papers are made available to the Members as soon as they are issued.

(R)

"Rules of Procedure" - Rules which regulate procedure, debate and the conduct of members in a Legislature.

(S)

"Schedule" - The Schedule is as much a part of the statute and as much an enactment as any other part; it must be read together with the Act for all purpose of construction.

"Select Committee on Bill(s)" - A Parliamentary Committee composed of members specially named and appointed from time to time to consider, inquire into or deal with Bills.

"Speaker" - The Speaker is the Principal Presiding Officer of the Lok Sabha. He is chosen by the House from among its Members by a simple majority of members present and voting. Within the walls of the House his authority is supreme, which is based on his absolute and unvarying impartiality.

"Speaker pro tem" - A member of a Legislative House appointed to perform the duties of the Office of the Speaker when the offices of both the Speaker and Deputy Speaker are vacant; the Speaker pro tem continues in office till the Speaker is elected.

(T)

"Table of the House" - In the pit of the two Houses of Indian Parliament, just in front of the table of the Secretary-General lays the table of the House. Papers which are required to be laid on the Table of the House in pursuance of constitutional provisions, Rules and Directions are formally placed on this Table.

www.ingramcontent.com/pod-product-compliance
Lightning Source LLC
La Vergne TN
LVHW021135160826
845679LV00023B/1922

* 9 7 9 8 8 9 4 7 5 3 9 3 5 *